From Inequality to Inclusive Growth

South Africa's pursuit of shared prosperity in extraordinary times

Edited by Jan Hofmeyr

THE INSTITUTE
FOR JUSTICE AND
RECONCILIATION

Institute for Justice and Reconciliation
www.ijr.org.za

2011 Transformation Audit
www.transformationaudit.org

Published by the Institute for Justice and Reconciliation
Wynberg Mews, 10 Brodie Road, Wynberg 7800, Cape Town, South Africa
www.ijr.org.za

Text © Institute for Justice and Reconciliation
Cover: © James P. Blair/National Geographic/Getty Images
Images © Jan Hofmeyr: pp. 1, 22, 46, 68, 94;
The Biggerpicture/Reuters: © Siphiwe Sibeko pp. 19/43, © Rogan Ward p. 39
Getty Images: © Richard du Toit p. 87

Copy-edited by Laurie Rose-Innes
Scorecards by Derek Yu
Designed and produced by COMPRESS.dsl www.compressdsl.com

Orders to be placed with either Blue Weaver Marketing and Distribution
Tel: +27 (21) 701 4477
Fax: +27 (21) 701 7302
E-mail: orders@bluweaver.co.za
or the IJR
Tel: +27 (21) 763 7137
E-mail: ijr@ijr.org.za

Authors to this publication write in their personal capacity.
Their views do not necessarily reflect those of their employers,
nor the Institute for Justice and Reconciliation.

Contents

List of tables and figures

Tables

Figures

Contributors

Patrick Bond directs the University of KwaZulu-Natal's Centre for Civil Society in Durban and is author of the new book *Politics of Climate Justice*.

Linda Chisholm is a director at the Education and Skills Development Research Programme of the Human Sciences Research Council. She is currently seconded as a special advisor to the Minister of Basic Education.

Arden Finn is a researcher on the National Income Dynamics Study within the Southern Africa Labour and Development Research Unit.

Vusi Gumede is an associate professor of development studies at the University of Johannesburg. He also teaches public policy at the Wits Graduate School of Public and Development Management.

Ebrahim-Khalil Hassen is a public policy analyst and the editor of *Zapreneur*.

Jan Hofmeyr heads the Policy and Analysis Unit of the Institute for Justice and Reconciliation.

Murray Leibbrandt is a professor at the School of Economics at the University of Cape Town and the Director of the Southern Africa Labour and Development Research Unit.

Neva Makgetla is Deputy Director-General: Economic Policy at the Department of Economic Development.

Chris Malikane is an associate professor at the School of Economics and Business Sciences at the University of the Witwatersrand. He is the Congress of South African Trade Unions' head of policy and also serves as commissioner on the National Planning Commission.

Saliem Patel is the executive director of the Labour Research Service, an independent NGO specialising in labour market research, education and information for trade unions.

Carol Paton is a journalist writing about politics, business and the economy. She has written extensively about employment for the *Financial Mail* and the *Sunday Times*.

Michael Spicer is the chief executive officer of Business Leadership South Africa, Vice-President of Business Unity South Africa.

Nick Taylor is a research fellow, and former CEO, of the Joint Education Trust.

Lucia Tiscornia is a master's student in peace studies at the Kroc Institute for International Peace Studies at Notre Dame University. During the second half of 2011 she was a research intern at the Institute for Justice and Reconciliation.

Eva Wegner is a post-doctoral fellow at the Southern Africa Labour and Development Research Unit, based at the University of Cape Town.

Russell Wildeman is Programme Manager of Idasa's Economic Governance Programme.

Derek Yu is a lecturer in economics at the University of the Western Cape.

Acronyms and abbreviations

AMW   average minimum wage
ANA   annual national assessment
ANCYL   African National Congress Youth League
AsgiSA   Accelerated and Shared Growth Initiative for South Africa
AWARD   Actual Wage Rates Database
BRICS   Brazil, Russia, India, China and South Africa
CIVETS   Colombia, Indonesia, Vietnam, Egypt, Turkey and South Africa
COSATU   Congress of South African Trade Unions
DBE   Department of Basic Education
DoE   Department of Education
DHET   Department of Higher Education and Training
EFAL   English First Additional Language
EHL   English Home Language
FEDUSA   Federation of Unions of South Africa
GEAR   Growth, Employment and Redistribution
HDI   Human Development Index
HPI-1   Human Poverty Index
IES   Income and Expenditure of Households
IIEP   International Institute for Educational Planning
IMF   International Monetary Fund
FDI   foreign direct investment
LRS   Labour Research Service
LSM   Living Standards Measurement
MPRDA   Mineral and Petroleum Resources Development Act 28 of 2002
MTBPS   Medium-term Budget Policy Statement

NEDLAC   National Economic Development and Labour Council
NGP   National Growth Path
NIDS   National Income Dynamics Study
NPC   National Planning Commission
NSC   National Senior Certificate
OECD   Organisation for Economic Co-operation and Development
PIRLS   Progress in International Reading Literacy Study
PSCBC   Public Service Co-ordinating Bargaining Council
PSLSD   Project for Statistics on Living Standards and Development
RDP   Reconstruction and Development Programme
SACCAWU   South African Commercial, Catering and Allied Workers Union
SACMEQ   Southern and Eastern Africa Consortium for Monitoring Educational Quality
SACTWU   Southern African Clothing and Textile Workers' Union
SADC   Southern African Development Community
SALGA   South African Local Government Association
SMME   small, medium and micro enterprise
TIMSS   Trends in International Mathematics and Science Study
UK   United Kingdom
UNESCO   United Nations Educational, Scientific and Cultural Organisation

Preface

In 2011, the longstanding debate about social and economic inclusion was fast-tracked to the top of the nation's agenda. As the global financial crisis deepened and citizens around the world took to the streets, the tragic and horrifying death of a South African protestor, Mr Andries Tatane – allegedly at the hands of the South African Police Service – reminded policy-makers that the time for merely talking about economic inclusion has come to an end.

Elsewhere in South Africa, strident rhetoric by factions of the youth culminated in a march for 'economic freedom' on the Union Buildings by thousands of angry young citizens demanding more effective measures to include them in mainstream society. The nationalisation debate also intensified as key social stakeholders engaged around the ways and means to upscale the state's role in creating a better life for its citizens at a more rapid pace than over the past 17 years.

However, economic growth and development cannot be the sole responsibility of policy-makers, or of development policy for that matter. It also needs to be driven by an engaged society, and particularly by those who have the means to do so. In South Africa, with its indefensibly high levels of poverty and inequality, there is an onus on affluent citizens and businesses to play a more substantive role in creating a more equitable society. The affluent – white and black – should know that their privileges will rest on increasingly tenuous grounds, in the absence of more direct engagement to counter the effects of a subdued economy on a society that is experiencing increasing financial strain.

Well-off white South Africans, in particular, who owe much of their privilege to the same source that accounts for the continued disadvantage of millions of black South Africans to this day, should play a more decisive role in this regard. Many have come to grips with this reality and are seeking ways to make a difference; yet, sadly, there are others who have failed to contribute. In the latter part of the year, Archbishop Emeritus Desmond Tutu reminded well-to-do (mainly white) South Africans of their historical privilege and their duty to pay some form of restitution to those at whose expense their wealth came. Tutu went to great lengths to assure white South Africans that restitution – whatever form it takes – must not be seen in a punitive sense, but as a means of reconstruction and healing. Several predominantly white interest groups did not see it this way and castigated the archbishop for his 'attack' on white South Africans.

Given this domestic and global context, publications like the Transformation Audit become even more vital for us to get a sense of where we find ourselves and where we ought to go. It serves as confirmation of the IJR's firm belief that national reconciliation is possible if justice is understood not only in a political sense, but also as a deeply material matter. Over the next few years, the IJR, through its Inclusive Economies Project, will increase its involvement in this field and, in addition to this publication, will engage with the issue of equitable development here and elsewhere in Africa in relevant forums.

This year's Audit makes for particularly incisive reading, and looks decidedly different from its predecessors. The aim has been to ensure that its contents become more accessible to those who require high-level insights in the fast-paced world of policy development and implementation. I would like to congratulate the Inclusive Economies Project team for their efforts in creating this outstanding publication, and hope that its contribution to the critical challenge of creating a more inclusive economy has a bearing far and wide in circles where the question of inclusivity is pondered.

Fanie du Toit
Executive Director, Institute for Justice and Reconciliation

Introduction

Jan Hofmeyr

Since 1994, the concept of 'transformation' has had a progressive connotation in South Africa. For the first 17 years after apartheid, it signified change from an inhumane system with unequal development to one that is more equal, inclusive and caring. In truth, though, the word does not exclusively denote positive change. A state can also be transformed into something other than what it intended to become if such change is not properly planned, sequenced and implemented. Importantly, planning also needs to be adjusted to prevailing and emerging trends.

This Transformation Audit was produced against the backdrop of continued global economic uncertainty. As in previous years, it continues its focus on four core areas, namely the macro-economy, skills and education, the labour market, and poverty and inequality. This year, it contains an additional chapter that presents selected public opinion data on matters of economic security, drawn from the IJR's annual SA Reconciliation Barometer Survey, which has been conducted nationally since 2003. As usual, the collection of contributions by some of the country's leading thinkers provides an overview of key trends and debates, but also asks pertinent questions about the appropriateness of prevailing development models. Do we still know where we want to go? If we do, how will we get there at a time when old certainties are increasingly challenged by economic, political and ecological events that previously have been unfathomable?

In a recent special report on Europe's ongoing debt challenges, *The Economist* cited the contention of a European central banker that, 'from the middle of a crisis, you can see how easy it is to make mistakes'.[1] This caution should also be heeded by our policy-makers across the political spectrum. *From Inequality to Inclusive Growth* seeks to provide sober insights on where we find ourselves as a nation, and to promote pragmatic thinking about how we navigate these challenging circumstances towards our goal of transformation that seeks a dignified life for all South Africans.

A volatile global economy

Towards the end of every year, financial publications dust off their crystal balls to predict trends for the ones approaching. These editions sell, because foresight is the most precious of commodities to their readerships from the worlds of finance and macroeconomic management. For the greater part of the

new century, their forecasts centred on opportunities and the direction of growth. The 'Great Recession' of 2008 brought an abrupt end to this; since then, the focus has shifted decidedly towards finding ways in which calamity can be averted. Volatility has become the trademark of our time. Prognoses have become more guarded, and those that have been published for 2012 seem to be even more cautious than in recent years.

The precious little consensus that does exist is distinctly on the downside, but just how much worse it can get seems to be anybody's guess. In the otherwise secular world of business journalism, many journalists have resorted to reminding their readers of the Mayan prophecy predicting the world's demise in 2012. Although most proceeded to dismiss the possibility, this seemed to be done with less conviction at a time where the unthinkable appears to happen with growing frequency.

In 2011, citizens in undemocratic and democratic states alike rose against the disproportionate privilege of their political and economic elites. The United States, the world's largest economy, saw its credit rating downgraded. In Europe, once the epitome of political and economic stability, politicians have been in a constant fire fight to avert a crisis that could ultimately lead to a significant reconfiguration or, at worst, dissolution of the European Union as we have come to know it.

The picture looks bleak. Some have labelled the status quo as the moment of truth for many Western economies, which sooner or later had to face up to the consequences of easy money and excessive spending for close to two decades. The new realities may have induced some humility in these states as they stumble from one crisis to the next, but this might not be a good time for *schadenfreude* amongst those that have always been frustrated by the West's economic hegemony, because global contagion will also infect states in the emerging (and, up to now, satisfactorily performing) BRICS and CIVETS groups.

Whereas private debtors were the first to fall victim to their unsustainable spending habits during the American subprime crisis, European nation states in 2011 have had to face up to the wrath of the markets for their 'bold' expenditure over a protracted period. Barely had the US fallout been contained than European governments (starting with Ireland in February) began to collapse one after the other under the weight of the continent's sovereign debt crisis. At the time of writing, the count stood at six, with three having fallen in the span of three weeks during November. A rattled George

Papandreou resigned as Greek prime minister on 11 November, after first having announced a surprise referendum on the country's harsh austerity package, and then caving in to pressure from his European counterparts to retract that option. The day thereafter, Italy's flamboyant, die-hard prime minister, Sylvio Berlusconi, was next to follow as he handed over power to banker, Mario Monti. A week later, Spain's socialist government of Jose Luiz Rodriguez Zapatero was ousted by Mariano Rajoy's conservative People's Party in a landslide victory. Already, eyes are turning to France, whose banks have been highly exposed to southern European debt, while it prepares for presidential elections.

At the close of 2011, everybody looked towards Germany, as the largest and most stable of the Eurozone economies, for answers. By the end of November, however, it appeared that investors doubted Germany's ability to steer through the crisis with limited damage, when it failed to obtain full subscription for €6 billion worth of government bonds that were released on the markets – another unpalatable first since the introduction of the Euro.

Although the European crisis deflected attention, the woes of the US economy continued on the other side of the Atlantic. Ironically, in the same week as President Barrack Obama urged European politicians to 'get their act together',[2] a US cross-party 'super committee' failed to agree on strategies to address the country's precipitous federal debt. This will curb Obama's plans for increased spending and, together with European austerity measures, will put a lid on the global growth that has been driven by emerging economies like China, India and Brazil.

At home the challenge will get bigger

Where does this scenario leave South Africa's developmental ambitions? The answer, in short, is: very exposed. Since its political liberation in 1994, the South African economy has largely mirrored average global trends. Despite its membership of the high-growth BRICS and CIVETS groups, the country has never been able to sustain the same levels of economic expansion that the other countries in the groups have managed to achieve over a protracted period. Nevertheless, even if South Africa's growth path were more closely aligned to the emerging economies of the global South, these economies, as indicated above, are not insulated from the crisis in the North.

Finance Minister Pravin Gordhan noted in September at the Southern Africa Volunteer Action Conference that the recent crises underscored the 'very interconnected and interdependent' nature of a global economy from which uncoupling was not an option.[3] In his 2011 Medium-Term Budget Policy Statement (MTBPS) a month later, he proceeded to outline how this intertwined relationship has a bearing on our present situation.[4] Gordhan predicted that the country would probably achieve a lower than expected growth of 3.1 per cent for 2011, followed by 3.4 per cent the following year, and 4 per cent the

year thereafter. In a very forthright analysis of the current state of the economy, the minister noted that the country's sound financial and fiscal institutions alone cannot shelter it from the impact of global economic instability on job creation, poverty and levels of inequality.

According to Gordhan, tackling those challenges will require 'an extraordinary national effort'. Yet, he bemoaned the fact that, if our primary developmental objective has been to create greater convergence between the living conditions of the poor and the rich, progress has been insufficient. Funding will always be in short supply, but the minister went to great lengths to underscore the need for more efficient expenditure, noting that consecutive increases in government expenditure over the years have translated into higher consumption and lower levels of capital spending. Thus, when government expenditure patterns are taken to their logical conclusion, it means that a focus on the present is crowding out investment for the future. This, by definition, is what unsustainability means.

The challenge of positive transformation, therefore, is not only one of addressing immediate needs, but also of ensuring that today's spending is part of a plan to reproduce development and prosperity tomorrow. Within our context, this means that expenditure on the challenges of the present – including those aimed at imbalances relating to our history of exclusion and discrimination – must be made with due respect for the required balance of investing in a society that over time will provide better education, create more jobs, offer better health care and see more people live longer in dignity. Investment requires patience, but in difficult times like these, populist pressure to throw caution to the wind is always likely to arise; hence, it is critical to anchor forward-looking policy within a national planning framework.

In addition to the obvious utility of providing clear parameters for the nature and sequencing of developmental strategy, planning documents also need to obtain the kind of prominence necessary, in the eyes of bureaucrats, business, labour and ordinary citizens alike, to galvanise energy and make sacrifices possible. They need to be the central reference points for development. To date, policy has been largely the outcome of fierce contests for the influence of exclusive interests in a crowded and highly charged policy space. The fact that these contests have occurred in democratic processes, in which outcomes have been accepted, bears testimony to the vitality of our democratic institutions. However, the outcomes themselves, more often than not, have failed to bring inclusive, win-win solutions for all stakeholders. Credible planning, forged through a common vision and legitimate processes, which bind the government, labour, business and civil society to outcomes, can go a long way in addressing this.

The 2010 Audit, *Vision or Vacuum*, contended that the country's current development model is not sustainable. It also made the case for the creation of a longer-term perspective that would harness the country's resources to bring substantive social transformation. The publication alluded to the New Growth Path (NGP) document, which was released by the Ministry of Economic Development in the latter part of 2010. Although the NGP has found expression in government documentation and strategies as a guiding instrument – most recently in the MTBPS – it still needs to gain currency as a central reference point for the broader set of policy stake-holders outside the government.

The NGP signified the government's intention to think critically about transforming the South African economy into one that sustains a higher growth trajectory, that is more inclusive and, importantly, also labour intensive. With regard to the latter, it sets the target of 5 million new jobs by 2020, but notes that this can be achieved only with sustained annual GDP growth of between 4 and 7 per cent, which is underpinned by a labour to capital ratio of 0.5-0.8 per year.[5] Given the current prognoses here and abroad for economic recovery (if things do not get worse before they get better), this will be difficult to achieve in the short to medium term. According to MTBPS projections, the lower margin of 4 per cent may be reached only by 2013, and as a result job creation is likely to remain under pressure. Clearly, there is a need for greater engagement around the document, also from outside the government, to ensure that the achievement of the original targets is kept within sight.

In 2011, the National Planning Commission (NPC) released two further notable documents aimed at charting South Africa's way forward into the future. The first, a Diagnostic Report, out-lined the major challenges that face the country up to 2030, as well as their root causes. The report, which was presented to President Zuma in June, identified nine core areas that deserve emphasis:

» creating jobs and livelihoods;
» expanding infrastructure;
» transitioning to a low-carbon economy;
» transforming urban and rural spaces;
» improving education and training;
» providing quality health care;
» building a capable state;
» fighting corruption and enhancing accountability; and
» transforming society and uniting the nation.

November saw the release of the NPC's draft National Development Plan (NDP), in which the commission provided a comprehensive 440-page response to the challenges that were outlined in the Diagnostic Report. Some proposals under-score what we already know about the need for responsible countercyclical fiscal and monetary policies, price stability, higher savings, investment in economic infrastructure and a dramatic improvement in our educational outputs. Others, such as suggestions to make the labour market more flexible to promote youth employment, are more controversial and at odds with what some within the ruling party and its alliance partners believe. Such bold engagement should have been

expected, given that all commissioners, with the exception of the Minister in the Presidency for National Planning, Trevor Manuel, represent diverse constituencies outside of the government. More important is the fact that a document has been put on the table that can guide more focused debate.[6]

Probably the most significant hurdle that the NDP will have to overcome is raised in the draft document itself: politics. In its chapter on the building of a capable state, the NDP contends that decision-making and implementation over the past 17 years often have been bedevilled by narrow political agendas. In response, it contains proposals that aim to insulate the state bureaucracy from undue intervention. Commissioners must have had the political fall-out around the African National Congress' (ANC) 2007 National Conference in Polokwane in mind when they flagged this concern in the report. Prior and subsequent to the 2007 conference, the heads of several departmental chiefs with strong political allegiances rolled, which inevitably resulted in delivery delays across govern-ment. This had an impact not only on critical social delivery clusters, but also on issues of national security, as members of critical agencies became embroiled in the leadership tussle between factions that supported Thabo Mbeki and Jacob Zuma. At the end of 2012, the ruling party will gather once again for its national conference – this time in Mangaung – and one hopes that a repeat of the events in Polokwane will be averted.

What is becoming clear within the present jittery global environment is that policy certainty is critical. The smallest hint of risk will be enough to drive nervous domestic and international investors away from potentially beneficial investment. Towards the end of 2011, international ratings agency, Moody's downgraded South Africa's credit rating to negative. While much bigger economies had to experience the same indignity this year, Moody's concern did not necessarily lie with matters of policy. In fact, the ratings agency in the past has expressed its satisfaction with the country's conservative fiscal approach. At stake rather was the question of whether it would be able to sustain it in the face of mounting popular and internal pressure from within the ANC and its alliance partners.

One does not need to subscribe to official policy or trust in the accuracy of international ratings agencies to realise that predictability is the key issue here. One way of dealing with this would be to continue to straddle the interests of everyone; an alternative would be to slow down the process towards the publication of the final NPD document. While it may be opportune for our government not to engage with potentially sensitive issues in a politically significant year, the short-term gains of postponing critical decisions will be overshadowed by the longer-term consequences of inaction. Some argue that we are paying the price for this already. The bold option would be to make strategic, but difficult, choices now to avoid delaying accelerated development any longer. This would not only provide predictability (and encourage employment-generating investment) but – if communicated properly – would also give South African policy stakeholders a common vision to pursue.

Chapter summaries

The chapter format of this year's Audit looks slightly different from that of preceding publications. Scorecards have been updated to provide a more longitudinal picture of developments within each focus area. In addition, statistics from selected emerging countries are provided, which allow for peer comparisons on selected indicators. As far as chapter contributions are concerned, we have opted to provide one comprehensive overview for each focal area, followed by two opinion articles that argue different positions on the same topical area. This change serves to provide readers with longer opinion pieces in which authors are afforded the opportunity to expand on arguments that are normally presented in abbreviated form in newspaper columns. The 2011 Audit also sees the addition of another chapter that reports on public opinion regarding personal economic security and the impact of development on ordinary people. Data have been obtained from the IJR's annual SA Reconciliation Barometer Survey.

Chapter 1: The macro-economy

The overview article of this chapter by Neva Makgetla deals with the challenges of economic policy-making in a complex domestic policy context, where the contest for influence is fierce, and, at the same time, highly exposed to a very fluid global environment. Makgetla notes that while policy stability has remained a trademark of the country's economic management for most of the democratic era, its vulnerability can be ascribed largely to a continued dependence on the mining value chain, and the exponential growth of the financial sector that has been driven by large inflows of portfolio capital. Neither of the two sectors has been good at creating employment, and when recession struck in 2009, the formal labour market shed nearly 6 per cent of employed South Africans.

Labour-intensive growth has become a clearly articulated policy priority in documents such as the Accelerated and Shared Growth Initiative for South Africa (AsgiSA) and the NGP. Both emphasise the need to diversify the economy in ways that would open up new opportunities for the marginalised majority, mostly through employment but also through support for small enterprises. Makgetla notes, however, that it is easier to conceptualise than to implement a development strategy that would sustain growth and simultaneously encourage employment creation and equity. She notes that much of this may have to do with historical distrust, which has made the search for common ground difficult. This, in addition, has been exacerbated by uneven implementation, resulting from varied exposure that different levels of government has had to specialised lobbying groups with their own particular needs.

This, Makgetla suggests, has been further accentuated by the fragmentation of economic policy-making between too many state departments, and has lent itself to endless debates and deadlocks between different government entities.

Despite the problematic nature of the country's 'resource addiction', mining and its downstream activities remain one of South Africa's primary revenue drivers. As a result, there has been a growing debate about how mining could be used more effectively to address South Africa's developmental challenges more directly. One suggestion, initially raised by the ANC Youth League (ANCYL), has been the nationalisation in the mining sector. Given mining's central role in the economy, this proposal has elicited much heated (and, some would argue, polarising) debate.

In the opinion section of this chapter, Chris Malikane, Congress of South African Trade Unions (COSATU) head of economic policy, makes the case for nationalisation by pointing out that investments in this sector would always be tenuous for as long as ownership of mineral wealth remains a contested issue. He bases his argument on the provision of the *Freedom Charter* that states that the country's mineral wealth 'shall be transferred to the ownership of the people',[7] noting that the experience of countries like Vietnam points to modern-day examples of how a nationalised mining industry can function in joint ventures with the private sector.

Michael Spicer, Vice-President of Business Leadership South Africa, which represents an association of leaders of the 80 largest South African companies and multinationals that do business in the country, argues that nationalisation will not serve the ultimate ideals of greater material dignity and opportunity for individuals. Spicer suggests that current proposals for nationalisation grossly underestimate the input costs of mining, which may ultimately become an onerous burden on a state that already suffers under capacity constraints. He concludes that much progress has already been made in terms of working towards greater equity, through the revised Mining Charter. In its new form, the charter is the product of protracted negotiation, and contains measurable targets that are worth pursuing over time, according to Spicer. In similar vein, he mentions the importance of the work of the Mining Industry Growth, Development and Employment Task Team, which is mandated with finding ways to ensure equitable inclusion in the growth of the mining sector.

Chapter 2: The labour market

The South African economy's brief dip into recession during 2009 has had a disproportionately devastating impact on the labour market. Already characterised by high levels of structural unemployment, the 2009 recession took with it close to a million jobs. The economy has not managed to regain the number of jobs lost.

The overview article in this section by Saliem Patel from the Cape Town-based Labour Research Service reviews the current state of the labour market and the challenges that unions face in serving the interests of their constituencies. Patel's review shows that the complexion and character of the South African labour market have not changed significantly since 1994, despite the many legislative gains that have been made in favour of the rights of workers. If anything, the uncertainty resulting from volatile markets at the time of writing in late 2011 has placed workers under even more pressure than in the past. Mass retrenchments, according to Patel, could become the catalyst for violent action, which unions would not be able to contain. It is, therefore, in the interests of all stakeholders to co-operate in the search for inclusive solutions to the country's unemployment question.

In recent years unions have frequently been accused of representing workers' interests to the detriment of the unemployed poor. In fact, some have argued that by insisting on greater labour protection they have exacerbated the plight of the poor. In the opinion section of this chapter, the question is asked as to whether trade unions can still be regarded as representing the interests of the country's working class as a whole. Independent analyst and writer, Ebrahim-Khalil Hassen argues that while they can still be regarded as doing so, unions will have to learn to adapt to rapidly changing circumstances. He notes that several innovations are required for trade unions to continue to legitimately claim to speak on behalf of the entire working class. Primary amongst these is the need to find new membership models, which take cognisance of the emergence of new social movements, as well as strategies that support self-organisation by the unemployed and atypical workers.

Financial journalist, Carol Paton notes that while unions have the potential to regain their status as the voice of marginalised people, they are largely failing to do so. What is required is a more pragmatic approach, devoid of ideology and revolutionary positions, to find practical solutions that address the plight of the poor. According to Paton, the zealous pursuit of unions to undo the practice of labour brokering provides an example of how they can become an obstacle that runs contrary to the objective of creating new employment. She, therefore, advocates soul-searching amongst union leaders, but also adds that it would be unfair of the government and the private sector to expect concessions from labour, without offering a *quid pro quo*.

Chapter 3: Education and skills

Before crises can be addressed comprehensively, they first need to be classified as such. Policy-makers are often cautious to do so, because such decisions have implications for prioritisation in a context of limited resources. Whereas education has, somewhat euphemistically, been described as a 'significant stumbling block' to South Africa's developmental aspirations during the first years of post-apartheid government, it is now broadly recognised as the most critical variable to unlocking higher levels of employment that are needed to reverse poverty and inequality.

According to Linda Chisholm, prioritisation and the actual policy-making around education is complicated, because performance in the classroom cannot be separated from the adverse social circumstances that many learners experience at home and in their communities. Therefore, policy interventions demand a comprehensive understanding of the dimensions of the problem. According to her, a greater recognition of the depth and breadth of the challenge in recent years has allowed for better mobilisation and rallying of significant sectors in society. This new momentum is in itself a significant achievement.

In her overview, Chisholm surveys the scale and the causes of the challenges involved, and proceeds to outline government responses at various levels. These steps have included: ongoing dialogue and consultation with prominent stake-holders in business and labour, but also with parents; due recognition for the growing demands of diversity in classrooms; improved alignment between interventions of the national and provincial education departments; curriculum reform, with particular attention to early childhood development; teacher recruitment; resource efficiency; greater accountability of teachers and managers within the education system; and the setting of appropriate targets at national, provincial and school level in those areas that require most attention.

Ultimately, the success or failure of these interventions becomes apparent in the results obtained by learners. In South Africa, the most publicised of these are the results of Grade 12 (matric) learners in their final year of schooling. In recent years, it has been asked increasingly whether a uniform standard provides an accurate reflection of school, teacher and learner performance. The question has been raised, furthermore, as to whether such standards do not have the unintended consequence of further exacerbating the already challenging circumstances of learners from disadvantaged backgrounds.

In the first of the opinion articles, Nick Taylor notes that targets have a dual purpose. On the one hand, they are measures of performance and, on the other, they set objectives to aim for. Ultimately, they are meant to provide an education that allows learners to seize opportunities in the labour market. Measures can be introduced in an attempt to ensure that targets are reached, but performance incentives may also lead to perverse outcomes when short cuts are taken. For example, pressure to perform can lead to the adjustment of aggregate figures, which gives a warped impression of actual educational achievement. This practice, which has also taken root in South African matric exams, defeats not only the developmental purpose of schooling, but also the economic imperative of a better-educated labour force.

In the light of this, Taylor argues for a more balanced set of performance indicators that include pass rates, but which are driven also by the imperatives of quality, equity and opportunity. Without measures that incorporate these values, pass rates will continue to render an inaccurate picture of progress (or otherwise) within the education system.

Russell Wildeman, in the second indicator-related piece, contends that the introduction of uniform school rankings, by means of league tables, would disadvantage poor schools. The intakes of schools in traditionally poor areas are characterised by a learner profile that has had less exposure to additional educational resources, and hence these schools start at a disadvantage to their more affluent peers. This also has a bearing on teaching outcomes, resulting in teachers in poor schools often being branded, unfairly, as lazy and inefficient. Wildeman proposes that more resources be invested in data-gathering that tracks school effects (the value that schooling adds to aggregate levels of education in schools with particular socio-economic backgrounds), as opposed to blunt uniform standards that value final outcomes but not achievement.

Chapter 4: Poverty and inequality

Ultimately, poverty and inequality remain the core indicators of South Africa's social transformation, because the struggle against apartheid oppression was, more than anything else, a struggle for human dignity.

Arden Finn, Murray Leibbrandt and Eva Wegner show in their overview article that while some inroads have been made in terms of poverty alleviation over the past 17 years, inequality levels have been exacerbated; and, today, South Africa is, arguably, the most unequal emerging state. Their exploration hones in on the primary drivers of inequality, and finds that the character of the South African labour market has managed to keep patterns of skewed distribution intact. The authors' analysis shows that employment rates in the top income deciles have remained higher than those in lower income groups. Since 1993, and especially since 2000, unemployment has actually declined in the upper categories. Those in lower income categories, however, have experienced a sharp increase in unemployment. Given the country's oversupply of unskilled and low-skilled labour, its overall unemployment rate has increased by a substantial margin, with significant consequences for equity. Without solving the labour market question, they argue, South Africa will not solve the inequality question.

These employment patterns are stubbornly entrenched, and the article asks to what extent fiscal redistribution has been successful in addressing the roots of inequality. Their focus falls on education as the primary driver of opportunity within the labour market. The data that they present show slow progress towards the objective of broadened access to quality education, despite high levels of resource mobilisation. In some instances, the performance of formerly disadvantaged schools has declined, and the gap between their performance and that of schools in privileged areas has actually increased. They ascribe this to various factors. Firstly, there is the unequal

starting point for measurement, due to the persistent legacy of apartheid underdevelopment. Secondly, and linked to this, is the nature of South Africa's compromise political transition, which constrained far-reaching corrective policy. Thirdly, they mention the scourge of corruption and maladministration within the government. Finally, it is argued that the equalisation of teacher salaries, which took on a political character in the first years after the transition, saw salary expenditure consume a disproportionate slice of the education budget.

Therefore, while the constraints on spending have been significant, the data lead the authors to ask whether education has indeed been a primary priority for the government. Following on this, they question whether there has been enough commitment to greater equity between schools that serve affluent and disadvantaged communities. The consequence of inequitable spending in schooling, they contend, is the inevitable reinforcement of inequitable development.

The final opinion section of this year's publication asks whether social development policy can contribute to rectifying unequal development at a time when resources are under particular strain. In recent years, the term 'developmental state' has been much bandied about in economic policy-making circles. In essence, the concept refers to a state that seeks to play an active role in promoting development through the alignment of policies in various spheres of government. What form it takes depends on the particular challenges, but ultimately the characterisation of a state as such depends on its capacity to effect change through the instruments at its disposal.

Patrick Bond maintains that the country's current develop-mental model – which has been fashioned according to the prescriptions of global financial institutions that have shown themselves to be out touch with developmental realities – has reached its expiry date. It requires a fundamental reconfiguration of thinking about how economies ought to function to address human needs. Using the issue of climate change, and its impact on the poor as a prism, Bond suggests that somehow the courage for bolder steps seems to be absent. In this regard, he notes that the NDP represents a missed opportunity to confront the country's development challenges head-on.

In the second opinion contribution to the chapter, Vusi Gumede reviews the South African state's developmental achievements over the past 17 years. He finds that although present-day South Africa is a decidedly better place to live in than its apartheid predecessor, its unequal development track record does not suggest that the term 'developmental' is an appropriate characterisation of our state. While progressing towards a stage where it could wield more influence over development, Gumede suggests that a more appropriate description at this stage may be that of a 'developmental state in the making'.

Chapter 5: Public opinion on human security

This final chapter is a new addition to the Transformation Audit. If we assume that the ultimate objective of economic transformation is an improved sense of well-being and dignity in citizens, then it is important to understand how they feel about their economic disposition and to track it over time. In a recent Organisation for Economic Co-operation and Development (OECD) publication, titled *Social cohesion in a shifting world*, it is argued that the perception as much as the reality of inequality in development is a driving factor of social instability.[8] Within this context, the new section serves to complement the macro picture that is presented elsewhere in this publication.

The opinion data are derived from the IJR's own SA Reconciliation Barometer Survey, which is conducted annually on a national basis with a representative sample of the South African population. The selected figures in this section show how perceptions of well-being have varied in recent years and how they have largely correlated with economic fluctuations.

From Inequality to Inclusive Growth

This collection of articles asks how we set goals and achieve them in a global climate that is hostile, unpredictable and a threat to painstakingly achieved gains. For close to two decades, South African researchers have done exhaustive analyses of the developmental challenges that this country faces. We have embarked on bold scenario exercises and, over the past two years, in particular, forward-looking strategies have been crafted to address these challenges. Courage is now needed to take decisions on which strategies to follow and which to jettison. Either way, the country needs clear objectives to pursue at a juncture where we cannot afford to waste time. As in previous years, this publication seeks to contribute in this regard by providing analysis and provoking debate by South Africa's foremost thinkers.

Notes

1. *The Economist*, Staring into the abyss, 12–18 November 2011.

2. See *The Guardian*, Euro bailout wrangles spook markets as fears of slump intensify. Available at: www.guardian.co.uk/world/2011/oct/25/euro-bailout-wrangles-spook-markets [accessed 29 November 2011].

3. Business Live (2011) *Human Development as Important as GDP: Gordhan*. Available at: www.businesslive.co.za/southafrica/sa_generalnews/2011/10/17/human-development-as-important-as-gdp-gordhan [accessed 27 November 2011].

4. National Treasury (2011) *Medium-Term Budget Statement 2011*. Available at: www.treasury.gov.za/documents/mtbps/2011/mtbps/speech.pdf [accessed 28 November 2011].

5. South Africa Government Online, *The New Growth Path*. Available at: www.info.gov.za/view/DownloadFileAction?id=135748 [accessed 29 November 2011].

6. Since the release of the NDP occurred at a time when this publication was being finalised, it does not contain a comprehensive response to the entire document. Where appropriate, authors have engaged with it in their contributions. In 2012, however, the IJR's Inclusive Economies Project will engage with individual proposals through its Policy Brief series.

7. *The Freedom Charter*. Available at: http://www.anc.org.za/show.php?id=72 [accessed 29 November 2011].

8. OECD (2011) *Perspectives on global development 2012: Social cohesion in a shifting world*. OECD Publishing.

Chapter 1

Economic Governance

Despite the deep economic and social
divisions facing South Africa, economic
policy between 1994 and 2010 showed
remarkable stability.

The Economy at a Glance

South Africa experienced robust GDP growth since the turn of the millennium, albeit at lower levels than most of its peer emerging markets. Lagging behind the global recession, it briefly dipped into a recession in 2009 that had a severe impact on the country's fragile labour market, but returned again to growth in 2010. As a result of tight fiscal management, the country has for most of the previous decade managed to reduce its budget deficit and recorded surpluses in the two years prior to the recession. Due to slow growth in the years since, government revenues have shrunk, resulting once again in a widening of the deficit. Against this background, the country's debt to GDP ratio has increased steadily by 9 percentage points from 27 per cent in 2008 to an estimated 36 per cent in 2011, to finance government expenditure.

3.1%

South Africa's projected GDP growth for 2011

SOUTH AFRICA YEAR-ON-YEAR GDP GROWTH SINCE 1994

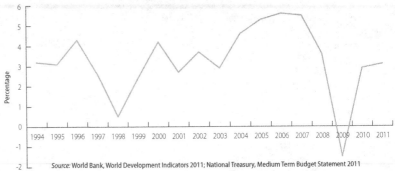

Source: World Bank, World Development Indicators 2011; National Treasury, Medium Term Budget Statement 2011

South Africa's gross debt to GDP ratio in comparative perspective								
	2005	**2006**	**2007**	**2008**	**2009**	**2010**	**2011 (est.)**	**Estimates start after**
Brazil	69%	67%	65%	64%	68%	67%	65%	2010
China	18%	16%	20%	17%	18%	34%	27%	2010
India	79%	75%	73%	73%	69%	64%	62%	2010
Indonesia	46%	40%	37%	33%	29%	27%	25%	2010
Mexico	40%	38%	38%	43%	45%	43%	43%	2010
Nigeria	29%	12%	13%	12%	15%	17%	16%	2009
Russia	14%	9%	9%	8%	11%	12%	12%	2010
South Africa	34%	31%	27%	27%	31%	34%	36%	2010

Source: International Monetary Fund: World Economic Outlook September 2011
Note: Gross debt consists of all liabilities that require payment or payments of interest and/or principal by the debtor to the creditor at a date or dates in the future. This includes debt liabilities in the form of SDRs, currency and deposits, debt securities, loans, insurance, pensions and standardised guarantee schemes, and other accounts payable. Thus, all liabilities in the GFSM 2001 system are debt, except for equity and investment fund shares and financial derivatives and employee stock options. Debt can be valued at current market, nominal, or face values (GFSM 2001, paragraph 7.110).

SOUTH AFRICA'S GDP PER CAPITA IN COMPARATIVE PERSPECTIVE, 2010

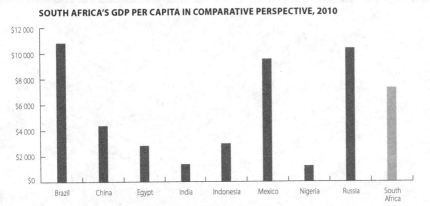

Source: International Monetary Fund: World Economic Outlook September 2011
Note: GDP is expressed in current US dollars per person. Data are derived by first converting GDP in national currency to US dollars and then dividing it by total population.

US$ 7 274

South Africa's GDP per capita income

GDP growth by main sectors of the South African economy

Sector	2007	2008	2009	2010
Primary	0.6%	-0.1%	-3.9%	4.3%
Agriculture	2.7%	16.1%	-3.0%	0.9%
Mining	0.0%	-5.6%	-4.2%	5.8%
Secondary	6.2%	3.0%	-7.1%	4.1%
Manufacturing	5.2%	2.6%	-10.4%	5.0%
Electricity	3.4%	-3.1%	-1.6%	2.0%
Construction	14.0%	9.5%	7.4%	1.5%
Tertiary	6.1%	4.5%	0.7%	2.2%
Wholesale and retail	5.3%	0.8%	-2.5%	2.2%
Transport	6.6%	3.4%	0.6%	2.9%
Finance	7.9%	7.3%	9.0%	1.9%
Government services	4.0%	4.5%	4.1%	3.0%
Personal services	5.6%	3.9%	-0.3%	0.6%
GDP growth	5.6%	3.6%	-1.7%	2.8%

Source: South African Reserve Bank, *Quarterly Bulletin* No.260, June 2011

South Africa's GDP growth in comparative perspective

	2006	2007	2008	2009	2010
Brazil	4.0%	6.1%	5.2%	-0.6%	7.5%
China	12.7%	14.2%	9.6%	9.2%	10.3%
India	9.3%	9.8%	4.9%	9.1%	9.7%
Indonesia	5.5%	6.3%	6.0%	4.6%	6.1%
Nigeria	6.2%	6.4%	6.0%	7.0%	7.9%
Russian Federation	8.2%	8.5%	5.2%	-7.8%	4.0%
South Africa	5.6%	5.6%	3.6%	-1.7%	2.8%

Source: World Bank: World Development Indicators 2010

5.0%
South Africa's official inflation rate for 2011

SOUTH AFRICA'S BUDGET BALANCE AS A PERCENTAGE OF GDP

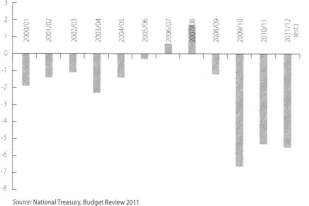

Source: National Treasury, Budget Review 2011

CPI INFLATION RATE, 2005–2011

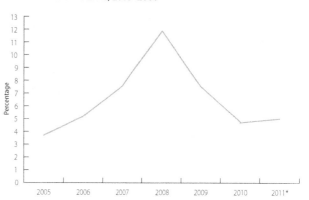

Source: Stats SA – www.statssa.gov.za, accessed 30/11/2011
Note: * Source for 2011: SA Treasury, MTBS 2011

BUDGET EXPENDITURE OF THE 2011/12 BUDGET (R BILLION)

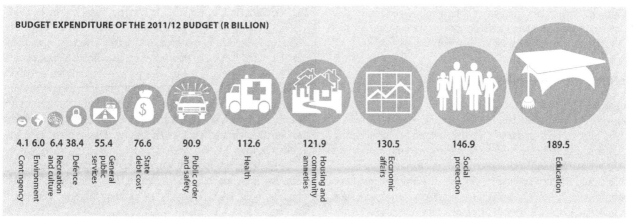

4.1	6.0	6.4	38.4	55.4	76.6	90.9	112.6	121.9	130.5	146.9	189.5
Contingency	Environment	Recreation and culture	Defence	General public services	State debt cost	Public order and safety	Health	Housing and community amenities	Economic affairs	Social protection	Education

Source: National Treasury, Budget Review 2011

REVIEW | 'If you want peace, fight for justice': Economic policy in a divided society

Neva Makgetla

In the course of South Africa's second decade of democracy, conflicts around economic policy intensified. While poverty levels declined, deep inequalities persisted, largely but not entirely along the lines of race, class and geography established under apartheid. That, in turn, provided fertile ground for disagreement about national economic strategies.

After 1994, the economy recovered from the very slow rates of growth and investment that had characterised the previous 15 years; yet, levels of joblessness and inequality continued to rank amongst the worst in the world. Mining and finance dominated economic growth, resulting in a deeply inequitable distribution of the benefits. Rapid employment growth emerged between 2000 and 2008, mostly in retail and services, but even more rapid job losses followed in the period 2008–2010. Thereafter, the fragility of the recovery in the global North constrained prospects for growth and employment.

Ultimately, the democratic state faced the dual challenge of making the economy more competitive while simultaneously improving conditions for employment and equity. In the late '00s, economic policy increasingly prioritised support for employment creation as central to enhanced equality. That laid the basis for more coherent economic strategies. Still, a deadlock over implementation remained a real risk. It arose largely from the fragmentation of the state, which ended up substantially mirroring the deep economic divisions in society.

This article first reviews trends in growth, investment, employment and equity since 1994. It then surveys some of the domestic and global factors underlying these trends. The third, and final, part summarises the implicit economic pact that led to extraordinarily stable economic policies for most of the democratic era, despite intense public debates.

Economic trends after 1994

In many ways, South Africa's economic record after 1994 looked like a poster child for democracy. After a decade of stagnation, growth and investment recovered to global norms. Fiscal redistribution provided new services and support for the poorest households, especially in the former bantustans. Nonetheless, participation in the formal economy remained extraordinarily inequitable. High levels of joblessness declined somewhat in the prolonged upswing of the '00s, but returned

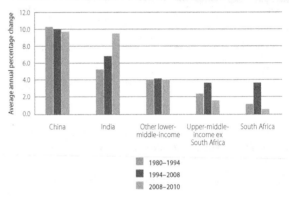

Figure 1.1.1: Growth in South Africa and other upper- and lower-middle-income economies, 1980–2010

Legend:
- 1980–1994
- 1994–2008
- 2008–2010

Source: Calculated from World Bank (2011)

to their original levels following extraordinary job losses in 2008–2010.

From 1994 until 2008, the South African economy grew almost exactly at the average for middle-income economies excluding China and India. In contrast, over the previous 15 years it had expanded at only half the norm for peer economies. The 2008 downturn saw a fall in GDP followed by a slower recovery than that of other middle-income economies.

Investment

The democratic era also saw a turnaround for investment, as Figure 1.1.2 shows. Investment fell from 27 per cent of the GDP in 1982 to 15 per cent in 1993. It remained fairly stagnant until the early '00s, but then climbed steadily to 23 per cent in 2008. The downturn meant that private investment dropped by close to 10 per cent between 2008 and mid-2011, although public investment – around a third of the total – climbed by 15 per cent. As a result, total investment dropped by 1.6 per cent and the investment rate fell to just under 18 per cent in the first half of 2011.

The improvement in growth and investment after 1994 was, however, not matched by a similar recovery in equity and employment. That, in turn, led to a steady increase in political strains.

Inequality

Reliable data on income distribution are difficult to obtain everywhere, because households find it hard to assess their income accurately, and a substantial share (in South Africa, typically between 5 per cent and 10 per cent) do not answer income surveys. Furthermore, Statistics South Africa's annual General Household Survey groups together all households earning over R20 000 a month, which accounted for the richest 8 per cent of households in 2010. As a result, estimates of income for the top decile can vary substantially. The Income and Expenditure Survey is more detailed but comes out only every five years, most recently in 2005/6. Finally, because statistics before 1994 largely excluded Africans, new survey systems had to be established, making the data for the late 1990s particularly untrustworthy.

Despite these caveats, the available surveys show that South Africa remained amongst the most inequitable countries in the world, with a Gini coefficient hovering just under .70.[1] The World Bank's World Development Indicators reported a Gini coefficient for only half of all countries in the '00s; of those, South Africa had the worst income distribution. The available surveys suggest that inequality worsened in the late 1990s (when the surveys were least reliable, however) but stabilised in the '00s.

Employment

The transition to democracy did little to alleviate the high rates of joblessness that emerged in the 1980s, although it brought a turnaround in the rapid deterioration in employment of the previous 15 years. As can be seen in Figure 1.1.4, the share of working-age people with employment fell steadily from the late 1970s through the mid-1990s. The boom of the '00s saw some improvement, with the creation of 2.5 million new jobs increasing the employment ratio to 45 per cent. However, the loss of around a million jobs in 2008/09, combined with the growth in the working-age population, meant that the employment ratio fell back to just over 40 per cent.

In sum, for most of the past decade only around two adults out of five in South Africa have been employed or self-employed. In contrast, the global norm is around three out of five. Unemployment was closely linked to the spatial inequalities left by apartheid. Some 35 per cent of the population, and 44 per cent of Africans, still lived in the former bantustans in 2010. Only 22 per cent of working-age adults in these areas had employment, however, compared to 48 per cent in the rest of the economy. Moreover, incomes for the employed tended to be lower than they were elsewhere. As a result, in 2010, the median household income in the former bantustans was

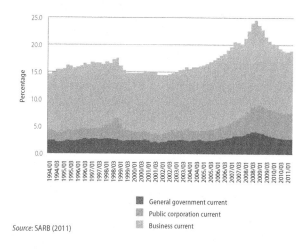

Figure 1.1.2: Investment by type of organisation as a percentage of GDP, 1994–2011

Legend:
- General government current
- Public corporation current
- Business current

Source: SARB (2011)

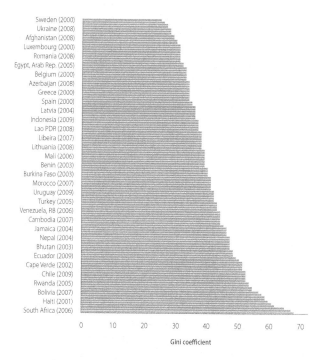

Figure 1.1.3: Reported Gini coefficients internationally and in South Africa, 2000–2009*

Source: World Bank (2011)

Note: *Only 130 out of 219 countries covered by the World Bank's World Development Indicators reported a Gini coefficient in the '00s. The year of the reported Gini is in parentheses following the country's name. Not all the names of countries appear due to lack of space.

Surveys show that South Africa remained amongst the most inequitable countries in the world.

> The economy's vulnerability resulted from the continued dependence on the mining value chain, combined with a surge in financialisation, driven by extraordinarily large inflows of portfolio capital.

R1 580, compared to R3 080 in the rest of the country (Stats SA 2011a for settlement patterns and median household incomes; Stats SA 2011b for employment status).

Unequal gains

Given growth with constant, although high, inequality, poverty as measured by international poverty lines declined substantially between 1994 and 2008. Again, the data for the 1990s are not fully reliable.[2] While not providing income data, the 1996 October Household Survey found that two-thirds of households spent less than R1 100, which was approximately equal to US$2 per person, or the international poverty line, for a household of five (Stats SA 1996). In 2009, in contrast, the General Household Survey found that only around a third of households lived on the equivalent amount. That was around R1 580 for a household of four, which was used because household size fell in the period (Stats SA 2010a). Moreover, the income data do not show the improvements in government services and housing in poor communities, which further enhanced living standards.

The disproportionate gains of the very well-off during this period, however, effectively overshadowed the real benefits for the poor, and fuelled broad discontent with economic outcomes despite improvements for the majority.

The downturn from 2008 saw an increase in poverty. According to the General Household Survey, the share of households living on less than US$2 a day per person increased slightly, to just over a third, from 2009 to 2010. Moreover, the median household income fell from R2 510 to R2 450 per month in nominal terms. Taking inflation into account, that meant a fall of 9 per cent (Stats SA 2010a, 2011a).

In short, while the transition to democracy brought a substantial economic dividend in terms of growth and investment, the deeply inequitable economy that was created under apartheid largely persisted. Moreover, the downturn from 2008 saw a substantial worsening in unemployment and poverty. In the following three years, despite some recovery, significant instability and generally weak economies in the global North meant that growth in South Africa also slowed, making it even more difficult to address mass joblessness and inequality.

Factors behind lasting inequality

The global downturn demonstrated the shortcomings of the growth path from 1994. In particular, the unusually large job losses – equal to 6 per cent of total employment – pointed to fragility in employment creation. Ultimately, the economy's

Figure 1.1.4: Share of adults with employment, 1970–2010*

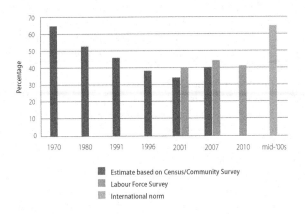

- Estimate based on Census/Community Survey
- Labour Force Survey
- International norm

Source: Calculated from Statistics South Africa. Census data for relevant years for RSA, Bophuthatswana, Ciskei and Venda. Downloaded from interactive data site (Nesstar facility) in August 2010; DBSA, data on population and employment in the RSA and TBVC, kindly provided in August 2010.

Note: *Before 1996, the Census did not fully cover Africans. Furthermore, the estimates tended to assume that virtually all adults in the former bantustans were employed as subsistence farmers. The figures here, therefore, represent estimates based on reinterpretations of the available data in line with more standard definitions.

Figure 1.1.5: Growth by sector, 1994–2010 (share of total value added in 2010 in brackets)

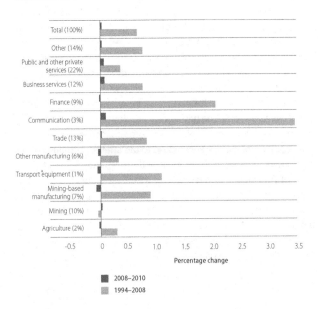

- 2008–2010
- 1994–2008

Source: Calculated from standardised industry data on value added at basic prices, downloaded from Quantec EasyData, October 2011.

vulnerability resulted from the continued dependence on the mining value chain, combined with a surge in financialisation, driven by extraordinarily large inflows of portfolio capital. The result was a persistently strong and volatile rand, which discouraged exports and made imports cheaper. This hampered diversification into new forms of production. Inequality skewed domestic demand, so that employment grew primarily in services for relatively well-off households and in the public sector.

From 1994 to 2010, the mining value chain provided more than half of all exports, but its overall growth was relatively slow. In contrast, the financial sector grew extraordinarily fast. It was outstripped only by the communications industry, which remained far smaller. The share of the financial sector in total value added increased from 7 per cent in 1994 to 11 per cent in 2008, before falling back to 9 per cent in the global downturn. Communications contributed only 3 per cent of value added in 2011. The financial sector accounted for almost a fifth of total economic growth after 1994.

Growth in the financial sector was underpinned by peculiarly high portfolio inflows, which followed the opening up of the economy from 1989. Between 1994 and 2008, portfolio inflows to the stock market equalled 2.9 per cent of GDP – a far higher proportion than for virtually any other middle-income economy. In this period, South Africa accounted for 0.5 per cent of global production, but received 1.0 per cent of all portfolio equity investment worldwide. In contrast, it received only 0.2 per cent of foreign direct investment (i.e. investment where the foreign partner obtains a controlling interest of at least 10 per cent). Foreign direct investment (FDI) equalled just 1.3 per cent of South Africa's GDP. While South Africa ranked first among the 47 upper-middle-income economies that reported on portfolio inflows relative to GDP, it found itself fifth from the bottom for FDI as a percentage of GDP (World Bank 2011; see also Ahmed, Arzeki & Funke 2007).

A comparison with Brazil, Russia, India and China (the so-called BRIC economies) underscores South Africa's unique position (see Figure 1.1.6). In these countries, portfolio investment ranged from 0.5 per cent of GDP in Russia to 1.1 per cent of GDP in India between 1994 and 2008. In contrast, FDI equalled 1.1 per cent of the GDP in India and 2.5 per cent in China.

As capital inflows boosted the value of the rand, producers of goods and services other than finance faced growing hurdles in both exporting and competing with imports. Between 1994 and 2010, exports of goods and services exceeded imports only in 2001 and 2002. In 2008, the trade deficit peaked at 7 per cent of GDP, before falling to 2.8 per cent in 2010.

High levels of portfolio investment also fed into a bubble on the stock market. By 2010, the market value of companies listed on the JSE was almost 300 per cent of GDP (an increase from 166 per cent in 1994).

The size of market capitalisation compared to GDP was uniquely high in South Africa. Of the 100 countries covered by World Bank data for 2010, the figure for South Africa was exceeded only by Hong Kong. In 2010, the average ratio of market capitalisation to GDP for the world as a whole was 90 per cent. The BRIC countries ranged from a high of 81 per cent for China to a low of 68 per cent for Russia (World Bank 2011).

Growth in the financial sector was also associated with rapid expansion in domestic credit (see Figure 1.1.7), with credit to the private sector climbing from 56 per cent of the GDP in 1994 to a high of 87 per cent in 2008 before dropping to 78 per cent in the downturn (see DTI 2011; Mohamed 2009).

The share of credit to business in total private borrowing rose from 40 per cent in 1994 to 55 per cent in 2003, but then fell back to around 50 per cent as bank loans to households boomed in the late '00s. Rich families dominated household borrowing, with the best-off 10 per cent of households accounting for around 90 per cent of all credit (almost entirely for houses and cars) in the mid-'00s (Stats SA 2006).

The growth of the financial sector was associated with a disproportionate increase in net operating surplus – returns to capital after depreciation – for the industry. From 1994 to 2008, the net operating surplus in finance rose at an average of 16 per cent a year, surpassed only by communications, where it climbed 24 per cent a year. In contrast, surpluses in agriculture, mining and manufacturing rose just 3 per cent a year, and in the rest of the economy around 6 per cent. The financial sector captured over a quarter of the increase in net operating surplus for the economy as a whole between 1994 and 2008.

The financialisation of the economy largely explained the relatively sharp impact of the 2008 downturn on South Africa.

Firstly, the financial institutions reduced their credit extension sharply with the global downturn. In real terms, loans to businesses fell by 9 per cent in 2008/09 before growing slowly by 0.5 per cent in the following year. This fall contributed to the decline in investment and growth. In addition, loans to households fell by 3 per cent in 2008/09 and then grew 3.3 per cent in the following year.[3]

Secondly, the dependence on short-term portfolio inflows left the country vulnerable to rapid changes in investor sentiment. The stock exchange experienced a sharp fall in value in 2008 as foreign capital fled to safer havens overseas, but the very relaxed monetary policies adopted in the global North in

Between 1994 and 2010, exports of goods and services exceeded imports only in 2001 and 2002.

response to the crisis soon saw a recovery. Revived short-term capital inflows led to a strong and highly volatile rand, which, in turn, depressed growth in the rest of the economy.

More fundamentally, large financial inflows combined with booming commodity prices in the first decade of the new millennium hampered diversification in the rest of the economy. The mineral value chain continued to dominate exports, accounting for around 60 per cent of merchandise exports from 1994 through 2010 (see Figure 1.1.8). The production of gold fell substantially, but platinum, iron ore and coal sales rose strongly. As platinum created far fewer jobs than gold mining, this shift contributed to an ongoing decline in employment in mining overall despite the rising value of exports.

Outside the mining value chain, only the auto industry substantially expanded its exports. It enjoyed very large tax subsidies, however, accounting (by various estimates) for between half and three-quarters of all industrial subsidies provided by the state.

Figures for profitability underscore the difficulties facing diversification, with relatively low gains in mining outside of mineral beneficiation and the auto industry. From 1994 to 2008, the net operating surplus in smelting and refining rose by 7.6 per cent a year, and in transport equipment, by 5.2 per cent. In the rest of manufacturing – mostly food processing, clothing, wood and paper production, appliances and capital goods production – the net operating surplus rose only 1.5 per cent a year in this period. In agriculture, the net operating surplus grew 4.0 per cent a year, falling from 9.0 per cent of the total in 1994 to 5.0 per cent in 2008.[4]

The 2008 downturn underscored the risks of continued over-dependence on mining. Smelting and refining saw a particularly sharp fall in profitability and production, due partly to the decline in export demand and partly to the soaring cost of electricity as South Africa reached the limits of its generation capacity. While commodity prices recovered relatively rapidly, the strong rand and high electricity prices continued to drag on the beneficiation sector. Indeed, the shift to expensive electricity necessitated a fundamental shift away from heavy industry, even as it benefited from high commodity prices. However, given the strong rand and comparatively low profitability in other sectors, it was difficult to identify viable alternatives.

The production structure that emerged from the growth of the financial sector and continued dependence on mining, generally, led to rapid expansion in employment in the '00s, but largely in sectors characterised by considerable insecurity. This pattern of employment creation largely explains the sharp fall in employment in 2008 and 2009.

Again, the data for the 1990s on employment are poor, making it hard to assess trends from 1994. Estimates suggest that agricultural employment shrank by half, or by more than a million jobs between 1994 and 2008, while mining jobs fell by around 100 000 and manufacturing employment remained virtually unchanged.[5] Meanwhile, most new jobs after 1994

Figure 1.1.6: Net flows of portfolio equity, public and private bonds and foreign direct investment as a percentage of GDP for the BRICS, 1994–2007 and 2008–2010

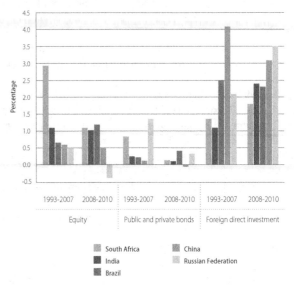

Source: World Bank (2011)

Figure 1.1.7: Credit to households and the rest of the private sector relative to GDP, 1994–2010

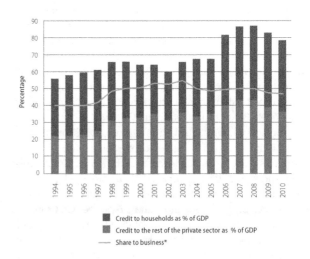

Source: SARB (2011)

Note: *The share to business is defined here as the share of total credit to the private sector that does not go to households.

The question became whether the fragmented economic policy institutions of the state could consistently support more vigorous efforts to encourage employment creation and equity.

were created in services and retail for high-end consumers, where employment is particularly sensitive to economic trends, and in the public sector. Retail, business and community services contributed virtually all net new employment between 1994 and 2008. Security guards alone accounted for 12 per cent of all new formal jobs created between 2002 and 2010 (Stats SA 2002, 2010c).

The slow growth of employment in the financial sector was particularly marked in the light of its rapid growth. The industry's contribution to GDP tripled between 1994 and 2008, but employment in the sector climbed by only 14 per cent, to make up just 4 per cent of non-agricultural employment growth. In other words, while the financialisation of the economy slowed growth and employment creation outside of the financial sector, finance itself did relatively little to generate new jobs.

The picture for smelting and refining was similar. The industry contributed 11 per cent of the growth in value added from 1994 to 2008, but lost jobs in the process. In 2008, it contributed an estimated 8 per cent of value added but only 4 per cent of employment.

Stagnant employment in the economy's growth industries contributed to a steady decline in the share of remuneration relative to profits in total value added. While employees in government and manufacturing captured a higher share of returns from 1994, overall, and in particular in mining, the share of remuneration in total value added fell in the democratic era (see Figure 1.1.9).

In sum, while growth and investment recovered between 1994 and 2008, they remained centred on mining and, increasingly, the financial sector. The result was that production and employment proved even more vulnerable to external shocks like that experienced in 2008. Relatively slow growth in more labour-intensive manufacturing, high-level services and agriculture meant that there was little qualitative change in the economic opportunities open to the majority of South Africans. In these circumstances, growth did little to address the deep inequalities left by apartheid.

Inequality and economic strategies

Despite the deep economic and social divisions facing South Africa, economic policy between 1994 and 2010 showed remarkable stability.[6] In effect, this can be understood as reflecting a durable social pact in which government policy provided something for all the major stakeholders. Persistent inequalities placed this pact under increasing pressure, however, as widespread expectations of more fundamental

Figure 1.1.8: Merchandise exports by industry, 1994–2010

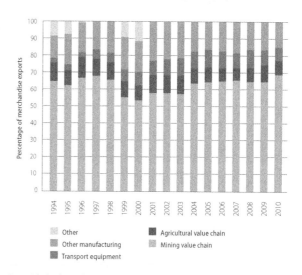

Source: Calculated using data on exports (2-digit SIC), downloaded from Quantec EasyData, October 2011.

Figure 1.1.9: Share of remuneration in total value added by major industries, 1994–2010*

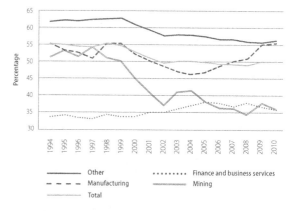

Source: Stats SA (2011c)

Note: *Remuneration includes payments to managers, which may include an element of profits.

Table 1.1.1: Summary of broad policy phases, 1994–2010

Policy document	Aim/central argument	Ownership	Employment	Government services	Economic infrastructure	Trade policy	Fiscal/ monetary
RDP (1994)	Growth through redistribution through the fiscus	Support SMMEs, land reform, housing subsidies	Result of broader development strategy	Improved services in black communities critical for equity and to stimulate demand	Not seen as a problem – emphasis on improving housing and related infrastructure in black communities	Open the economy and support exports through supply-side measures	Maintain existing ratios – meaning, above all, budget deficit to GDP
GEAR (1997)	Reassure capital especially by reducing the budget deficit	Privatise large state-owned enterprises	Result of accelerated economic growth and pay restraint in the public sector	Expenditure constrained by deficit target	Same	Same	Reduce budget deficit to 3 per cent
Post-GEAR (2000)	More expansionary fiscal and monetary stance	No explicit shifts	Result of broader development	Relatively rapid expansion, especially in social grants	Same	Same	Expansion in government spending primarily due to more efficient tax collection and reduced interest rates; inflation targeting introduced to relax monetary policy
AsgiSA (2005)	More inclusive growth based on government infrastructure spend, sector strategies and skills development	Greater support for SMMEs and skilling, and stronger and more strategic approach to competition policy	Accelerate through sector strategies, SMMEs and skills	Same	Core economic infrastructure seen as major constraint on growth	Increasingly protectionist in response to Doha demands	Same, plus call for more competitive exchange rate
Crisis response (2008/09)	Counter-cyclical package plus efforts to limit formal-sector retrenchment	Support for major companies	Active labour market policies plus targeted sector rescues	No reduction despite 10 per cent drop in revenues	Maintain infrastructure programmes despite financing problems	Same	Counter-cyclical fiscal strategy and call for more competitive exchange rate
New Growth Path (2011)	Government must reduce unnecessary costs to business but more vigorously support economic equity, especially through employment creation	Intensify strategic competition policy aimed at reducing costs on intermediate and wage goods; support for small-scale agriculture and social economy	Accelerate, above all, through diversification into more labour-inten-sive activities (light industry, agriculture, high-end services)	Review to ensure more consistent support for employment creation	High public investment as key growth driver	Increasingly shift toward region and global South especially given slowdown in traditional partners	Same; much greater emphasis on local procurement as a driver of diversification

Note: RDP = Reconstruction and Development Programme; GEAR = Growth, Employment and Redistribution; AsgiSA = Accelerated and Shared Growth Initiative for South Africa.

The fragmentation of the state itself made rigorous implementation of new policies difficult, while the global economic downturn reduced the resources available to finance new initiatives.

change remained unfulfilled. The question became whether the fragmented economic policy institutions of the state could consistently support more vigorous efforts to encourage employment creation and equity.

We can define phases in the state's broad approach to development largely in terms of major policy documents. As Table 1.1.1 shows, every phase had in common a commitment to maintaining the core elements of a market economy while gradually bringing about greater equity.

The following areas of continuity and change in economic policy stand out.

» The RDP contended essentially that improvements in government services to black communities would in themselves ensure a more inclusive economy. This theme increasingly gave way to an emphasis on measures to reform the production structure and ownership, mostly through various subsidies combined with targeted government procurement. The shift emerged together with a growing emphasis on employment creation in the rhetoric of the documents.

» At least until AsgiSA, the government generally took the core formal economy for granted, focusing its efforts on ensuring greater equity without causing major disruptions. It effectively saw the main concession to business as its protection of property rights. It, therefore, felt free to abruptly end many subsidies, including on economic infrastructure. The result was rising costs in key industries, especially for electricity and transport, combined with a decline in the quality of economic infrastructure. AsgiSA reversed this tendency by emphasising the need to address core constraints on business. The New Growth Path strongly emphasises the need to reduce unnecessary costs to enterprise while maintaining pressure for diversification in ways that would support employment creation.

» Social services remained largely delinked from economic needs, in contrast to the RDP's argument that they should be shaped to support economic development. This emerged, for instance, in the location of RDP housing far from economic opportunities, the failure to address core quality issues in education in poor communities, and the escalating health care costs that raised employment costs. Furthermore, the bureaucratic provision of services to individuals and households, with very little opportunity for more transparent or collective decision-making and responsibility, created fertile ground for anger and unrest over perceived unfairness and shortcomings.

» The strategy, as perceived by the public and stakeholders, usually diverged quite fundamentally from the written texts, which generally included many programmes that were never implemented. For instance, GEAR included a host of proposals around redistribution and equity, including restraint on public servants' pay to permit more rapid expansion in public sector employment, and AsgiSA specified strong sector strategies as a major vehicle for employment creation.

» Only the crisis response in 2008 and the New Growth Path began to include measures around emissions as an important part of economic strategy. However, the issue appeared mostly in terms of green jobs rather than as part of a fundamental shift away from an emissions-intensive economy.

In effect, the stability of economic policy resulted from an implicit social pact through which the state managed: the divergence between economic power, still located predominantly in large businesses; the political power wielded by the majority of voters, who remained mostly poor and largely jobless; and the social and lobbying strength of black businesspeople. It, therefore, provided the following:

» For business, only incremental change in the structures of ownership, production and residential areas, combined with a strong commitment to maintaining property rights and core economic infrastructure.

» A combination of social and housing grants to improve conditions for the most marginalised. By 2010, a fifth of all households and two-fifths of households in the former bantustans said that social grants were their main source of income (Stats SA 2011a).

» For the urban working-class, labour rights on the European model, significant improvements in infrastructure and desegregation of historically white institutions and areas.

» For black business and graduates, vastly expanded opportunities through BEE policies in the private sector and employment practices in the public sector.

This social pact was maintained through state policies, rather than being formalised as an agreement to pursue a common development strategy that would bring costs as well as benefits to participants. In this context, policy debates tended to revolve around a zero-sum approach, rather than a search for mutually beneficial compromises. In essence, they reflected the efforts of different stakeholders to modify the underlying social pact in their favour. Participants regularly threatened to resort to power, with business invariably warning of capital flight, while labour organised general strikes and community representatives pointed to rising civil unrest.

The government did not consciously design the social pact to mirror the economy. Rather, the extreme fragmentation of economic policy-making meant that it largely reflected the balance of economic, political and social power in the broader society.

Economic policy-making was divided amongst a host of state entities: sectoral economic departments at national level; co-ordinating departments such as the Treasury, the Economic Development Department and the Department of Rural Development and Land Reform; the Reserve Bank and other regulators; the development finance institutions and state-owned enterprises; and local and provincial governments.

Given this institutional fragmentation, it was easy for policy-makers to end up representing, not the majority in a democratic sense, but rather their key stakeholders. As a result, efforts to implement broad policy changes often got bogged down in inter-departmental debates.

By 2011, the weaknesses in the compromises that emerged after 1994 became increasingly clear, in part because of the sharp losses suffered by the majority in the economic downturn. Calls for nationalisation of the mines and expropriation of farms reflected frustration with the slow pace of change for the majority. The government responded by promising to do more to prioritise the needs of ordinary South Africans, through increased efforts to support employment creation, as reflected in the New Growth Path. However, the fragmentation of the state itself made rigorous implementation of new policies difficult, while the global economic downturn reduced the resources available to finance new initiatives.

Some conclusions

Both AsgiSA and the New Growth Path provided reasonable responses to the economic challenges facing South Africa. In effect, they emphasised the need to diversify the economy in ways that would open new opportunities for the marginalised majority, mostly through employment but also through support for small enterprise. However, it proved much easier to conceptualise a development strategy that would sustain growth while encouraging greater employment and equity than to implement it.

In large part, this situation reflected a vicious cycle common to deeply unequal societies. The divisions resulting from economic injustices in themselves make it more difficult to ensure consistent implementation of national strategies, as stakeholders lobby government departments to meet their specific needs. In South Africa, this weakness was accentuated by the fragmentation of the democratic state, which lent itself to endless debates and deadlocks between different government entities.

Notes

1. The higher the Gini coefficient, the more inequitable the economy. Statistics South Africa's 2005/6 Income and Expenditure Survey, which provides the most reliable income distribution data, used a somewhat unconventional calculation method to come up with a Gini slightly over .70. Using the more common international method, the figure was just under .70. Statistics South Africa's General Household Survey data for 2010 also give a figure of around .70, but the figure is very sensitive to how one estimates income for households earning over R20 000 a month. The data for both surveys are available from the interactive Nesstar database on www.statssa.gov.za.

2. Various authors give different figures for poverty trends, although they agree on a substantial decline. See, amongst others, Stats SA (2010b) and Presidency (2009), which should be treated with caution because some of the data are clearly mislabelled (for instance, the document refers to an Income Expenditure Survey 2008, but the survey was limited to 2005/06).

3. Calculated using data from SARB interactive data site on credit extension to the private sector and households, deflated using the CPI (accessed October 2011).

4. Calculated using Quantec EasyData figures for net operating surplus by standardised industry in constant 2005 rand (accessed October 2011).

5. Figures for employment from 1994 are from estimates for total employment in standardised industries by Quantec EasyData (accessed October 2011).

6. This analysis originated in research by the author for the Centre for Development and Enterprise in 2010.

OPINION | Nationalisation of mines

A NECESSARY STEP TOWARDS ECONOMIC LIBERATION

Chris Malikane

The mining sector has experienced phenomenal growth over the past ten years. Between 2002 and 2010, the rate of return on capital employed rose from 5 per cent to 18 per cent. Average price increases of leading revenue earners for 2010 – coal, copper, iron ore and gold – ranged from 26 per cent to 111 per cent (PwC 2011). These are massive real earnings per unit of minerals produced.

South Africa ranks seventh internationally in terms of coal and iron ore production, and fifth in terms of gold production. Yet, for all its mineral wealth, the country has little to show in terms for production output. Several peer countries, including some that also bore the brunt of colonialism, are outperforming South Africa, not only in terms of output volumes, but critically also in terms of developmental indicators, such as employment, poverty and inequality. These countries have one thing in common: significant state ownership in the mineral extraction sector. While others are steaming ahead on the road of economic development, South Africa seems to be caught in a rut of low growth and slow development.

The most perplexing part about the debate on nationalisation is that those who oppose nationalisation essentially seek to suppress it. The popular line is that nationalisation puts off investors. Not only is this a myth, it is also problematic in that it is not sensitive to the political economy that continues to define modern South African society. In addition, nationalisation's detractors tend to resort to scaremongering, conjuring up images of disaster, often based on selective evidence. In the process, they also present a false perspective regarding the performance of nationalised enterprises, and their role in economic development.

While acknowledging the scale of the inequality, poverty and unemployment that continue to afflict South African society, opponents of nationalisation sow fear about its implications. It will 'kill the goose that lays the golden eggs', and is unaffordable, they say. Instead, they propose job-creation and education as panaceas to our problems.

Such arguments sidestep the crucial point that is at the heart of the calls for nationalisation. The history of South Africa is the history of wholesale dispossession, the perfection of methods of extreme exploitation and gallant struggles of resistance against these evils. It is important to underline this fact,

because it places the debate about nationalisation in its concrete historical context. The call is not from some young man who woke up one day and thought it would be nice to sloganeer about nationalisation. This call can be found in the most important documents of all national liberation movements, particularly trade unions, that continue to envision a socialist South Africa.

Several reasons have been advanced against nationalisation, and alternatives have been proposed. This contribution furthers the argument that nationalisation is both necessary for industrialisation and important for sustainable job-creation. It exposes the counterposition of education and job-creation, on the one hand, and nationalisation, on the other, as a diversion from the real issues. Lastly, it concludes that, more than anything, the resistance to nationalisation is informed by deep-seated greed, which is founded on colonial exploitation of Africa's resources.

Nationalisation: a primer

Nationalisation is the transfer of privately owned assets into public ownership. In a democratic dispensation, the identification of the public with the state is resolved to a large extent, because the government that is at the head of the state is based on the will of the people. It is in this context that the clause in the *Freedom Charter* stating that 'the mineral wealth beneath the soil, the banks and monopoly industry shall be transferred to the ownership of the people as a whole' should be understood. Here, 'the people as a whole' are represented by the democratic state, the only structure that can justly claim such authority.

No class of people or section of the population can claim authority, unless it is based on the will of the people. Over the past 17 years, South Africa has undergone profound political changes. There is a democratic government that can justly claim to represent the people as a whole politically. However, the democratic government virtually disappears when it comes to economic transformation, particularly the ownership and control of assets in the economy on behalf of 'the people as a whole'. Over this period, attempts to shift ownership and control of the economy to a group of black people, the black bourgeoisie, not only have failed to deliver tangible socio-

> The true value in the nationalisation of the mines lies in downstream processing of mineral resources, the process of industrialisation.

economic upliftment to the vast majority of the people, but they have failed to meet the targets that were initially set.

This failure prompts us to recall the *Freedom Charter's* words that 'only a democratic state, based on the will of the people', can secure the birthright of the people; only a democratic state can secure the transfer of mineral, financial and industrial wealth to the ownership of the people as a whole. The idea of giving groups of black people ownership over critical aspects of the economy is a diversion from the *Freedom Charter*, because it places these groups above the democratic state, as representative of the people as a whole on matters of economic ownership and control of strategic sectors.

It is, therefore, illegitimate: (a) to equate black economic empowerment (BEE), which is a programme ostensibly aimed at de-racialising ownership and control, with a programme of democratisation of ownership and control; and (b) to extend BEE to sectors in which it should not be applied. The *Freedom Charter* calls for de-racialisation of the economy: 'people shall have equal rights to trade where they choose, to manufacture and to enter all trades, crafts and professions'. However, this kind of de-racialisation, which refers to the entrepreneurship of individuals or groups of individuals among the people, is envisioned to occur in 'all other industry and trade' (i.e. other than that which is supposed to be 'transferred to the people as a whole').

In short, the *Freedom Charter* calls for public ownership of mineral wealth beneath the soil, the banks and monopoly industry. The reason why it was deemed necessary to include this clause in the *Freedom Charter* was because it recognised that the apartheid government that claimed authority over the people was founded on robbery, injustice and inequality. The wholesale dispossession of the indigenous African population meant that major industries had to be placed in public owner-ship in order to address this historical injustice.

Those who oppose the nationalisation of the mines, in particular, are quick to point out that the *Freedom Charter* calls for nationalisation of mineral wealth beneath the soil, and that this has been achieved by the Mineral and Petroleum Resources Development Act 28 of 2002 (MPRDA). However, this is flawed, because mines are inseparable from mineral resources. No mine can exist without mineral resources; the current valuation methods for mines are based on discounting net cash flows from selling mineral wealth over the lifespan of the mine. Therefore, nationalisation of mineral wealth beneath the soil without nationalising the mines is impossible, because mines are the means of production through which minerals are extracted from the soil. Furthermore, large parts of the mining sector are dominated by monopolies or oligopolies,

which exert significant economic power; for example, the leading producers' market share in mineral production ranges from 24 per cent to 78 per cent.

Nationalisation for industrialisation

The true value in the nationalisation of the mines lies in downstream processing of mineral resources, the process of industrialisation. Opponents of nationalisation isolate the sector from the rest of the economy; they talk about creating jobs through 'growing the sector'. However, the only way to sustainably create jobs is to create linkages between domestic downstream manufacturing and the mining sector. Any other view is archaic and unsustainable. Economies grow more by adding value to raw minerals, or by producing high-value-added output, than by increasing physical output. It is in this context that the slogan, 'nationalisation for industrialisation' becomes important. It is also for this reason, and in this context, that nationalisation provides a platform for broad-based job creation.

In this part of the paper, it is argued that post-colonial countries that have industrialised did so on the basis of state ownership of large segments of the mining sector. In this regard, it is worth looking at the fast-growing economies of India, Brazil and Vietnam. Before proceeding, it should be noted that private ownership of mining production leads to severe industrial distortions. There is widespread monopoly pricing of raw minerals, especially import-parity pricing, in the South African economy, which is made possible by high global demand for these commodities. The effect of this has been to stifle the growth of downstream manufacturing, which India has successfully managed through its extensively nationalised mining sector.

In its national mineral policy, India states that 'the strategy for development of any mineral should naturally keep in view its ultimate end uses' (IMM 1993). The policy goes on to state that 'a thrust is to be given to exploitation of mineral resources in which the country is well endowed so that industries based on these resources can come up to meet the needs of industrial materials for which we have now to depend on external sources' (IMM 1993). In other words, the state in India intervenes to guarantee an unhindered supply of materials to industries, thereby protecting industrial development from market fluct-uations. Consequently, the state in India accounts for 88 per cent of mineral production. With its heavily nationalised mining industry, India has emerged as the second fastest-growing economy following China, with a robust manufacturing sector. The Indians do not put faith in private ownership and control of their natural resources, because these are their exhaustible natural heritage and should be deployed in a way that will deliver maximum national development (which almost always does not coincide with profit-maximisation).

The leading mining company in Brazil is Vale, which used to be state-owned but was privatised in 1997, and which is the second largest mining company in the world. The circumstances surrounding the privatisation of Vale remain controversial and had nothing to do with inefficiency. Nevertheless, Brazil continues to be characterised by heavy state-ownership of critical sectors, such as petro-chemicals and banking. In fact, the basis of Brazil's industrial vitality lies in the former state-owned companies such as Vale, the National Steel Company and Petrobas. There is no doubt that state-ownership marked a significant turning point in Brazil's industrialisation. Although the state has withdrawn in industrial sectors, the remaining state-owned enterprises continue to be the mainstay of Brazil's industrial strategy.

In its mining plan for 2030, Brazil is pushing aggressively for downstream linkages. Interestingly, this move is said to unsettle the omnipresent Vale, which now controls 80 per cent of mineral production in Brazil. Vale is intent on maximising shareholder value while the Brazilian government seeks to strengthen and broaden linkages between the mining sector and downstream industries (GBR 2011). The privatisation of Vale is perhaps one of the biggest privatisation blunders in history, and makes the unfortunate privatisation of South Africa's Iron and Steel Industrial Corporation (ISCOR) fade in comparison. Brazil and India are not the only countries where state ownership has produced significant economic development. Vietnam is touted in some circles as a country that has turned the corner and abandoned state ownership. This is not true. State ownership in Vietnam is dominant and remains the hallmark of Vietnam's economy. In some countries (e.g. Spain, New Zealand and Indonesia), state ownership of mining is in a targeted sector.

What is critical to note, however, is that the argument for nationalisation based on industrialisation makes economic sense, because countries that grow the fastest are those that produce high-value-added goods, not those that rely on increasing physical quantities. Value is added to raw materials as they move down the value chain. In a situation where raw materials upstream are owned by the private sector, the private sector would seek to gain maximum returns and pocket all the profits, thereby stifling the growth of downstream high-value-added production. Nationalisation, on the other hand, is premised on the idea that it is high-value-added sectors that should benefit the most. By avoiding crude profit maximisation

at the beginning of the value chain and securing the availability of raw minerals at affordable prices, value is unlocked downstream to a greater extent than had the profits been locked upstream, thanks to multipliers, the externalities, economies of scale and scope effects that are inherent in downstream manufacturing.

The current patterns of ownership and control in the mining sector are harmful to South Africa's long-term economic development. For example, South Africa ranks seventh in coal production, second in manganese production and seventh in iron-ore production. South Africa accounts for 75 per cent of the world's manganese resources. Yet, the country ranks nineteenth in steel production. South Africa accounts for 52 per cent of ferromanganese imports into the USA. This, on its own, is indicative of the scale of damage and lost opportunity that the current patterns of ownership and control have on the country's long-term development potential. It is estimated that South Africa exports 73 per cent of its crude minerals. Of the 27 per cent that remain to be processed, 80 per cent are exported after processing. This vividly illustrates the extent of the disconnection between the mining value chain and downstream manufacturing, which is what happens when a country places the extraction and exploitation of its mineral wealth in the hands of the private sector.

Overall, there is overwhelming evidence that fast-growing economies with sophisticated manufacturing have succeeded on the basis of extensive state-ownership and control of mining. This political economy explains to a large extent the structure of South African manufacturing as well, which is driven predominantly by the formerly state-owned coal and oil company, SASOL and ISCOR. Both have strong links with mining; they owned coal and iron-ore mines. The existing strengths of the South African economy are due largely to state ownership of upstream sectors. Today, if we were to remove the erstwhile state-owned petro-chemical and basic iron and steel sectors from manufacturing, very little would be left. What does all this demonstrate? The evidence is clear: all fast-growing, emerging market economies are characterised by heavy state ownership of upstream sectors, including mining.

Education and job-creation: alternatives to nationalisation?

If education and jobs were a substitute for nationalisation, the *Freedom Charter* would not have had distinct clauses in this regard. The opening of the doors of learning and culture would have been enough, and white domination would collapse purely under the weight of education. However, there is no

The current patterns of ownership and control in the mining sector are harmful to South Africa's long-term economic development.

> There is overwhelming evidence that fast-growing economies with sophisticated manufacturing have succeeded on the basis of extensive state-ownership and control of mining.

precedent in history where a country educated itself out of colonialism. Neither is there a country that has pursued job-creation in order to address colonial dispossession. It simply does not make political-economic sense. The *Freedom Charter's* call for the doors of learning and culture to be opened and for free medical care cannot be substituted for the transfer of strategic sectors to the democratic state.

In fact, if job-creation were to be used as an index of economic liberation in the true sense of the word, the apartheid era would rank as economically more empowering than the current dispensation because, then, the unemployment rate was not as high as in the post-apartheid period. In any case, even from a micro-analytical point of view, it is becoming evident that there are growing numbers of educated black people who perform sophisticated functions in the economy. Yet, the rate at which this black intellect and labour is exploited is not matched by the rate of economic transformation in terms of black ownership and control of the economy. Within the existing structures of colonial ownership and control, the more black people get educated, the more they get exploited, and the deeper inequality becomes.

At a more profound level, the counterposition of job-creation and nationalisation is disingenuous because it denies the link between current patterns of ownership and control and high levels of unemployment. Just to illustrate the point, the privatisation of steel producer ISCOR has subjected the manufacturing sector to massive input price hikes based on import-parity pricing. Similarly, manganese, which is an important ingredient in steel production, is also subject to import-parity pricing. Steel-intensive manufacturing firms, especially in the machinery and equipment sectors, find themselves uncompetitive and excluded from the market. However, in countries where industrial development and, hence, sustainable productive employment are taken seriously, essential inputs such as steel and petro-chemicals are made available to downstream firms in such a way as to maintain manufacturing competitiveness. The bottom line is that profits are not maximised upstream; they are maximised downstream, where job-creation is intensive.

Nobody can deny the progress that has been made over the past 17 years in increasing the pool of educated black people. On the other hand, nobody can deny the increase in inequality across the board. Similarly, nobody can deny the scale of job-creation over the past ten years, but nobody can deny the poor quality of these jobs, which have been mainly in private services and the wholesale and retail trade sectors. We know that these sectors do not drive growth in fast-growing,

emerging market economies. Such economies are driven by the electrical equipment, machinery and transport equipment sectors, not by the types of sectors that have been growing in South Africa. The interesting part is that they import raw materials from South Africa to sustain their manufacturing sectors. For example, the share of South African manganese exports to Brazil is a staggering 49 per cent, and Brazil is the ninth largest steel producer globally. Ninety-three per cent of South Africa's platinum group metals are exported, while these could be used to support downstream manufacturing, including the electronics and automotive sectors.

Those who insert education and health in the discussion of ownership and control of the country's strategic industries are disingenuous. In fact, the crisis in education and health is itself due to the existing patterns of ownership and control of the economy. The fundamental economic relationship between the black working class and the white capitalist class has never been one between humans. A significant part of what would be regarded as profits in the economy arises from the fact that the working class has limited access to quality health care and education, among other social services. The low cost of reproduction of labour-power in South Africa, and the reduction of working class livelihoods to animalistic levels, is reflected in the form of massive accumulation of wealth by a minority of the population. In other words, the socio-economic conditions of the black working class itself provide the solid foundation for accumulation.

Conclusion

Efforts to sidetrack the debate on nationalisation through selective use of facts will not work. No serious scholar can argue that post-colonial economies that are fast-growing are not supported and powered by nationalised sectors. Opponents of nationalisation must come up with better arguments. If the *Freedom Charter* is the starting point, it is clear that no group of black people can claim ownership and control of what belongs to the people as whole: the mines, banks and monopoly industries. This means that BEE deals in these sectors are illegitimate, because these sectors are supposed to be transferred to democratic state ownership. If the *Freedom Charter* is outdated, opponents of nationalisation must say so, and provide the country with a different vision.

Opponents of nationalisation raise the spectre of capital flight and lack of foreign investment in South Africa as a consequence of nationalisation. This is a myth. Many countries that have state-owned or nationalised mines and industries (not least of which is Vietnam) enter into joint ventures and partnerships with private investors. Such arrangements can be structured in line with prevailing circumstances. In fact, when the state that owns the national assets is democratic, as in South Africa, it is safer for investors to invest. What is not safe for investors is when they enter into deals with illegitimate owners of a country's national resources. Clearly it is an anomaly for foreign investors to embrace a group of white people who mortgage our mines and other strategic sectors, when it is well known that South Africa has an unresolved post-colonial situation.

Lastly, the insertion of issues of health and education in the debate is a non-starter. Those of us who argue for national-isation do not see a trade-off between the various clauses of the *Freedom Charter*. Instead, we see them as complementary: no state can claim to be fully democratic unless it secures the birthright of the people, which is enshrined in the *Charter*. Furthermore, the issue of nationalisation is not about mining communities and good corporate social responsibility; these can be achieved easily by a nationalised mine. What is at issue here is the resolution of the underlying national question: the wholesale colonial dispossession of black people and the African majority, in particular. This dispossession remains the foundation upon which South Africa stands, and it is the foundation into which South Africa will fall, with or without foreign investors.

BURDENING THE STATE DOES NOT SERVE THE CAUSE OF ECONOMIC LIBERATION

Michael Spicer[1]

In late June 2011, the African National Congress Youth League (ANCYL) formally adopted two sets of policy proposals to shape our country's future: nationalising the mines and expropriating land without compensation. This brought into sharper focus a 'debate' about nationalisation that had been carried in the media for more than a year, and that generally amounted to little more than unsubstantiated assertion and populist sloganeering. The proposals, therefore, are deserving of a more reasoned response from all who have a vested interest in South Africa's future.

This article is a response to the policy proposal relating to the nationalisation of mines, and the ideas associated therewith. It is not focussed on the people or personalities proposing these ideas, as this generates more heat than light, and detracts from the underlying challenges facing the country and appro-priate responses to them.

Three sets of questions should be asked of all public policy:

1. What will the likely benefits of the policies be for the nation?
2. What will be their likely costs?
3. What alternative policies might as or more effectively achieve the proposed policies' intended goals?

Nationalising the mining industry

In order to respond to these questions, one needs to under-stand the ANCYL's reasons for promoting nationalisation in the mining industry. In the final document of the League's 24th National Congress, nationalisation of the mining industry and expropriation without compensation are described as two of the '7 cardinal pillars of economic freedom in our lifetime'. Titled, *A clarion call to economic freedom fighters: programme of action for economic freedom in our lifetime*, it sets out five arguments in favour of the nationalisation of mines:

a. Increased fiscus and therefore more resources for education, housing, healthcare, infrastructure development, safety and security and sustainable livelihoods for our people.
b. More jobs for our people, because State owned and controlled Mines will increase local beneficiation and industrialisation of Mineral resources. This will in turn reduce the high levels of poverty, which is consequent of joblessness.
c. More equitable spatial development, because State owned and controlled mines will invest in areas where Mining is happening.

93 per cent (or R407 billion) of the value of expenditures by mining companies remains in South Africa to benefit local industries and citizens.

d. Better salaries and working conditions in Mines because State owned Mines will increase the Mining wage and improve compliance to occupational health and safety standards.
e. Greater levels of economic and political sovereignty as the State will be in control and ownership of strategic sectors of the economy, which produces minerals resources needed across the world. (ANCYL 2011: 12)

The document asserts several benefits deriving from nationalisation, including increased tax revenue, more jobs, improved spatial development, better salaries and working conditions, and greater political and economic sovereignty of the state *vis-à-vis* domestic and international private capital. Are these assumptions accurate, however? The section below considers each in more detail.

Increased tax revenue

In 2010, the mining industry paid R17.1 billion in direct corporate tax. R16.2 billion was paid to shareholders, the providers of capital (which enabled the original investments that gave birth to our mining sector). Nationalisation implies that the government would get the R16.2 billion in dividends, to add to the R17.1 billion already received in direct corporate tax. Leaving aside the extraordinary cost of acquiring the mines, dealt with below, this would be true only if the state were able to fund the R17 billion deficit between the income (R424 billion) and expenditure (R441 billion) of the sector. On these numbers, the National Treasury would be worse off; and this scenario does not even take into account the impact on skills retention, operating efficiencies of the private sector, and foreign direct investment (FDI) and portfolio flows to South Africa. A survey of jurisdictions around the world where mines have been nationalised overwhelmingly indicates a deterioration in respect of all the above factors.

Perhaps the key issue here is the perception that mining companies are just 'dirt diggers' that export all the benefits offshore, with no value addition or benefits accruing locally. The reality is quite the opposite. In 2010, the mining industry's total expenditure was R441 billion. This included the procurement of goods and services, the payment of wages, capital expenditure, depreciation, corporate taxes, dividends and interest payments. It is estimated that only R34 billion (or 7 per cent of the expenditure) went offshore in the form of dividends, interest and payment for goods and services not provided in South Africa. In other words, 93 per cent (or R407 billion) of the value of expenditures by mining companies remains in South Africa to benefit local industries and citizens.

In addition, the scale of local downstream beneficiation is very large. All of South Africa's cement, 94 per cent of our electricity, 80 per cent of our steel, 30 per cent of our liquid fuel requirements, and most of our plastics, polymers, waxes, explosives, fertilisers, and so on are made in South Africa using South African-mined products. The country accounts for 20 per cent of the world's production of platinum catalytic converters, while many other minerals are further beneficiated in the country. Estimates suggest that R200 billion in extra sales value, and more than 150 000 jobs, are created in downstream beneficiation industries using locally mined minerals. This undermines the myth that no beneficiation of minerals is happening in South Africa.

We also need to take a long-term view. If governments were required to provide all the resources for mining, from the most basic exploration for new ore sources, to mine construction, mine maintenance and expansion, and ultimately for environmental rehabilitation at the end of mining operations, it seems highly implausible that they would earn more by owning mines than by regulating them. Governments are driven by politicians with their eyes (in democracies) on regular and short-term electoral cycles. Consequently, they find it extraordinarily difficult to plan for and invest in the kind of long-term cycles that govern the mining industry, which often exceed 50 years and span exploration, feasibility studies, the building of shafts and infrastructure, production, expansion, closure planning and rehabilitation. This is why governments typically underinvest in maintenance and expansion, and focus more on extracting revenues. The Zambian nationalisation story is a vivid illustration of sustained underinvestment over decades, reducing the value of a rich, world-class asset to almost zero at the point of its privatisation in the 1990s.

Very recently, the Zambian minister of mines confirmed this truth, saying that during the dismal period of nationalisation, the copper mines cost the country $1m per day, while under privatisation they were now earning the state $1m per day, a swing of 200 per cent.

Another important factor to bear in mind is that the debate on nationalisation is occurring in South Africa at a time when the state is turning to the private sector to help fund its massive R900-billion infrastructure roll-out for roads, ports, electricity and transport, because it simply does not have sufficient resources to cover all the demands of its core activities or, indeed, the capacity to run these facilities.

This is why the worldwide trend is away from state ownership of mining; the focus of most governments these days is on efforts to optimise revenues from privately run mining companies.

> Major black-owned mining companies and black economic empowerment (BEE) participants would be among the losers in the case of expropriation without compensation.

More jobs

Putting more South Africans to work is a goal we all share. There is a compelling case to challenge both the public and private sector to increase employment wherever they can, although the government's new growth path rightly requires the overwhelming majority of employment creation to be by the private sector (and implicitly by new firms, as economic growth accelerates).

The mining sector currently employs 500 000 people directly and creates another 500 000 jobs through the expenditure multipliers and industries that either use mining inputs or supply inputs to the mining sector (i.e. 12 per cent of total employment in the formal sector). In mining, as in other sectors, however, creating more sustainable jobs depends on growing the sector, finding, developing and exploiting more mineral resources through increased and better exploration, producing more from existing resources (better technology and productivity) and/or marketing existing production more effectively.

Does comparative experience suggest that state-owned mines do any of these three things better than privately owned mines? The international evidence, again, is overwhelming that it is the private-sector mining companies that best create long-term, sustainable employment through productive investment. Chile and Venezuela make good examples. In Chile where the private copper mining industry has grown in the last few decades to several times the size of the dominant state-owned company, Codelco, the state has publicly criticised the latter for its efficiency. Venezuela, one of the very few countries recently to have taken the nationalisation road, vividly illustrates a national oil company comprehensively underperforming its private-sector counterparts in both employment and production.

Improved spatial development

Again, all South Africans should agree that we need to change the spatial character of the South African economy, where poor people often live long distances from their places of employment. But how can state ownership of mines (the location of which is determined by where ore bodies are found) change this? The section on taxes above suggests that the government will have fewer resources to correct the spatial imbalance, rather than more, if mines are nationalised. Yet, at present, the government is struggling to use the considerable tax revenues and royalties generated by the industry to provide effective services in mining communities.

Better salaries and working conditions

Salaries are determined by collective bargaining, and occupational conditions are governed by law and regulation. Unions help in determining the first of these, and the department of mineral resources the second.

In 2010, wages and salaries accounted for R78.4 billion, compared again to R16.2 billion in dividends and R17.1 billion in taxes. If salaries are to go up (when sales remain constant) what will go down? The evidence elsewhere in the world is that when governments cannot find extra resources from the fiscus to pay salaries to which they are committed, and cannot or will not reduce the number of employees to make up the shortfall, they resort to the printing press, thereby progressively devaluing the wages their employees earn in real terms (through fuelling inflation – where everyone loses).

Greater economic and political sovereignty

The state holds all of South Africa's mineral resources in 'custodianship', and decides through a licensing system who is able to explore and exploit them. This was one of the fundamental achievements of the Mineral and Petroleum Resources Development Act 28 of 2002 (MPRDA), which changed the previous system of private and public ownership of mineral rights into a state custodianship system. Via the MPRDA and Mining Charter, the industry has been opened up, and a considerable degree of access to ownership and management of mines for historically disadvantaged South Africans has been created. How much greater sovereignty is achieved by also owning the private mining companies that do this?

What about the costs?

We need to consider, firstly, the costs of taking ownership. Would this be done without compensating any present owners? Through revenue distribution, black South Africans are beneficiaries of about half of the institutional holdings in mining shares, and they, as well as their white counterparts, thus stand to lose large portions of their savings and pensions, which would be expropriated by the state in the name of enhancing their welfare. Furthermore, if foreign owners (substantial in all mining sectors, and often with holdings of more than 50 per cent) were not compensated, governments, both from fellow BRICS states – Brazil, Russia, India and China – and the traditional developed world would in all likelihood invoke international treaties to protect their interests. South Africa's membership of BRICS would be in jeopardy immediately, and it would be in danger of relegation to a pariah status similar to that held during the apartheid years.

Major black-owned mining companies and black economic empowerment (BEE) participants would, of course, be among the losers in the case of expropriation without compensation.

The market capitalisation of mining companies listed on the JSE is R1.9 trillion or 43 per cent of the total market capitalisation of the JSE. In the case of part or full compensation, therefore, the South African government would be required to move very significant resources from present essential applications. In other words, less infrastructure, less health, less education and less welfare spending. There are significant trade-offs that the government has to balance, and the diversion of resources for investment in mining would mean that other vital expenditures would suffer. Of course, the government might seek to raise such resources, in part or wholly, by dramatically increasing individual and corporate taxes. The effect of this would be to reduce investment and employment elsewhere in the economy, leaving the country worse off than before.

Why would anyone want to spend R1.9 trillion in state resources (which would massively add to the country's debt levels) when the benefits of expenditure, downstream beneficiation and employment are already substantially created by the mining sector in South Africa. The cost-benefit analysis of nationalisation just does not make economic sense.

More important than this once-off cost is the cost of forgoing non-state investment in the future of our mining industry. A mine is a factory of which the construction is never finished. Mines are capital-hungry economic machines. South Africa is a capital-scarce economy and, at present, the state lacks the resources even to fulfil its core mandates optimally. Within the nationalisation scenario, there is a very strong likelihood that our mining industry would sink rather than grow if it were to have access only to state investment. This is especially the case in terms of the recruitment of skilled South African mining personnel by international mining companies in a context of significant skills shortages. The lesson of history is that citizens of democracies are not inert pawns to be moved around at will by power-driven politicians. Many scarce, highly skilled employees, such as engineers and managers, would exercise their right to choose to work where they would be compensated best.

There are other important, but perhaps less tangible costs. These include the fact that: state ownership of such a large industry denies the opportunity not only of entrepreneurship through venture capitalism, but also of business ownership to all citizens; access to the technology, innovation and best practice of global investors is limited; and regulatory conflicts emerge as the government becomes both an economic player and a regulator.

Are there alternative policies that might work as well or better?

The Mining Charter, a document whose intention was to govern the race, gender and, indeed, broader transformation of this

sector, was reviewed and revised in September 2010. The new Charter sets out specific targets with regard to racial ownership, equity procurement, equity enterprise development, beneficiation, employment equity, human resources development, mine community development and housing and living conditions. Specific timelines are attached to each of these targets, sometimes year by year.

There are few, if any, other parts of the economy with a more detailed plan for transformation.

The revised Charter was painstakingly negotiated between the government, trade unions representing mine-workers, and the representatives of shareholders. Such a social compact, in a country where all social actors constantly refer to the need for such compacts, is worthy of analysis and debate.

A second stakeholder process is underway in this industry, which aims to grow the economic pie that is available to all South Africans by exploiting the country's untapped mineral wealth (by some reckoning, the largest in the world). This is the Mining Industry Growth, Development and Employment Task Team (MIGDETT). The objective of this process is to ensure the long-term growth and meaningful transformation of South Africa's mining industry, as well as the equitable inclusion of all stakeholders in that growth. A dialogue between proponents of this process and those who argue for nationalisation should be of benefit to both sides, and to all South Africans. Minister Pravin Gordhan, in his Medium-Term Budget Statement of 25 October 2011, made his sentiments on the nationalisation issue very clear when he said regarding the mining industry:

> Energy constraints, inadequate transport capacity and uncertainty in the regulatory environment have held back progress. In contrast, mining production expanded by 30% in Australia, and 44% in Brazil between 2003 and 2010. This has provided a huge boost for investment, tax revenues, jobs and incomes in these countries. Minister Shabangu's engagement with the Chamber of Mines on increasing investment in our mining resources is therefore to be welcomed.[2]

Resources that lie beneath the soil represent potential, not actual, wealth. Mere slogans and poor policy will ensure that such wealth remains dormant, and that South Africans are deprived of its benefits.

Notes

1. This article is adapted from a piece by Michael Spicer and Bobby Godsell (*Business Day* 1 July 2011).

2. Interestingly, these remarks were echoed even more forcefully by Minister Trevor Manuel at the Sunday Times Top 100 Awards dinner the same evening (see Manuel 2011).

The Labour Market

Wage increases in South Africa (in contrast to demands) have been alarmingly timid over the past decade.

Chapter ● ● 2 ● ● ● ●

forward not
forgetting

Our Solidarity

Peoples of the world
together join to serve
the common cause
so it feeds us all for ever
Workers of the World
uniting thats the way
to lose your chains.
Black or white or brow
or yellow leave your
disputes behind
when starving or w
forward no

The Labour Market at a Glance

High levels of unemployment remain the South African economy's Achilles heel. At the end of 2011, formal unemployment stood at around a quarter of the population. This is significantly higher than any of its emerging market peers. The crisis in the labour market is most pronounced amongst young South Africans, with just over 70 per cent unable to find employment. Given the precarious position of workers, strike action has often been protracted and costly to the economy, peaking in 2010 with an extended public sector strike that amounted to about 20 million working days lost.

NARROW UNEMPLOYMENT RATE BETWEEN 2001–2011

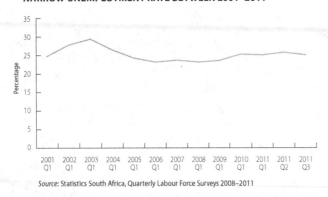

Source: Statistics South Africa, Quarterly Labour Force Surveys 2008–2011

NUMBER OF FORMALLY EMPLOYED SOUTH AFRICANS ('000)

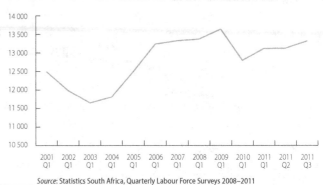

Source: Statistics South Africa, Quarterly Labour Force Surveys 2008–2011

South African unemployment in a comparative perspective					
	2007	**2008**	**2009**	**2010**	**2011**
Brazil	9.29	7.90	8.10	6.70	6.70
China	4.00	4.20	4.30	4.10	4.00
Egypt	9.21	8.78	9.52	8.99	10.41
Indonesia	9.11	8.39	7.87	7.14	6.80
Mexico	3.71	3.97	5.46	5.37	4.50
Nigeria	4.50	4.50	4.50	4.50	4.50
Russia	6.10	6.40	8.40	7.50	7.30
South Africa	22.23	22.91	23.94	24.91	24.51

Source: International Monetary Fund, 2011

Note: Unemployment rate can be defined by either the national definition, the ILO harmonised definition, or the OECD harmonised definition. The OECD harmonised unemployment rate gives the number of unemployed persons as a percentage of the labour force (the total number of people employed plus unemployed). [OECD Main Economic Indicators, OECD, monthly]. As defined by the International Labour Organisation, unemployed workers are those who are currently not working but are willing and able to work for pay, currently available to work, and have actively searched for work. [ILO, http://www.ilo.org/public/english/bureau/stat/res/index.htm]. Estimates start after 2010.

40.9%
Proportion of sector workers in skilled positions

EMPLOYED SOUTH AFRICANS AS A PERCENTAGE OF THE TOTAL WORKING-AGE POPULATION (15–64)

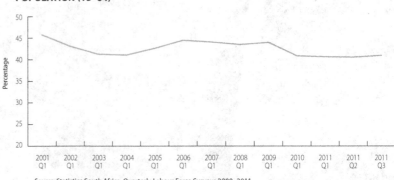

Source: Statistics South Africa, Quarterly Labour Force Surveys 2008–2011

YOUNG PEOPLE AGED 15–34 AS A PERCENTAGE OF UNEMPLOYED SOUTH AFRICANS

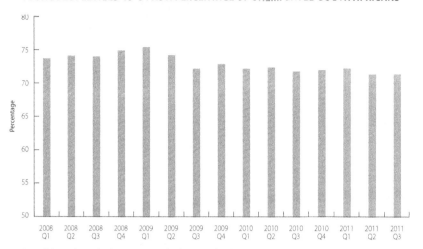

Source: Elaborated using data from Statistics South Africa, Quarterly Labour Force Surveys 2008–2011

NUMBER OF WORKING DAYS LOST* DUE TO INDUSTRIAL ACTION (MILLION)

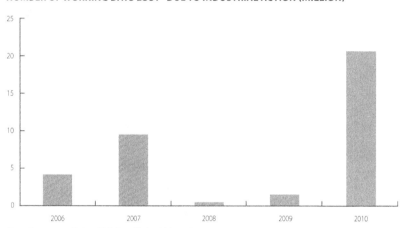

Source: Department of Labour, 2010 Annual Industrial Action Report
Note: * Working days lost = the number of workers on strike or lockout multiplied by the length of the work stoppage.

Working days lost by industry in 2010 (actual days)	
Sector	Days
Agriculture	108
Mining	361 113
Manufacturing	384 980
Electricity	7 681
Construction	3 787
Wholesale, retail trade	394 584
Transport	640 757
Financial Intermediation	15 196
Community Services (Civil Service)	18 866 531

Source: Department of Labour, 2010 Annual Industrial Action Report

NUMBER OF WORK STOPPAGES AS A RESULT OF INDUSTRIAL ACTION

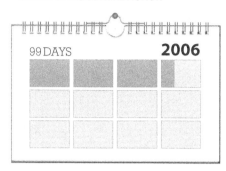

99 DAYS — 2006

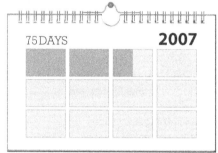

75 DAYS — 2007

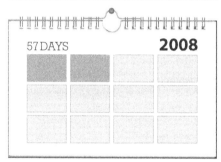

57 DAYS — 2008

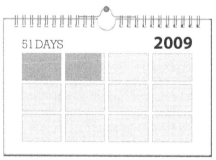

51 DAYS — 2009

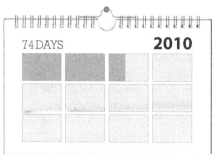

74 DAYS — 2010

TWO

REVIEW | Employment under pressure: Inclusive strategies are in everybody's interest

Saliem Patel

. . . .

2010 saw one of the most protracted and highly charged public service strikes since this country's transition to democracy, with an estimated one million workers taking to the streets. Negotiations started in April and were concluded only in October, culminating in Resolution 4 of 2010 in the Public Service Co-ordinating Bargaining Council (PSCBC). Amongst its provisions were a 7.5 per cent salary hike and an R800 per month housing allowance.[1]

On 16 August 2011, another agreement was struck between the single employer, the state, and unions in the PSCBC, this time without any strike activity. Apart from the wage offer of 6.8 per cent, backdated to 1 May 2011, the remainder of the new agreement was about the need to negotiate numerous outstanding and new demands.[2]

The outstanding issues included medical aid, housing allowances, a minimum service agreement and a remuneration policy, each with different processes and proposed dates for resolution. The new demands covered time off for shop stewards, overtime, review of a previous agreement on pensions, performance management and development systems, compliance with the Occupational Health and Safety Act 85 of 1993, and the delinking of housing allowances from spouses. Importantly, the issue of outsourcing, which has become a standard item on the agendas of unions across all sectors, was included.

The document also stated an intention to reach a long-term agreement for the period 2012–2015, but several factors may delay its adoption. These include the large number of unresolved issues, their complexity, union members' mounting dissatisfaction with the approach of and offers from the state over the past two years, and the number of unions involved in the public sector. Gauging from the number of other negotiations that started early in 2011 and are still to be concluded, all indications are that settlements will be difficult to attain. In the case of municipalities, the employer, the South African Local Government Association (SALGA), implemented a unilateral decision on wage increases that led to protests and strike action. At this stage, therefore, the eventual outcome of the process remains anybody's guess.

However, in the interest of forward planning and projection, informed guesses are better than mere speculation. This article reviews labour market indicators and industrial action patterns of the recent past, in search for clues of discernible trends. It concludes that recent trends in the context of economic stagnation lean towards an approach by all social partners that focuses on self-interest with short-term gain. Social dialogue, therefore, needs to be prioritised in order to prevent a scenario where the cost of stagnation is borne by the poor, and, conversely, to ensure that benefits are distributed evenly where gains have been made. Failure would result in the battle of redistribution spilling over into the streets once again – this time in growing numbers and intensity.

Striking a bargain

It is often assumed that there are too many strikes in South Africa, and from an economic point of view one strike is always one too many. Companies lose profits and employees lose wages. Leslie Owen, from the University of KwaZulu-Natal, believes that the incidence of strikes in South Africa is comparatively much lower than elsewhere, when measured in terms of the number of days lost per one million of the population. He shows, for example, that in 2008 South Africa trailed countries like Denmark, France and Italy in Europe; Brazil, Peru and Argentina in Latin America; India and Korea in the East; and Canada in North America in terms of strike activity.[3] All these states are vibrant democracies, and collective bargaining is a function of democratic labour relations. Freedom of association, the right to collective bargaining and the right to strike, despite short-term economic consequences, build stable democracies with more predictable and sustainable economies.

Owen's contention is supported by the Department of Labour's *Annual Industrial Action Report 2010*, which notes that strike activity has been low over the past three years, when compared to the 99 stoppages in 2006.[4]

Yet, an assessment of stoppages alone can create a false impression of the actual impact of strikes. It is also important to take sector and union size into consideration when making such an assessment, as is demonstrated in Figure 2.1.1. Industrial action by one large union, therefore, may have as much impact on the economy as action by a large number of small unions. The 99 stoppages in 2006, for example, resulted in the loss of 4.1 million working days, and the 75 stoppages in 2007 amounted in 9.5 million working days. When looking at the comparable figures for 2010, the full extent of last year's strike is put in perspective: 74 work stoppages resulted in 20.6 million working days lost. This is more than double the number recorded in 2007. For both of these years, the high number of days lost can be attributed to public sector strikes. Indeed, the 2010 figure represents the highest ever number of working days lost in one year. Public service action accounts for 90 per cent of this. It is estimated that 18 million working days were lost when approximately one million employees went on strike for 18 working days each.

In 2009, the transport industry topped the list with the highest number of industrial action incidents, but in 2010 it was overtaken by the mining industry (see Figure 2.1.2). The number of incidents in the manufacturing industry doubled, due largely to the fact that prior agreements in the sector had reached their termination date and had to be renegotiated in 2010. The long-term agreement of 2008–2010 within the Metal and Engineering Industries Bargaining Council, for example, came to an end and, as a result, new negotiations had to commence.

The lowest number of strike incidents occurred in agriculture, construction and energy. Fewer incidents in the first two can be attributed, by and large, to lower levels of unionisation and the precarious forms of employment in these sectors; in the case of energy, Eskom's monopoly and regulations around its status as an essential service account for the relative lack of strike activity in this sphere. It is important to note, however, that in 2010 over 3 000 workers in the sector embarked on a strike, because of frustration with the offer of a 5 per cent wage increase at a time when Eskom executives were being paid salaries regarded as excessive and not in line with their actual performance.

Due to the first-ever nationwide strike in the construction industry, it also recorded unusually high levels of working days lost in 2009 (see Figure 2.1.3). The strike action was the result of greater co-operation between trade unions affiliated to different federations that began working together in 2007 around the infrastructure development for the 2010 World Cup.[5] The campaign for decent work in this sector raised awareness among union members and developed a sufficiently strong and co-operative relationship to mobilise and co-ordinate a national strike.

It was in the mining industry that most industrial action incidents occurred during 2010. The number of incidents does not necessarily correspond with the number of working days lost; as shown in Figure 2.1.3, the number of working days lost in the mining industry was surpassed by the manufacturing, wholesale and retail, transport, and community services industries in that year.

The significant year-on-year increase in the retail and wholesale industry between 2009 and 2010 was due to the September 2010 strike at Pick n Pay, which has a total staff

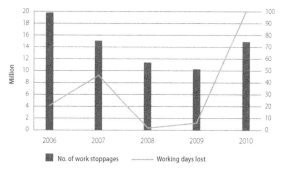

Figure 2.1.1: Number of work stoppages and number of working days lost, 2006–2010

Source: DoL (2011)

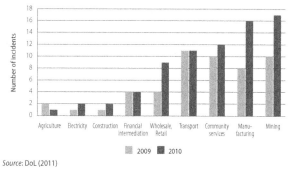

Figure 2.1.2: Number of incidents by industry, 2009–2010

Source: DoL (2011)

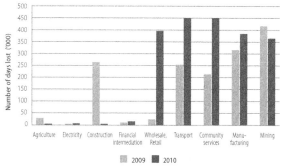

Figure 2.1.3: Working days lost by industry, 2009–2010

Source: DoL (2011)

complement of 50 000 employees. Other notable action within this industry included the South African Commercial, Catering and Allied Workers Union (SACCAWU) protest in May 2010 against the DisChem chain's refusal to recognise the union. This was not the first time that the union has had to fight for recognition; in 2008, another major retailer, Woolworths, refused to respect its status as a representative of workers. This industry is not amenable to unionisation, and, to date, SACCAWU's longstanding demand for a bargaining council has fallen on deaf ears.

Another apparent feature noted in Figure 2.1.3 is the smaller year-on-year variance in the number of working days lost in the mining and manufacturing industries during 2009 and 2010, compared to that of other industries during the same period. This is due to the number of negotiations that unions are involved in annually in these industries, albeit with different employers from year to year.

The number of working days lost between 2009 and 2010 increased exponentially from 1.5 million to 20.6 million. As noted above, this was due to the duration of, and the number of employees involved in, the 2010 public sector strike. Given this dramatic increase, the obvious question to ask is what impact it has had on the economy. Figure 2.1.4 shows that 7 045 days were lost for every 1 000 employees in the community and social services industry for 2010, an average of 7 days lost per employee. This is the same number of public holidays we have on an annual basis, without counting the religious holidays also regarded as public holidays. In 2009, the number of days lost per employee in the same industry was a miniscule 82 days per 1 000 employees, or an average of 40 minutes lost per employee for the entire year. Over the two years, the average would come down to 3.5 days lost per employee per annum. This year, an agreement was reached in the public sector without a nationwide strike, which would lower even further the average number of days lost per annum in the industry over three years. In short, the level of strike activity in the industry that recorded the highest number of days lost in 2010 is not as high, and its impact more muted, than one might have expected.

Figure 2.1.4 shows that the mining industry lost just over a day per employee per year to strike action in both 2009 and 2010. While the transport industry came close to this level in 2010, the average in 2009 was lower, at one-third of a day lost per employee per annum. The numbers are very low in the agriculture, construction, financial, and retail and whole-sale industries, although there are variations from one year to the other.

Figure 2.1.4: Number of days lost per thousand employees, 2009–2010

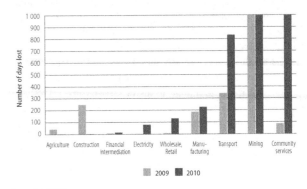

Source: DoL (2011)

	Year	Wage (R)	AMW increase (R)	AMW increase (%)	Inflation (%)	Real increase (%)	Real wage (R)	Real increase/ decrease (R)
	2003	1 940			5.8			
	2004	2 015	75	3.9	1.4	2.4	1 987	47
	2005	2 236	221	11.0	3.3	7.6	2 169	154
	2006	2 429	193	8.6	4.6	4.0	2 336	90
	2007	2 639	210	8.6	7.1	1.5	2 466	37
	2008	2 819	180	6.8	11.5	-4.7	2 514	-125
	2009	2 939	120	4.3	6.6	-2.3	2 754	-65
	2010	3 305	366	12.5	4.3	8.2	3 179	240
Estimate	2011	3 569	264	8.0	5.0	3.0	3 404	99
9 years	2003–2011		1 629	84.0	55.3	28.7	2 497	261
8 years	2003–2010		1 365	70.4	47.9	22.5	2 375.7	436
5 years	2006–2010		876	36.1	38.0	-1.9	2 382.0	-47
3 years	2008–2010		486	17.2	19.2	-2.0	2 763.8	-55

Table 2.1.1: Average minimum wage (AMW) across all bargaining units, 2003–2010

Source: Actual Wage Rates Database (AWARD) of the Labour Research Service (LRS) [6]
Note: Inflation calculated from the Statistics South Africa (Stats SA) Consumer Price Index (CPI) [7]

Demanding a strategy

Wage demands on employers have been growing by between 15 and 20 per cent in recent years. When compared to the low rate of inflation over the past two years, this appears to be excessively high. During this period, unions have also put increased emphasis on non-wage demands, which range from housing and medical allowances to job security and the use of labour brokers. However, an analysis of these settlements suggests that this is more part of union strategy to start high and leave room for downward negotiation. Employers, in turn, use the same strategy in reverse, and place counter-demands of retrenchments, reducing wages and cutting benefits on the table.

Wage increases in South Africa (in contrast to demands) have been alarmingly timid over the past decade. Contrary to the notion that demands are driven by high wage expectations, it appears that the demands are being led by growing fears of reduced real income. Table 2.1.1 is revealing on a number of levels.

It shows that, on average, nominal monthly wage increases since 2003 have been below 10 per cent per annum, except for 2005 when it was 11 per cent and 2010 when it was 12.5 per cent. In real terms (percentage increase minus inflation), annual increases of the monthly wage were less and there was an actual reduction in wages of 4.7 per cent and 2.3 per cent in 2008 and 2009 respectively. This has seriously affected the long-term pattern for improvements to minimum wages, and has had equally severe short-term implications for incomes.

Over the period 2003–2010, there was a nominal increase of 70.4 per cent in the average minimum monthly wage, but when inflation is factored in, this drops significantly to a real increase of 22.5 per cent or R436 over the entire period of 8 years – an annual average increase of R54 per annum or R4.50 per month.

Between 2006 and 2010, the average minimum monthly wage actually declined by R47 in real terms for the entire period, or on average by R9.40 each year. The annual real loss grows to an average of R18.33 a year over a three-year period between 2008 and 2010. In this time, the average minimum monthly wage decreased by 2 per cent or R55 in real terms.

It is estimated that the average minimum monthly wage will increase by about 8 per cent in 2011, as a result of the most recent settlements. If we assume an inflation rate of around 5 per cent for 2011, then the losses experienced in 2008 and 2009 will be overcome. The average minimum monthly wage would increase by R99 from the previous year and by an average of R9 per annum over the period 2006–2011.

A closer look at Table 2.1.1 reveals the tyranny of percentages, and how low wages for the majority of South African workers really are. This fact is borne out in successive household surveys by Stats SA. The latest results at the time of writing, released in August 2011, show that the expenditure of two-thirds of South Africa's households is R2 500 or less. This differs by racial group, with 80 per cent of African households, 50 per cent of coloured households, 30 per cent of Indian households and 13 per cent of white households falling in this category. [8]

The approach to cushion the real wage losses of workers by adding non-wage demands has not been successful. Employers have used strategies, such as outsourcing or threats of retrenchment, to curtail any real improvement to benefits and conditions of work. In fact, numerous negotiation rounds have been bedevilled by employers attempting to convert what is regarded as overtime work into normal hours. When taken to its logical conclusion, it amounts to reduced remuneration for workers working overtime, and a lower wage bill for the company.

Such measures remain highly contested, and both sides are working tirelessly towards an improvement in their bargaining position by legalistic means. Trade unions and employers alike are campaigning strongly for amendments to the labour laws. Unions have been calling for legislation to ban or restrict labour broking, thereby extending the wage and non-wage benefits of the main company or contractor to employees who currently work for labour brokers. Employers, on the other hand, are campaigning for a relaxation of labour laws that would allow for lower retrenchment costs, which, if achieved, would make the practice of labour broking redundant.

Employment and unemployment

An assessment of the South African labour market cannot ignore the racial and gender dimensions inherited from apartheid. They remain intact and, arguably, much of the marginal gains that have been made since 2003 have been eroded by the brief recession of 2009. Before proceeding to look at these dimensions in more detail, we first consider the more general employment patterns of recent years.

The comparative data in Figure 2.1.5 show that there were 624 000 more jobs in the first quarter of 2011 than there were at the same time ten years ago in 2001. This is a growth of 62 000 jobs per annum. To put this annual figure in perspective, it is sobering to note that it amounts to only 10 per cent of the number of pupils who wrote the 2010 Grade 12 examinations. Another disconcerting fact is that today there are 139 000 fewer women in the labour market than ten years ago, while the number of men increased by about 760 000 during the same period.

The figure further shows that while 2001–2008 was characterised by higher employment growth, its benefits have since been eroded by the economic crisis that began in 2008 and impacted on employment in 2009. Employment peaked during the first quarter of 2009 at 13.64 million, but then dropped dramatically to 12.8 million in the first quarter of 2010 – over 800 000 jobs were wiped out in one year! By the first quarter of 2011, this figure had increased slightly again by 300 000 to 13.1 million, but it still remained 500 000 shy of the 2009 figure. As far as the gender profile of job shedding during this period is concerned, the data show that 360 000 fewer women were employed in the first quarter of 2011 than at the same time in 2009. The comparable figure for men is 140 000.

Another disturbing fact, which is brought to the fore in Figure 2.1.6, is that only 40.6 per cent of working-age South

Figure 2.1.5: Number of men and women employed, 2001–2011

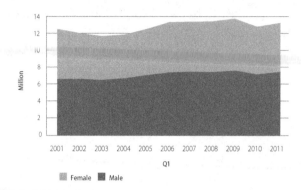

Source: Stats SA, *Quarterly Labour Force Survey* (for 2008–11) and the *Labour Force Survey: Historical Revisions* (for 2001–2007)

Figure 2.1.6: Percentage employed of total working-age population, 2001–2011

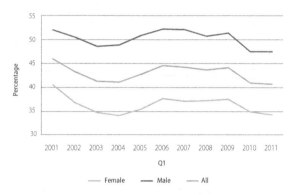

Source: Stats SA, *Quarterly Labour Force Survey* (for 2008–11) and the *Labour Force Survey: Historical Revisions* (for 2001–2007)

Africans were employed during the first quarter of 2011. Ten years ago, in 2001, the comparable statistic was 45.8 per cent. This decline of 5 per cent is cause for serious concern, because it suggests that the economy is far from able to absorb greater numbers than those who annually enter the labour market.

When viewed from a gender perspective, the realities presented in Figure 2.1.6 are unambiguous. In South Africa, only 34.2 per cent of working-age women are employed, while the comparative figure for men is 47.4 per cent – a difference of 13 per cent in the first quarter of 2011. Another important dimension of the gendered nature of work emerges when we evaluate employment by occupation. In South Africa, 1 out of every 7 working women is a domestic worker, while 1 out of every 24 men finds himself in this occupation (Patel 2011). Many women remain trapped in low-paying occupations. In *Labour Market Dynamics 2010*, related data, which have been broken down in terms of sex and occupation, reveal that whereas 738 000 men were employed in a managerial position, less than half the number of women (312 000) found themselves in this category.[9]

A demographic breakdown of the labour force shows that black Africans (78.2 per cent) make up the vast majority of employed workers, followed by white (9.6 per cent), coloured (9.3 per cent) and Indian (2.9 per cent) workers. However, as a proportion of the total working-age population, employed black Africans trail far behind the other groups. Only 36.2 per cent of this group find themselves in employment, compared to 49.5 per cent of the coloured, 52.5 per cent of the Indian and 63.8 per cent of the white groups.

An analysis of employment in terms of racial representation at the level of occupations points out that apartheid characteristics are entrenched in the labour market. Lehohla (2011) notes that in 2010 there was a much higher percentage of white employees (60.6 per cent) in skilled positions, compared to any other racial group. For Indian employees, the figure stood at 47.1 per cent, while for coloured and African employees it was 23.1 per cent and 15.9 per cent respectively.[10]

During the first quarter of 2011, there were 3.7 million unemployed black Africans, which translates into 85.7 per cent of the total number of 4.36 million unemployed in the country. Other groups constitute much less of this total number, with coloured, Indian and white unemployed at 436 000, 64 000 and 124 000 respectively. The unemployment rate was 25 per cent early in 2011; however, a demographic analysis again highlights entrenched apartheid characteristics. Figure 2.1.7 shows that unemployment within race groups remains extremely high for both the African and coloured groups, at 29 per cent and 22.6 per cent respectively, and much lower for the Indian and white groups, at 11.5 per cent and 5 per cent respectively.

Unemployment is the major concern in the labour market and is regarded as the cause of numerous social ills. It stood at 25.2 per cent in the second quarter of 2010. Stats SA's

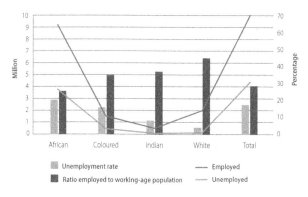

Figure 2.1.7: Employment and unemployment by racial group, 2011

Source: Stats SA (2011) *Quarterly Labour Force Survey,* July

South Africa remains unable to produce faster, cheaper and in greater volumes ...

Quarterly Labour Force Survey of July 2011 shows that unemployment abated to 25 per cent in the first quarter of 2011; however, it again increased to 25.7 per cent in the second quarter, instead of abating as the economy grows.[11]

Productivity, unit labour cost and economic growth

Everybody is looking towards the transformation of the economy to stem unemployment and restructure apartheid employment patterns. However, low productivity, high unit labour cost and sluggish economic growth, especially in labour-intensive industries, give the impression that the cart is indeed before the horse. After so many years, South Africa remains unable to produce faster, cheaper and in greater volumes, while numerous other countries have done so.

As shown above, the levels of strike activity are muted and wage increases have barely kept up with inflation; hence, unions and their members can hardly be held responsible for this situation. Another indictor – the wage gap – reveals that a worker earning the minimum wage will have to work for 154 years to earn what the average director of a South African company earns in just one year. This worker will have to work an extra 100 years on top of that (255 years) in the case of the average remuneration of a CEO (see LRS 2011). Clearly, our economy lacks balance and equity, and it seems as if true transformation has been sacrificed for inflated bonuses.

Adrian Saville, investment officer at Canon Asset Managers argues that 'productivity is our best currency' and opposes the idea that the rand should be devalued to make South Africa more competitive. He views labour productivity as the key to global competitiveness, with the qualification that labour productivity does not necessarily have to be based on the Chinese model of low wages. On the contrary, he suggests that 'the focus should be on promoting productivity and sharing gains in productivity', and that those looking for quick fixes 'would be surprised to find that this world of higher productivity and higher incomes correlates with a stronger Rand, greater global competitiveness of South African firms and higher standards of living for South Africans generally' (Saville 2011).

The possibility of another recession so quickly after the previous one of 2008/09, and the grave consequences it will have especially for manufactured exports, unfortunately may push back long-term solutions in favour of quick fixes. The rand has devalued slightly over the past year and the debate continues with a slant towards the increasing cost of imports.

If productivity and shared productivity gains should be the focus, recent trends show the contrary. The Reserve Bank has indicated that the percentage growth of economy-wide labour productivity slowed down quarter on quarter throughout 2010 and that this trend continued in the first quarter of 2011. In addition, the rate of salary increases also receded faster than productivity growth, which resulted in slower growth in unit labour cost from 7.7 per cent in the fourth quarter of 2010 to 5.3 per cent in the first quarter of 2011. In manufacturing, however, productivity growth accelerated as a result of increased output at lower employment levels (see SARB 2011).

In general, there are increasing concerns about the sustainability of South Africa's economic recovery. Although it was sustained throughout the four quarters of 2010, growth remained sluggish, resulting in GDP growth of 2.8 per cent for the year, after the economy shrank by 1.7 per cent in 2009. While growth for the first quarter of 2011 was 4.5 per cent, it declined to 1.4 per cent in the third quarter (Stats SA 2011). The Treasury revised its growth forecast downwards to 3.1 per cent from the initial 3.4 per cent for this year, with a caution that the continuing debt crisis in Europe could have severe repercussions locally.[12]

Skills and stimuli

When unemployment is a major feature of the labour market, it is expected that a political solution will be sought to increase the potential of job creation and to ensure that skills are acquired for employment. It is widely acknowledged that the level and quality of education present a major impediment to higher levels of employment in South Africa (see Stats SA 2011). Sufficient and appropriate economic stimuli by way of direct and indirect subsidies by the government to transform the labour market are also lacking. Unfortunately, an analysis of current data reveals unsatisfactory results.

Average education levels of the labour force are low, with 52 per cent having less than a full secondary education (there being substantial variations across racial groups) – 58.7 per cent of the employed black African population, 50.6 per cent of the employed coloured population, 25.6 per cent of the employed Indian population, and 14.5 per cent of the employed white population fall into this category. While 15.7 per cent of the employed population have a tertiary qualification, the racial variations are once again notable, with 11.5 per cent of the black African group, 10.7 per cent of the coloured group and 24.1 per cent of the Indian group having tertiary qualifications – far less than the 42.6 per cent of the white group with such a qualification (Stats SA 2011).

These figures reveal only the level of education attained by the employed, and this should not be confused with the quality of education attained. Over the past decade and a half, significant resource investments have been made in the country's education system. This is yet to bear fruit, and, as contributions elsewhere in this publication suggest, it will take much more than just monetary investment to turn the system around.

In recent years, much has changed in the thinking around government involvement in employment creation. Since the 1980s, policy-makers generally frowned on the idea of increasing state involvement in stimulating economic activity and employment. Today, the contrary is true and it is no longer a challenge to orthodoxy to suggest that the state is not doing enough in this regard.

Intervention in the form of bank bailouts, export subsidies, protection of vulnerable economic sectors, employment subsidies and even governments bailing out other governments have become increasingly commonplace since 2007. In South Africa, government subsidies have been provided for certain sectors, such as the motor industry and the government's expanded public works programme, to stymie unemployment. The onset of the economic crisis has resulted in broader and more targeted stimuli in the form of tax rebates for investment in strategic industries related to the New Growth Path strategy, as well as employment subsidies, such as the Jobs Fund for the creation of new jobs, and the training layoff scheme for reskilling and preventing large-scale retrenchments. In addition, the introduction of a youth subsidy will be targeted at skilling young people (aged 15–34 years), who make up 72 per cent of the unemployed (see Stats SA 2011). Finding the first job, and gaining job experience, appears to be a big challenge to employability (National Treasury 2011). Whether a lowering of the wage cost of young people will increase labour demand in the economy for this section of the population will be tested when the subsidy comes into effect next year. The government has allocated R5 billion over the next three years for its implementation.

The government's target for all these initiatives is the creation of 5 million jobs by 2020 – an average increase of 500 000 jobs per annum. This is 100 000 fewer than the number of pupils sitting for the Grade 12 examinations in 2011, and will be inadequate for bringing down the rate of unemployment even if these interventions are successful.

Accords and discord

The concluding paragraph of the declaration at the bargaining conference of the Southern African Clothing and Textile Workers Union (SACTWU) in March 2011 reads as follows: 'Conference called on all SACTWU members throughout the country to effectively prepare themselves for the upcoming round of substantive negotiations in our industry, and to be on high alert to confront employers head on, should they refuse to grant us our demands.'[13] Early in October, seven months later, newspaper headlines lauded a 'landmark' deal in the textile sector. The highlight of the agreement was that wages for new employees could be 30 per cent lower than for currently employed workers. The condition attached to this was that 5 000 jobs should be created by 2014. It was seen as a win-win agreement, as employers seeking to expand their workforce would pay less, the union would potentially benefit by more employment as it could increase its membership, and the development of the country, which is struggling to compete with cheaper imported goods, could be enhanced.[14] This agreement is significant, however, as its sets the precedent for other sectors to follow. An important concern remains that new workers will be bound by an agreement that they were not party to, and which would see them earning less than others at the same level.

Another accord that has made headlines is an agreement between the government, labour and business on 31 October 2011, which seeks to save and protect jobs by setting a 75 per cent local procurement target for employers. This accord will be hard to monitor, given limited access to company and government procurement data.[15] The significance of the accord lies elsewhere, namely in the creation of a space to develop common ground around inclusive and coherent strategies to counter the adverse impact of global conditions on the local economy.

Results and prospects

The labour market indicators discussed above broadly reveal that post-apartheid legislation and policy have not effectively changed the gender and racial characteristics of the labour market as it was under apartheid. Nevertheless, it is not worse. Furthermore, the country has achieved less frequent, and reduced levels of, industrial action (with the exception of public sector strikes in 2007 and 2010). The higher wage demands, together with an increasing range of non-wage demands from unions across the federations, and the inability of management to address these adequately, raises the possibility of heightened levels of industrial action.

Economic prospects appear very uncertain, with continuing economic stagnation in industrial countries, which is underpinned by a financial crisis in the Euro zone. These countries are important trading partners of South Africa and our economy is highly dependent on exports to them. If the crisis

It is widely acknowledged that the level and quality of education present a major impediment to higher levels of employment in South Africa.

persists, a decline in exports will lead ultimately to retrenchments, which will put trade unions on the back foot, given that 50 per cent of the jobs lost in 2009 have not been regained, and wages have not improved in real terms over the past six years. When jobs are on the line, more violent forms of action can occur, even if unions condemn this.

At this stage, there is insufficient evidence to suggest that the government, business and labour have reached a new consensus on how to address the unequal gender and racial characteristics of the labour market, to reshape the economy to meet the needs of employment and social protection, and ultimately to reposition South Africa in the global economy. This, however, is a long-term agenda. A good start would be to ensure that immediate and narrow stakeholder interests, which are being squeezed by a flailing global economy, do not overshadow our longer-term developmental objectives.

Notes

1. Home page of the PSCBC web site (http://www.pscbc.org.za/) downloaded 28 August 2011.

2. The agreement, Resolution 2 of 2011, can be downloaded from the PSCBC web site.

3. Owen (2011). His sample includes the following countries (and strike days per million of the population): Denmark – 373 820; Uruguay – 292 166; Brazil – 75 095; Peru – 52 446; France – 40 179; Canada – 26 534; Argentina – 21 034; Korea – 17 285; India – 14 432; Italy – 12 460; South Africa – 10 151; Turkey – 9 985; USA – 6 365.

4. DoL (2011). See Chapter 4 for statistics on strike activity.

5. For more information on the dynamics and settlement of the construction sector strike, see Cottle (2011).

6. The AWARD was started by the LRS in the mid-1990s to capture wage and non-wage data from collective bargaining agreements. It captures information from agreements entered into between union/s and a company (bilateral agreements), bargaining council agreements (often made up of more than one union and more than one company) and sectoral determinations, which are legislated minimums for certain kinds of work rather than agreements between unions and companies. The database can be accessed online and data are updated continuously. AWARD can be accessed through the LRS web site – www.lrs.org.za.

7. CPI inflation is obtained from Stats SA, which releases monthly inflation data for the country. Inflation data prior to 2008 were revised by Stats SA; consequently, the revised CPI was used for that period. The information is available at www.statssa.gov.za.

8. Stats SA (2011) *General Household Survey*, 2010.

9. Lehohla (2011) – see Table 3.5 on page A-12 of the publication's appendix.

10. Lehohla (2011:11) – see Figure 4.9 in the publication.

11. Stats SA (2011). See table A on page vi.

12. See the speech by the minister of Finance to Parliament presenting the Medium-Term Budget Policy Statement, 25 October, at http://www.treasury.gov.za/documents/mtbps/2011/mtbps/speech.pdf [downloaded 28 October 2011].

13. See SACTWU web site – http://www.sactwu.org.za/pr-and-news/184-nbc2011 [downloaded 28 October 2011].

14. See *Business Day Online* – http://www.businessday.co.za/articles/Content.aspx?id=155236 [downloaded 28 October 2011].

15. See *Business Report*, 1 November 2011.

OPINION | Are labour unions still serving the interests of the entire working class?

REINVENT TO REMAIN RELEVANT: THE CHALLENGE FOR UNIONS AS THE VOICE OF THE WORKING CLASS

Ebrahim-Khalil Hassen

Introduction

Have trade unions become an obstacle to the achievement of South Africa's developmental goals? The balance of opinion in contemporary public policy debates seems to suggest that this is the case. Trade unions, so the conventional argument goes, represent full-time workers, entrench their advantaged position and, in so doing, replicate an economic system characterised by high inequality and high unemployment. Unions, as is to be expected, reject this notion. The view, across union federations, is that they are still the drivers of a redistributive agenda, which speaks for the voiceless poor and challenges the unjust structural underpinnings of employment and distribution patterns. Far from becoming an obstacle to societal change, trade unions argue that they remain as relevant as ever in supporting a more egalitarian society.

This article has two themes. The first is the ongoing, important role that trade unions play in representing their members and in advancing South Africa's economic transformation agenda. In the parlance of the Congress of South African Trade Unions (COSATU) 'transformative unionism' shapes the choices, campaigns and conflicts that unions engage in.

However, the criticism of the trade union movement raises significant challenges that cannot go unanswered. Innovation in several areas of union activity is urgently required to foster the unions' role in achieving a more inclusive society. The methods and means of reimagining trade unionism are the subject of the second theme.

Insider-outsider

Trade unions in South Africa have made major gains since 1994. These have included significant improvements to labour legislation, the entrenchment of collective bargaining in several sectors and social dialogue forums – especially the National Economic Development and Labour Council (NEDLAC) –

which have transformed many aspects of apartheid labour relations. In winning these gains, some have asked whether unions have not become 'insiders' of the very system they criticise? More bluntly, have trade unions been co-opted into a system that they once criticised and, thereby, become part of the problem? The 'insider-outsider' hypothesis argues that trade unions have indeed become 'insiders', and contribute (perhaps inadvertently) to shutting the door on 'outsiders'.

Jeremy Seekings and Nicoli Nattrass (2006: 375) provide a compelling background statement to this argument:

> The post-apartheid distributional regime displays strong continuities from its predecessor, the late apartheid distributional regime, because the biggest losers under both have remained politically weak. The unemployed, especially the rural poor without easy access to urban land markets, were unable to use their electoral strength to secure pro-poor reforms, in part because it was unclear precisely what reforms would be pro-poor in the longer term. The powerful political constituencies in post-apartheid South Africa, on the other hand, were able to mobilize effectively and secure beneficial policies including lowered tax rates and raised wages and salaries for working people with skills.

The argument is important because, taken to its logical conclusion, it provides a response as to why inequality remains so high in South Africa. In more accessible terms, Nic Dawes (2011) refers to this as the 'great carve-up'. His view is that that the economy has been carved up between government, big business and organised labour (the insiders), each of which has received an economic benefit, but at the expense of the poor and unemployed (the outsiders). In essence, the proposition is advanced that the social accord created at the end of apartheid (what Seekings and Nattrass call the 'post-apartheid distributional regime') saw trade unions

> Through regaining their organisational strength, trade unions could play a more progressive role, instead of being viewed as insiders that have been co-opted into the system.

become part of this deal, and that in securing gains for their members, they entered into a compromise that has perpetuated unemployment.

Seekings and Nattrass take the analogy further, arguing that two types of social accord are possible. The first, an 'insider accord', is focused on tweaking the implicit social accord crafted after democracy, which would detail the parameters of wage increases, exclusion for firms unable to pay the agreed wage increases, and improvements in skills training and education. The second, an 'outsider-friendly accord', would include labour market reforms to encourage labour-intensive firms and sectors, support to areas that negatively impact on employment, and changes that benefit the unemployed through measures like public works or a basic income grant. Importantly, such an envisaged package would also include the removal of taxes on employment. In a country with such high levels of inequality and unemployment, the shift from an insider accord to an outsider-friendly accord is a tempting prospect, even if one disagrees with the argument underpinning the shift.

Importantly, the recommendations in both accords are focused on the trade unions making significant compromises and the government providing social security and other reforms; but there are no substantive compromises on the part of big business. In other words, business as an insider would be incentivised to provide more jobs through the compromises reached, and their contribution would be larger numbers of low-skilled jobs. Trade unions have rejected this model. At its 4th Central Committee meeting held in 2011, COSATU criticised this as being unfair, likening it to 'class suicide' (COSATU 2011).

The structuring of possible accords points to weak redistributive channels. It is revealing that the primary transfer occurs from the middle strata to the lowest strata, and not from the top to the middle or lowest strata. The trade union defence of its role in economic policy has been anchored on this feature of the 'insider-outsider' hypothesis. Their core argument has always been that a more just social dispensation would entail a steadier stream of resource and wealth transfer from the top end of the income distribution to the lowest end.

More to the point, trade unions have argued that there are clear linkages between the organised working class and the unemployed in the day-to-day interactions in the economy. South Africa has a high dependency rate (which measures the number of people a working person supports). The National Planning Commission (NPC) provides the most recent estimate, indicating a dependency ratio of 3.9 people for every one

worker (NPC 2011). Thus, there is sufficient evidence of existing redistribution channels from the organised working class to the unemployed, through workers that support unemployed members of society. This is significant, because it challenges the simplistic 'insider-outsider' dichotomy, which assumes little or no solidarity between organised labour and the unemployed.

A more disconcerting truth for trade unions is that the living standards of workers have not improved significantly, despite worker militancy in several sectors. Labour's share of the economy has declined (COSATU 2010). More importantly, settlements on wages and salaries have not been significantly high. Data provided by the National Treasury, for instance, clearly shows that the real wage increase across the economy between 2008 and 2010 was 14.2 per cent (National Treasury 2011). At face value, the increase seems high, but if one considers that labour's share of the national economy has declined, one can infer that other actors in the economy have done significantly better than workers (even those represented in collective bargaining arrangements). Here again, the distributional issues are important, as they show that the higher income earners have benefitted more than workers. Simply stated, organised workers have not managed to attain increases to wages and salaries that would entail the carving up of a small economic pie.

Trade union activity is not limited to collective bargaining. All union federations in South Africa regularly campaign on matters of public policy. COSATU, as the largest federation, leads the way with its focus on changing economic and social policy in South Africa. Solidarity, a union representing mostly white workers has a programme to train apprentices and regularly comments on the impacts of policies such as affirmative action. The Federation of Unions of South Africa (FEDUSA), the second largest trade union federation in South Africa, has a distinctly pro-market stance, and advocates a set of public policy positions to this end. There are, thus, disagreements between trade unions on the exact public policy prescriptions, but there have been contributions to wider public policy issues and debates that suggest a more comprehensive focus than merely representing union members.

Collective bargaining arrangements, too, have placed greater emphasis on smaller firms, the introduction of flexibility to support productivity, and linking employer and employee demands. In the motor industry, there have been several agreements supporting continued work at factories; in the mining sector, there are similar examples. More recently, the agreement in the clothing sector to introduce lower entry-level wages in exchange for increased employment, suggests that the unions are finding more innovative ways to address the challenges that South Africa faces.

The picture is not all rosy, however, with Webster and Von Holdt (2005) showing that restructuring at the workplace after democracy has taken various forms of co-operation, but in several instances also authoritarian restoration (where managers actively seek to assert their authority, as opposed to pursuing co-operative arrangements). There are instances, moreover, where small business players have been unable to meet the commitments reached at bargaining councils, especially when agreements are extended to non-parties to the bargaining council.

The details of innovative wage settlements, and the impact of these on small business, are beyond the scope of this article. However, they do show that the insider-outsider paradigm, which portrays unions as an obstacle to South Africa's developmental goals, is a highly problematic simplification of a much more complex relationship between workers and owners.

Bureaucratisation and politics

There is also a more left-leaning critique of trade unions, which is comprised of three major arguments.

Firstly, the victory of democratisation and the consequent changes to labour laws have turned trade unions from activist organisations into more bureaucratic organisations. In a challenging book, titled *Paradox of victory: COSATU and the democratic transformation in South Africa*, Sakhela Buhlungu (2010a) argues that with democratisation trade unions have lost the organisational muscle they once had. Buhlungu (2010b: 60) says of trade unions:

> In South Africa, the crisis of the industrial union model is best illustrated by its inability to cope with labour market changes, such as the segmentation of the labour market into a core workforce, comprised of workers in permanent positions with benefits and relative security of tenure, and a peripheral workforce, made up of workers in precarious forms of employment.

The argument being made is similar to that advanced by Seekings and Nattrass, but the political project is different. For Buhlungu, trade unions need to regain their militancy to fight fights that are focused on social justice. In other words, through regaining their organisational strength, trade unions could play a more progressive role, instead of being viewed as insiders that have been co-opted into the system. However,

Buhlungu points to the increasingly inward-looking focus of trade unions as limiting their ability to organise and represent outside of formal workplaces. It is a valid criticism, even if somewhat overstated.

COSATU, in particular, has consistently retained close linkages with civil society, as part of its political programme. Its campaigns on fiscal policy, social security and economic policy have prioritised coalitions with a wide range of civil society actors. More to the point, over the last decade, it has consistently managed to bring out the numbers onto the street for campaigns focused on poverty and unemployment. Over a period of three years in the mid-'00s, it held one-day strikes under the theme, 'Crush poverty! Create quality jobs!'. Moreover, its anti-privatisation strikes campaigned for public service delivery by the government, and not as an extension of markets in the provision of public goods and services.

Secondly, the politics of the tripartite alliance have largely played a disciplining role in respect of the organised working class. The relations between alliance partners are difficult to decipher, even for insiders to this process, as there is a constant shifting of positions. Here again, the criticism has merit, especially as it has the potential to divide COSATU. Steven Friedman (2011) makes the point that the 'economic freedom' march by the African National Congress Youth League (ANCYL) had the impact of dividing COSATU affiliates. Friedman further stresses that layering the agenda of workers with politics in the ANC could result in significant weakness and paralysis in the trade union movement.

Trade unions, themselves, are divided by their distinctive political strategies. While COSATU continues to maintain strong relations with the ANC, FEDUSA and several independent unions are fashioning themselves as a 'non-political' trade union centre. There are profound disagreements, thus, amongst the major trade unions on how to engage with the dominant ANC.

Thirdly, new forms of organisation, such as social movements, are emerging outside of the trade union movement. Webster and Von Holdt (2005) argue that trade unions need to find innovative strategies to engage with these new actors and their modes of protest, which are located in communities but linked to the wider changes in what they call 'the world of work'. The relationship between community struggles and wider economic conditions is important to understand in order to grasp why and how such new forms of organisation are beginning to emerge.

COSATU has attempted to engage with social movements and self-organisation efforts by workers on the periphery, primarily by offering support and adopting sympathetic resolutions at its congresses. However, it has not yet managed

The Insider-outsider paradigm is a highly problematic simplification of a much more complex relationship between workers and owners.

> To ensure that trade unions continue to play a wider role, they must first ensure that the arguments they make reflect a wider social reality, and not just the perspectives of their members.

to build strong and sustainable linkages with social movements; nor has it managed to find ways to organise atypical workers. This is an area of weakness that must be addressed, and is given expression in the following rhetorical flourish by Zwelinzima Vavi (2009):

> It must unite unionised and the un-unionised workers, it must bring together blue collar and black professionals. It must unite the workers with permanent jobs with those employed by the labour brokers. The campaign must have clear demands and time frames how these should be realised by when.

COSATU, thus, recognises the challenges that it faces in building a broad alliance that could support a more egalitarian social outcome. However, it would need to undertake significant changes to achieve these outcomes; this is discussed in the final section.

New directions

Thus far, the substantial weaknesses of the rigid 'insider-outsider' hypothesis have been raised, but contextual realities also point to the significant challenges to their relevance that trade unions have to face up to. If it is to sustain its progressive and transformative role, the organized working class will have to adapt to these new realities. How then can it continue to play this role?

The debate about the youth subsidy provides signposts to the answer of this question. Trade unions opposed a proposal from the National Treasury to provide a subsidy for employers to employ young unemployed workers. Their concerns stemmed from the risk of creating a 'dual labour market' for members, but also the fear that the inherently skewed structural nature of unemployment would remain unaddressed. The arguments find empirical support in an important paper by Burger and Von Fintel (2009) who suggest that structural reforms are needed to address structural unemployment; hence, the extension of a youth subsidy would be a meek response. In other words, to ensure that trade unions continue to play a wider role, they must first ensure that the arguments they make reflect a wider social reality, and not just the perspectives of their members.

Secondly, unions must develop policy proposals. In the case of the youth subsidy, trade unions have focused on industrial policy, and on public works programmes. The coherence of the policy positions needs to be improved. However, as shown in COSATU's New Growth Path documents, there is a very conscious effort to speak to smaller business players and seek alliances.

The NPC's Diagnostic Report (2011) also cites Burger and Von Fintel's (2009) analysis of the deeply structural nature of youth unemployment. The depressing conclusion is that the average unemployed 25-year-old youth will still be unemployed at the age of 35 or 45. Yes, there are welcome commitments to expanded public works programmes, and significantly detailed proposals to improve education in the national plan, but the deeper question of how the excluded are to connect with opportunity remains an unmet challenge.

Thirdly, the experiments to organise informal traders, build social movements and even explore new forms of union membership must be sustained. The current membership model for trade unions is beginning to look old in the face of significant changes in the world of work. For instance, informal workers are rarely organised in the workplace, lack regular income to pay monthly fees and often prefer self-organisation. Similarly, social movements are diverse, located in communities or around a specific issue, making old coalitions difficult to implement in the current context. The trade unions must find ways of giving voice to these new forms of organisation, even if it means self-organisation outside of the trade union movement, or membership systems that are flexible enough to accommodate atypical workers. The debate on the youth subsidy showed that trade unions need to build these relationships, not only to garner support, but because the debate on economic transformation must include those outside the formal economy.

Conclusion

Trade unions continue to play an important role in our society, one that is guided by an egalitarian outcome. Attempts to sustain the 'insider-outsider' hypothesis reflect a significant challenge to the role that trade unions argue that they play. Ultimately, though, this hypothesis lacks the substantive evidence to be sustained. The criticism that trade unions are facing a significant challenge to their continued role as social actors capable of representing the 'working class as a whole', however, has merit, because that role is not preordained but rather is constructed in the day-to-day work of trade unions.

TRADE UNION STRATEGIES ARE NOT HELPING THE POOR AND UNEMPLOYED

Carol Paton

The problem with South Africa's economy is that too few people work. While this is a statement of the obvious, the low level of participation in economic activity is remarkable in comparison with other economies. In South Africa, only 41 per cent of adults between the ages of 18 and 60 years do work of any kind, whether full-time, part-time or informal (see Figure 2.3.1).

In comparable developing countries like Brazil and Malaysia, the rate of participation in the economy by working-age adults is around 66 per cent. In developed economies, such as the US and UK, it is 70 per cent.

South Africa's high and sustained rate of unemployment is almost unparalleled anywhere in the world, according to the Organisation for Economic Co-operation and Development (OECD) 2010 country survey. One quarter of the workforce is unemployed and looking for work; at least a further 5 per cent are discouraged from looking for work at all; and the broad rate of unemployment has been well over 30 per cent since the 1990s (OECD 2010).

That this must change is something on which everyone agrees. Job-creation, say the government, business, labour and political parties, is South Africa's overriding priority. However, the debate on creating jobs has been mired in political conflict and has made little progress. Anyone arguing for increased flexibility in employment conditions has been labelled anti-worker, anti-poor and anti-transformation. With a political zeal that has eliminated the possibility of reasoning and genuine engagement, organised labour has defended every inch of space won under the labour regime that came into being in the1990s.

At the other end of the political spectrum, the mission to reverse labour's gains in order to increase labour market flexibility has been held up mistakenly for many years by free market champions as the panacea for our unemployment problems. However, as countless analyses have shown, the reasons for unemployment are deep and historical, and cannot be attributed to any one cause or to the actions of any one social actor. In particular, it has been pointed out in several authoritative studies by, among others, the International Monetary Fund (IMF) and the OECD, that labour laws – those governing hiring and firing – are not the cause of high unemployment.

Misconception, fear and resentment have poisoned the

Figure 2.3.1: Youth and adult employment ratios in South Africa and selected emerging market economies

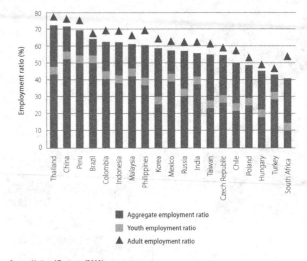

Source: National Treasury (2011)

The reasons for unemployment are deep and historical, and cannot be attributed to any one cause or to the actions of any one social actor.

atmosphere for engagement. The result is that in achieving what is undeniably its most important goal, South Africa remains no closer to finding solutions than when the transition to democracy began 17 years ago.

The trade union movement must take its share of responsibility for the stalemate. Its ideologically laden and outdated theoretical analysis of the unemployment problem and how to solve it is one of the roots of the impasse.

In the past five years, many excellent analyses have diagnosed the unemployment problem from a variety of standpoints. The National Planning Commission (NPC), the National Treasury, the International Panel on Growth (popularly known as the Harvard group) and the OECD have all produced high-level studies on South Africa's economic weaknesses, all outlining a similar picture.

The problem has been summed up as follows. While South Africa's colonial economy, shaped by the extraction of minerals and the development of agriculture, produced large volumes of cheap, black labour to work on the mines and farms, the demand for low-skill jobs was too weak over time to absorb the growing labour force. For most of the twentieth century, the mines and farms employed large numbers of low-skilled people, but there was a very large decline in jobs in these sectors over the past 20 years.

The loss of jobs in mining and agriculture was not compensated for by the growth of manufacturing, which during apartheid was both highly protected and capital intensive. In fact, employment in manufacturing began to decline in 1982 and, by 2004, had fallen by 21 per cent (Hausmann 2008).

So, while the country's development path created masses of low-skilled labour, employment opportunities for this group began to decline markedly from the 1980s. This coincided with the beginning of the end of apartheid and the lifting of restrictions on the movement of black people that had been at the heart of the system. In other words, as most of these studies point out, there was a very large reduction in the number of unskilled jobs at a time when the demand for exactly that sort of work was growing rapidly.

Combine this with the fact that apartheid had all but destroyed the capacity for subsistence and peasant agriculture – which, in many developing economies, continues to provide livelihoods during industrialisation – and South Africa's massive unemployment problem is put in perspective.

What these analyses tell us is that the unemployment situation is deep, historical and structural. On a political level, it is important to acknowledge this, because it means that no social actor – whether trade union, business or government – can be held solely responsible for the development path the economy has taken.

From the 1980s, a further bias against labour-intensive production developed, with employment growth shifting towards skills-intensive sectors such as services. It is widely agreed that the shrinking of employment in manufacturing is probably the most important single factor in the economy's failure to absorb labour in sufficient quantities, but it is here (in the manufacture of goods that can be exported), where relatively low-levels of skill are required, that jobs need to be created. According to the Harvard group, for instance, this is important not only in order to ensure that the growth that South Africa produces is sustainable, but also because 'such a pattern of growth is needed to create the kinds of jobs that use the human resources that the society has at its disposal' (Hausmann 2008: 4).

This means encouraging the growth of industries and firms that can employ large numbers of people in low-skill (and, unfortunately, low-pay) jobs. Preferably, the goods they produce must be made for export, which means again that the wage component of the cost of production must be globally competitive.

COSATU's typical response to these reports has been to dismiss them as ideologically biased. In September 2010, the union federation published an in-depth analysis of its own – *A growth path towards full employment* – in which it advocated a range of radical policies (COSATU 2010a).

Although internally coherent in an abstract, theoretical way, the policy ideas take no account of global economic realities. The argument is that to overcome the exclusion from economic participation of the vast majority, the growth path must have redistribution (which includes higher wages for the employed) as its central organising principle. Since this approach is at loggerheads with 'global forces', an 'active state is required to drive economic development'.

Thus, fiscal policy, for example, should involve higher taxes on the wealthy and on companies, permanently higher spending on social infrastructure, and comprehensive social security. Social security should include a basic income grant for those unable to work and the guarantee of employment 'for everyone of working age who is willing to work and able to work'. Industrial policy would include the nationalisation of strategic industries and the creation of state-owned enterprises in a range of sectors.

All of this would be financed by the creation of a state bank to buy government bonds and by bringing the South African Reserve Bank under state ownership and control, so that its balance sheet could be accessed for 'developmental purposes'.

Only in Utopia would such policies be viable. In the real world, where private investment is central to economic growth and employment, and the resources of the state are limited,

It is widely agreed that the shrinking of employment in manufacturing is probably the most important single factor in the economy's failure to absorb labour in sufficient quantities.

policies like these have no place. The only function that they do serve is to propagate the fiction among workers that old-fashioned socialism could be revived if only enough political will were generated and sufficient pressure exerted. The relevance and importance of what has become the most frequently recommended policy solution – that higher employment lies in the fostering of a low-wage manufacturing sector – is, by definition, excluded by COSATU from the debate.

Much of COSATU's analysis and rhetoric argues that the wage struggles of the employed are where the battle for the redistribution of wealth is fought. The poor and marginalised, who are unfortunately not part of this relationship, should be looked after by the state, it is asserted. These arguments are frequently employed to provide a revolutionary justification for the entrenchment of South Africa's historically segmented labour market, in which a small group of insiders enjoys opportunities from which the outsiders are excluded. And because wages for workers in South Africa are low, relative to the cost of living, and the inequalities between rich and poor are vast, it is an argument that has easily seen off any ANC policy-maker bold enough to raise the issue of wage levels.

There is indeed great moral and political difficulty in asking workers to accept low wages in the interests of restructuring the economy. However, weighed against the objective of drawing more people into work, it is not as immoral as is often contended. Rather than closing down the discussion, union leaders would do well to look for a practical solution to the question of how the burden of a lower-wage structure could be generalised more equally across society.

To make it possible for trade unions to even contemplate such a discussion, it is important that other social actors make certain acknowledgements.

The first is that while manufacturing wages in South Africa are high by developing country standards, the high cost of living and the poor quality of public services means that workers live poor quality lives. The NPC (n.d.) notes that South Africa's hourly manufacturing wage is five times that of Sri Lanka, India, Philippines and China, and three times that of Russia, Brazil, Turkey and Hungary. Nevertheless, as COSATU think tank, the National Labour and Economic Development Institute (NALEDI) points out, the average wage of an unskilled worker (covered by bargaining council agreement) amounts to R1 909.00 per month, which is below the estimated R2 428.00 per month required to provide nutrition and other basic needs for a family of four (COSATU 2011).

Further complicating the picture is that South Africa's 'high wages' came about not by virtue of large or disproportionate

gains made at any point by black workers (something analysed by the OECD 2010 survey), but rather as a result of a combination of changes in labour supply and demand during the 1990s, as well as the wage bargaining system and union power, which stopped wages from falling as much as they would have needed to for the market 'to clear'.

The second acknowledgement that should be made (by business, in particular) is that the excesses of corporate pay have made a discussion on low-wages for workers politically untenable. Not only that, but the escalation of executive pay – which has been rising much faster than wages – is fuelling an unfeasible level of inequality.

One suggested mechanism that could lower wages without making workers poorer – that of a wage subsidy for youth – initially made by the Harvard group has been rejected out of hand by COSATU unions. The wage subsidy – formally proposed by the National Treasury in February 2011 and due to be implemented on a limited scale in April 2012 – will displace older, expensive workers with cheaper, younger ones, according to COSATU.[1]

This is not necessarily true. While there is the danger of some degree of substitution (older, unsubsidised work-seekers are less likely to be favoured in the competition with younger, subsidised work-seekers), existing employees would remain protected by labour legislation and would not be easily substituted.

A wage subsidy for youth doing entry-level, low- or semi-skilled jobs has another advantage for South Africa's particular problems. Due to union power and the collective bargaining architecture, there is strong evidence that entry-level wages are particularly high and problematic.[2] Drawing on analyses by the OECD, the Treasury states that starting wages for entry-level workers in South Africa are 62 per cent of the average formal sector wage; in OECD countries (which also have high starting wages compared to developing countries), starting wages are 37 per cent of average wages (see Figure 2.3.2).

Since workers with or without work experience cost the same to hire, employers have opted unsurprisingly for those who have worked before, putting youth at a disadvantage and (because of enduring, structural unemployment) at risk of a lifetime of unemployment. The social costs of this phenomenon are high.

COSATU's fear of the proposal, however, lies in the possibility that it might just work. Among some workers, and even one union – the Southern African Clothing and Textile Workers' Union (SACTWU), which recently agreed to such an arrangement – lower entry-level wages make sense, if it

means that more people can work. The economic theory of wage elasticity says that it should (the demand for labour should rise when the wage rate falls), and SACTWU's agreement with employers is premised on an anticipated 5 per cent rise in employment. If the increase in employment does not happen over a three-year period, the agreement to employ entry-level workers at lower wage rates will fall away.

Other COSATU unions have responded with outrage to the SACTWU agreement. However, it means that, together with the limited roll-out of the wage subsidy next year, there are two experiments in the field, which will assess the actual and not just theoretical effects of lower wages on labour demand.

A second suggestion for solving the 'high-wage, high-unemployment' problem is an agreement at a society-wide level. Numerous in-depth studies, including the Labour Market Commission in 1996,[3] the national Growth and Development Summit in 2003,[4] the New Growth Path document (DED 2010) and the OECD country study (2010) have all arrived at the same point after grappling with the same intractable problems.

However, COSATU has declared that a pact would be 'suicide', on the grounds that elsewhere in the world similar agreements on wages typically have involved a moratorium on industrial action, which led to the demise of union membership and power: 'If we did sign such an agreement, five years down the line workers would create a new federation, once they see the impact a wage freeze has had on their lives' (COSATU 2010b).

Again, objections of this sort are ideological rather than pragmatic and are based on the principle of self-preservation, which COSATU does not want compromised.

In contrast to the evidence in favour of creating economic activities that would suit the human resources that it has at its disposal, COSATU has done its best to propel the economy in the opposite direction. The campaign for 'decent work' – defined by COSATU (but not by the government) as work that is permanent and has social security benefits – illustrates this trend.

Over the past three years, advocating decent work has entailed a concerted campaign to ban labour brokers, third-party agents that have provided contract employees on a flexible basis with great success. Banning labour brokers, which would mean that employers would have to appoint such workers permanently, is a high-risk strategy for employment. An impact study commissioned by the Cabinet expressed concern that the 'major source of job creation over the past 14 years could be outlawed' (Benjamin & Bhorat 2011).

These are difficult issues for both trade unions and the country to negotiate, but no progress will be made unless

Figure 2.3.2: Ratio of minimum wage to average wage of full-time workers in selected countries

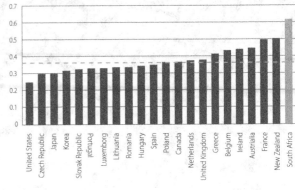

Source: NPC (n.d.)

ideological positions are softened, revolutionary theories are put aside, and pragmatic and practical solutions are looked at. Nowhere is this truer than within the trade union movement, which has continued to take its guidance from outdated theories with an uncertain Utopian destination.

It is unreasonable, however, to expect workers and union leaders to make the necessary leap to a new way of thinking on their own. Others in society need to make it happen by, among other things, spreading the burden of poverty more equitably, committing to reducing inequality, and uplifting the poor and working classes through good quality social services that could compensate for a lower-wage structure. Two issue-based social accords – one on increased skills training, and a second that has set a 75 per cent local target for government procurement – concluded this year between the government, business and labour are excellent examples of how to share responsibility among social actors to promote better employment outcomes. A social accord on productivity would be the next place to look for even greater progress to be made. Trade unions should agree to engage rather than object for abstract ideological reasons.

Notes

1. The wage subsidy proposed by the National Treasury will subsidise employers who take on new workers between the ages of 18 and 29 and who earn less than R60 000 per year. For the first 12 months, the subsidy will be 50 per cent of the wage to a maximum of R12 000, tapering off in the second year towards zero. Existing young workers will be subsidised for 12 months, at a rate of 20 per cent, tapering off to zero.

2. One reason for South Africa's high starting wages is the bargaining council system, which sets minimum wages across sectors. While big employers and big labour tend to belong to councils, wage agreements can legally be extended to non-parties. In OECD countries, legal extension of agreements to non-parties has been found to be particularly bad for employment outcomes. Empirical research on bargaining councils backs this up, showing that firms covered by bargaining councils pay wages that are 10 per cent to 21 per cent higher than similar firms that are not covered (Magruder 2010).

3. *Restructuring the South African Labour Market, Report of the Presidential Commission to Investigate Labour Market Policy* (1996). Available at: http://www.polity.org.za/polity/govdocs/commissions/fintoc.html.

4. *Growth and Development Summit Agreement*, June 2003. Available at: http://www.nedlac.org.za/summits/presidential-summits/growthanddevelopment-summit/agreement.aspx.

Chapter 3

Skills and Education

> While schools cannot fix the ills of society, this should not lead us to dismiss their importance in countering the effects of poverty and inequality.

Skills and Education at a Glance

An underperforming education system continues to be a major obstacle to increased employment in a labour market that is strongly skills-biased. At present less than 20 per cent of South Africa's labour force is in possession of a tertiary qualification (degree or certificate). Despite significant budget allocations (education still remains the single largest line of government expenditure), progress has been slow. While access to educational institutions has increased, the quality of outcomes remains disappointing, when compared to the country's emerging market peers, but also when measured against that of several other African states.

89%

Youth literacy rate for South Africa

LITERACY RATES

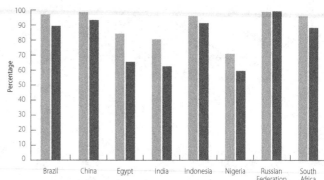

Total youth (15–24) literacy rate % 2004–2008*

Total adult literacy rate % 2005–2008*

Source: The State of the World's Children 2011, UNICEF, Tables 1 and 5

Note: * Data refer to the most recent year available during the period specified in the column heading.

SACMECQ III DATA FOR MATHEMATICS AMONGST GRADE 6 STUDENTS

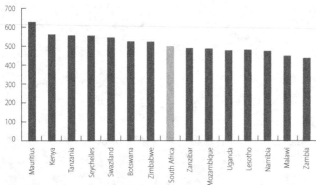

Source: SAQMEC Website: www.saqmec.org/downloads/sacmeqIII/WD01_SACMEQ_III_Results_Pupil_Achievement.pdf

Note: SACMEQ stands for Southern and Eastern Africa Consortium for Monitoring Educational Quality; This is an African study done on Grade 6 students; SACMEQ III data were collected during the fourth quarter of 2007.

SACMECQ III DATA FOR READING AMONGST GRADE 6 STUDENTS

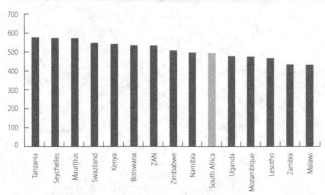

Source: The State of the World's Children 2011, UNICEF, Tables 1 and 5

2011 National Senior Certificate (NSC) results in perspective				
National performance	2008	2009	2010	2011
Number of candidates	533 561	552 073	537 543	496 090
Number of passes	334 239	334 716	364 147	348 117
Percentage of passes	62.6%	60.6%	67.8%	70.2%
Mathematics	2008	2009	2010	2011
Number of candidates	300 008	290 407	263 034	224 635
Number of passes (30% +)	136 184	133 505	124 749	104 033
Percentage of passes (30% +)	45.4%	46.0%	47.4%	46.3%
Physical sciences	2008	2009	2010	2011
Number of candidates	217 300	220 882	205 364	180 585
Number of passes (30% +)	119 206	81 356	98 260	96 441
Percentage of passes	54.9%	36.8%	47.8%	53.4%

Source: Department of Basic Education: Report on the National Senior Sertificate Examination 2011 – Technical Report

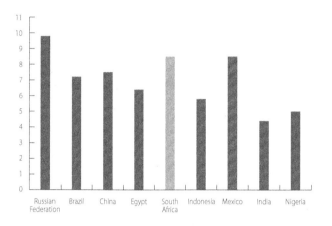

MEAN YEARS OF SCHOOLING OF ADULTS (25 AND OLDER)

Source: UNDP 2011

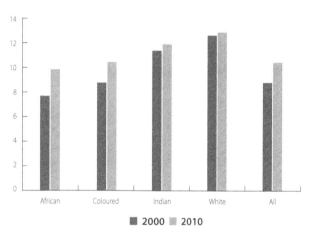

EDUCATION OF EMPLOYED SOUTH AFRICANS BY RACE (AVERAGE NUMBER OF YEARS)

■ 2000 ■ 2010

Source: OHS 1995–1999, LFS 2000-2007, QLFS 2008–2010

EDUCATIONAL ATTAINMENT OF NARROW LABOUR FORCE

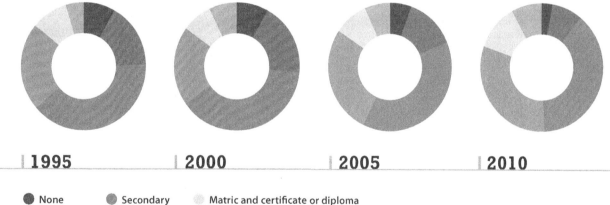

| **1995** | **2000** | **2005** | **2010** |

● None   ● Secondary   ● Matric and certificate or diploma
● Primary   ● Matric   ● Degree

Source: OHS 1995–1999, LFS 2000–2007, QLFS 2008–2010

Formal sector workers in highly skilled occupations					
	African	Coloured	Indian	White	National
2000	19.2%	18.8%	32.4%	50.1%	27.1%
2005	19.7%	21.4%	35.6%	50.1%	27.0%
2010	21.2%	28.9%	46.1%	60.2%	30.2%

Source: OHS 1995–1999, LFS 2000–2007, QLFS 2008–2010

30.2%
Proportion
of employed
South Africans
in highly skilled
occupations

REVIEW | The challenge of South African schooling: dimensions, targets and initiatives

Linda Chisholm

. . . .

The crisis in South African schooling is not new. It predates the achievement of democracy in 1994 and has been an ongoing refrain in public discourse since 1994. What is new is the emerging consensus on its dimensions and causes. Since the 1990s, both the government and donors have invested substantial resources in understanding what exactly the problems may be. The government has not been slow to respond to such findings, but in the welter of everyday crisis-talk, these responses have gone largely unnoticed and are rarely analysed and discussed. The resulting public debate is the poorer for it.

It is important to analyse these directions, however, and to understand them, as they form part of a wider palimpsest of debates and approaches not only in South Africa but also globally. The crisis discourse surrounding education and the policy approaches adopted locally resonate with international debates. The discourse is one of comparative learning performance and what to do about it. This article accordingly considers what some of the research informing government thinking shows on the dimensions and causes of the education quality challenge, what the government is doing about it, how it fits into broader international debates and what it means.

The challenges in schooling

Dimensions

The quality of education, linked to equity in the system, was identified as the main challenge facing South African education since the early 1990s. Its principal manifestation until recently was matric results. However, as international and provincial assessments of children's literacy and numeracy skills lower down in the system gathered momentum, so the full extent of the problem in South Africa was also laid bare through scholarly and popular syntheses and elaborations of the evidence relating to underperformance (Reddy 2006; Howie 2007; Howie & Plomp 2008; Fleisch 2008; Bloch 2009; Taylor & Yu 2009). Despite improvements in more equitable spending, relieving poor schools of fee burdens, introducing school nutrition, increasing the number of children attending Grade R classes, achieving near-universal enrolment in the compulsory phase of schooling and dramatically expanding the number of qualified teachers in the system, learning outcomes are still abysmal by any measure (DBE 2011a).

Recent assessments provide ample evidence. The United Nations Educational, Scientific and Cultural Organisation (UNESCO) and Southern African Development Community (SADC) collaboration in the form of the Southern and Eastern African Consortium for Monitoring Education Quality (SACMEQ) has enabled comparison of Grade 6 literacy and numeracy capabilities across the SADC region at two key points in 2000 and 2007 (see IIEP, UNESCO & SACMEQ 2011). South Africa does well on gender equality and a gradual reduction of its high repetition rates over the period, but there is no change in the overall trend for South African pupils' *reading* achievement and a negligible improvement in their *mathematics* achievement. South Africa performed below the SACMEQ mean in both reading and numeracy. South Africa also performed worse than other much poorer countries in the region, such as Swaziland and Tanzania (IIEP 2010). One of the most telling findings is the association between household poverty and learning achievement. As UNESCO pointed out in its analysis, 'children from the wealthiest households in South Africa are ten times as likely as children from the poorest households to score well on reading. This is more than double the comparable wealth differential for Namibia', which has a similar level of achievement to that of South Africa (UNESCO 2011: 87).

Most disturbing of all, however, have been the results of the education department's own annual national assessments (ANAs), first conducted in 2009 and again in 2011 (DBE 2011a). The tests were administered in all Grade 1–6 classes across the country, and the Human Sciences Research Council verified the results and conducted an analysis of learners' responses. The ANAs not only document and confirm the wide disparity in test scores between schools located in different socio-economic contexts, and progressive deterioration in results from Grades 1 to 6, but also provide insight into what children are getting wrong and, consequently, are not learning to do (DBE 2011b). The latter is instructive.

On the whole, children simply did not understand what they were being asked, even when they were responding in their home language. Handwriting, even beyond the Foundation

Far too many learners are stigmatised as failures, leaving school without literacy and numeracy capabilities, and heading for unemployment and bare survival in a society and global world that thrives on and rewards high-level education and skills, knowledge and innovation.

Phase, revealed a lack of writing practice. Children were unable to answer simple grammar questions, including spelling of commonly used words, the proper use of prepositions, plural forms, tenses and opposites. Reading comprehension was limited, as was the children's ability to write their own text from given prompts. A Joint Education Trust school-effectiveness study (see Taylor 2011) has provided similar in-depth information on reading. The study estimates that, on average, South African children perform writing of any kind in language classes once in about four days, despite the curriculum providing time for language teaching every day.

In the ANA numeracy tests, children were unable to perform basic numeracy operations, such as subtraction, multiplication and division, involving whole numbers. They had seriously limited or distorted conceptions of fractions and could not translate a problem given in words and write it in a way that enables them to solve the problem. Common mathematical misconceptions seem to be shared by teachers and students (Carnoy, Chisholm & Chilisa forthcoming; Taylor 2011).

Not surprisingly, in part as a consequence of such little learning, there are high repetition rates in the lower grades and high drop-out rates in the higher grades. So, although South Africa can be proud of its high enrolment and attendance rate, as well as the achievement of gender parity in enrolment and performance, its repetition rates are much higher than the international norm, especially among boys in the lower grades, and far fewer girls excel academically than should be the case (Motala & Dieltiens 2010). Over-age learners are much less likely to persist in school and much more likely to repeat and drop out. Such 'silent exclusions', where children are nominally enrolled but learn very little and are at risk of dropping out, are significant in the Western Cape, in particular, but learners across the country are affected (Lewin 2008; CREATE n.d; Gilmour & Soudien 2009; Lewin 2009; Meny-Gibert & Russell 2009). These access issues mask the deeper quality challenge of providing 'meaningful access' to learners.

For those who do survive to matric, the certificate is still their gateway to the labour market. Matric is now less of a gate-keeper than it was under apartheid: while the number of candidates increased from 518 225 in 1996 to 537 543 in 2010, the number of passes increased even more from 278 487 to 364 573 over the same period. The employment and earnings prospects for those with a matric remain higher than for those without and higher still for those with some form of tertiary education. It is even better for those with a matric and pro-

ficiency in English (Casale & Posel 2010). Of consistent concern has been the small numbers passing mathematics and science and qualifying for higher study in these subjects. From 2009, the old higher and standard grade distinction was phased out and mathematics literacy, a subject intended to provide basic mathematical skills to a broader range of students, replaced mathematics standard grade. The result was that many students who could be taking and passing mathematics at a higher level have tended to opt for mathematics literacy instead (Simkins 2010). Again, proficiency in English is a good predictor of success in the matric exam.

The cumulative consequence is that far too many learners are stigmatised as failures, leaving school without literacy and numeracy capabilities, and heading for unemployment and bare survival in a society and global world that thrives on and rewards high-level education and skills, knowledge and innovation. The hidden depths and dimensions of these lived realities and their underlying causes can be glimpsed through Jonathan Jansen's regular public interventions and riveting weekly column in *The Times* (Jansen 2011).

Reasons

Explanations and reasons pivot around whether such out-comes are seen as principally contextual or school-based. Government explanations tend to link poor results to school functionality. School functionality, in turn, is seen as the consequence of a variety of linked issues. The National Planning Commission (NPC) has summarised an emerging consensus that acknowledges the role of inequality and contextual factors but sees school and classroom-based issues as decisive in the functionality of a school and its results. School functionality is linked to a combination of leadership, management and administration, teaching, resourcing and support-related issues. Without dismissing all the factors that have a bearing on poor performance, the NPC's assessment is that 'the main problems in schools lie in teacher performance and school leadership' (NPC 2011: 15). The idea is that if a school is dysfunctional, its school leadership and classroom practice need attention, in the first instance. The view that a combination of factors rather one cause is necessary for a full explanation and understanding of the problem is borne out by analyses of the SACMEQ III results.

To understand why the education system reinforces current patterns of poverty and privilege instead of challenging them, Van der Berg (2011: 08) refers to a 'double burden' that

> Linguistic, race, class, culture and gender differences often compound the barriers to learning that learners face in classrooms.

learners from poor communities in South Africa face – the burden of poverty and 'the burden of attending a school that still bears the scars of neglect and underfunding under the apartheid dispensation'. What matters in schools are the management of resources, the number of teachers and teacher quality, textbooks, classroom practices, discipline and management, assessment and feedback and home background. On resources, IDASA's Russell Wildeman goes so far as to say that while they are important, their availability and efficient use will not by themselves bridge the education quality gap in South Africa (Wildeman 2010). He, too, points to classroom factors as mattering most in learning outcomes.

Although education is the highest item of budgetary expenditure in South Africa, and per capita expenditure has increased substantially in both nominal and real terms since 1995, government expenditure on schooling as a percentage of the country's GDP declined from 4.9 per cent in 1995 to 4.1 per cent in 2009, and education's share of government expenditure declined from 22 per cent in 1996/97 to 17.7 per cent in 2009/10 (DBE 2011a). This is much less than, for example, Botswana, Kenya and Namibia spend on education. Thus, global spending allocations are not as extravagant as is often claimed. Even so, the annual auditor-general's provincial reports show significant under-spending and financial management challenges in several provinces (see PMG 2011). The availability of resources at school level has as much to do with household income as with how it is managed at provincial and school level, and with systems that militate against equity.

School leadership and teacher performance, as the NPC (2011) mentions, are critical in-school factors accounting for school functionality and literacy and numeracy achievements. Honing in on these issues, more specific analyses of teacher quality have linked it to what teachers know, their ability to convey complex concepts and ideas and their commitment and motivation to teaching, otherwise known as content and pedagogical-content knowledge. When they are unsure and unconfident of what they know and have to teach, teachers will then also be unlikely to teach it well, will avoid teaching those parts of the curriculum they find difficult and will seek to find ways of spending less time in the classroom (Carnoy et al. 2011; Taylor 2011).

The 'critical shortfall' of learners passing mathematics and science at higher levels seems to be linked to poor levels of teacher content and pedagogical-content knowledge, the small number of teachers who are actually able to teach these subjects, and the fact that many teachers qualified to teach scarce subjects do not actually teach them, while teachers not qualified to teach mathematics and science do teach these subjects (Paterson & Arends 2009; Simkins, Rule & Bernstein 2007; Simkins 2010). The issue of shortages is one of quantity and quality, across the system, and is part of a wider problem in the recruitment, retention, education and deployment of teachers faced in the system as a whole.

A link is also often made with the language of learning and teaching. Learners who are proficient in English are more successful in matric as well as later in the labour market (Casale & Posel 2010). This is something that schools and parents recognise and that results in their choosing English as the language of learning and teaching, even though home-language proficiency in the early years is critical for later success, and despite teachers' English proficiency being weaker than their home-language proficiency. Moreover, UMALUSI (the education quality-assurance council) has drawn attention to the fact that the issue in home-language teaching in African schools is that standards and expectations are low and that until this changes the transfer to English will be ineffective. The priority here, therefore, is improving home-language instruction, a matter principally of teacher education and resources. However, it is made more difficult when student-teachers do not take up bursaries to specialise in the teaching of home languages and when classrooms, especially in urban areas, have a variety of languages in them and a common language has to be found. The curriculum review of 2009 (DBE 2009) argued that the transition from home language in Grade 3 to English as a language of learning and teaching in many African schools in Grade 4 gave rise to learning difficulties that would be solved by starting with English in Grade 1, such that both the home language and English as the first additional language would be taught simultaneously. English would not substitute for the home language but would be taught alongside it.

The problem to be addressed, in the perspective sketched above, is located in the classroom and centres on classroom practice. Both contextual and school-based issues have a bearing on classroom practice, but it is seen as capable of change with the correct policies and strategies in place. In searching for reasons or underlying causes of the problem in South African schooling, the tendency is not to go for mono-causal but to favour complex yet focused explanations that enable key issues specific to classroom practice to be addressed.

What the government is doing about it

Dialogue, debate and participation

The dimensions and cluster of reasons discussed above all point to what needs to be done. There is no single, overarching policy intervention that will solve all problems; a range of small changes across different areas relating specifically to the school-based factors, however, will make a big difference (Carnoy et al. 2011). In addition, an approach committed not only to improving learning outcomes but to social justice and democracy more broadly also requires 'processes of dialogue, consultation and debate' (Tikly 2011: 11) and a more substantial engagement with diversity in South African classrooms (Sayed & Ahmed 2011). The National Education Policy Act 27 of 1996 provides for consultative processes in the determination of national policy, and a national framework for inclusive education does exist. However, what are national commitments in practice?

In this respect, the role of the teacher unions has come under scrutiny. The NPC itself has acknowledged that educational issues 'cannot be fixed without the active participation and engagement of teachers, their unions and parents' (NPC 2011: 15). This is in line with the commitment by the ruling party to ensure that education becomes a 'societal issue,' an issue that engages, mobilises and harnesses all sectors of society towards addressing the crisis in education and improving teaching and learning in schools. When wage talks stalled in 2010 and the teacher unions went on strike at a critical juncture in the year for matriculants, national mobilisation in support of the matric class of that year was overwhelming. Supplementary tuition activities mushroomed and have continued in many cases. In this vision of learners being at the centre of a society-wide national educational effort, labour peace is considered preferable to labour conflict. Unions and government acting together is considered more beneficial to the overall goals of education than a showdown between them that can result in vitiating rounds of labour conflict.

In pursuance of education becoming 'a societal matter', a national Accord on Basic Education was launched in October 2011. The Accord is a partnership between the Department of Basic Education (DBE), business and organised labour. It is explicitly intended to mobilise support for schools in the light of the ANA results and their analysis to identify schools most in need of assistance (see DBE n.d.). While the government considers dialogue essential, there is evidence that unions, teachers and analysts do not think there is sufficient consultation and dialogue on key policies. Official forums and channels exist for such dialogue, but the time frames of research, consultation, policy and implementation frequently conflict and produce tensions, as evidenced in recent curriculum revision processes. Conflict and co-operation exist in tension with one another in a society and sector that is highly divided but increasingly focused and united on the key priority of improving classroom practice.

Dialogue, consultation, debate and participation go beyond dialogue between the government, business and unions and include the involvement of parents and other members of civil society. One of the aims of the ANA is to help parents understand better how their children are performing and how they can help them to improve. This is based on the perspective that lack of information constitutes a key blockage in the system, and providing such information will help the 'consumers of education' (parents) make demands on the 'producers' of education (teachers and principals) to improve the quality and supply of it. Here, the assumption is that education quality will improve only when the demand for and expectation of better quality education are higher than they are currently. This is a model that underestimates how social class works in education and schooling in South Africa; low levels of literacy among parents historically have tended to reinforce rather than help parents to challenge power differentials between themselves and school principals and teachers. Since the unintended consequences of education have a habit of undermining the good intentions, it is important to monitor and assess whether this aim is met or not and with what consequences.

Where projects have been undertaken independently to mobilise communities in the interests of education, they have resulted in the successful establishment of reading clubs, homework centres, matric catch-up classes and campaigns for school libraries (Kgobe 2011) as well as innovative projects that use 'mentoring as an alternative model for teacher training' (Bloch et al. 2011: 37). The Western Cape, especially, has been the site for numerous reading club initiatives, including the Vulindlela reading clubs and Learning-to-Read project, which trains volunteers to teach and assist with the teaching of reading in schools. Perhaps the most visible and successful of such mobilisation initiatives has been the NGO, Equal Education, which campaigns for school libraries and librarians, and conducts various forms of youth leadership training and educational programmes as a means not only of mobilising communities but of enabling youth and interested supporters to become active agents in their own educational and social development. Through its Bookery project, Equal Education has been able to start libraries in schools. Such projects can be no substitute for government responsibility but are a vital part of a democratic society in which citizens are also able to take the initiative to ensure the realisation of broader social and educational goals.

Diversity

Recognition of diversity is as central to South Africa's formal commitment to democracy as is its commitment to debate, dialogue, consultation and participation. Yet, policy activity in education, according to Sayed and Ahmed (2011: 111), 'suggests a failure to substantially address this link' between diversity, equity and quality. Classrooms in South Africa have become much more diverse than they were. Linguistic, race, class, culture and gender differences often compound the barriers to learning that learners face in classrooms. At least one province, KwaZulu-Natal, has made major strides in improving its results by placing an inclusive framework at the centre of its education implementation strategies. Thus, it can work.

> The message is going out that the expectations are higher than the outcomes that are being delivered, and that turning education around requires concrete plans and action from everyone at all levels in the system.

Nevertheless, despite the existence of national and provincial frameworks for inclusive education, many provinces, districts, principals and teachers are inadequately trained to recognise and address differences and specific needs. Research on the experience of migrants, for example, shows that regardless of policies, frameworks and curricular intentions, a lack of awareness of rights and xenophobic or discriminatory practices still prevail in many schools. This suggests a need for ongoing dialogue between researchers, teachers and policy-makers at national and provincial level to design appropriate interventions. Fataar (forthcoming) offers vivid insights into different learning dispositions that children bring to schools and the 'suppressions of learning' that occur in those spaces.

An approach to quality that takes diversity seriously might differentiate 'one-size-fits-all' policies that are generally framed in the interests of the middle class (Soudien 2004). It would support the approach popularised by the McKinsey report among policy-makers on *How the world's most improved school systems keep getting better* (Mourshed, Chijioke & Barber 2010). The report essentially argues for the principle of differentiated strategies for different schools and classrooms on the basis that all systems have different starting points and all can improve. By extension, an approach that takes diversity in the classroom seriously needs to think about structured teaching and learning strategies that take different starting points and experiences of learners in classrooms seriously. The issue is complex and requires careful attention.

Target-setting approach

Policies to redress inequalities in order to improve the quality of education have been central priorities since the mid-1990s. They have not produced the desired outcomes. Responding to the mounting evidence of implementation failure across a wide range of sectors, but education most importantly, the administration voted into office in 2009 not only made education 'an apex priority' but also introduced an intersectoral approach focused on target-setting, monitoring and evaluating the implementation of activities to enable the achievement of goals and targets. The approach of the DBE is informed by this broader governmental approach. The Minister of Basic Education has signed a delivery agreement to improve the quality of education. Her success will be measured by the achievement of national targets set for literacy and numeracy in Grades 3, 6 and 9 and for mathematics and science in matric. By 2014, it is expected that at least 60 per cent of learners in the early grades will be able to perform at the required level. Targets have been mapped for each province against their

ANA 2011 results, and provinces will set targets and design interventions for districts and schools.

The DBE has developed an Action Plan to 2014, which sets in place the priorities, strategies and activities to ensure achievement of the targets. Activities are organised around four themes: improving early childhood development; the quality of learning and teaching; undertaking regular assessments to track progress; and improving and ensuring a credible, outcomes-focused planning system. It identifies specific cross-cutting activities for the national, provincial and school levels to take up in accordance with constitutional responsibilities. The focus of the national department is on policies, frameworks, norms and standards, and monitoring and evaluation, whereas that of the provinces, is on actual implementation.

National and provincial alignment and co-ordination

The system is designed constitutionally to allow considerable decision-making and diversity of approach at provincial and local level. In effect, this has meant that while some provinces such as Gauteng, the Western Cape and, to some extent, KwaZulu-Natal have surged ahead in designing and implementing specific literacy and numeracy implementation strategies in line with the overall approach, others such as the Eastern Cape, Limpopo and Mpumalanga, with their more difficult inheritances, have been less successful. Thus, provincial and urban-rural inequalities are reinforced. The Eastern Cape is a case in point. Here, financial and administrative collapse of the provincial educational administration at the beginning of 2010 led to the establishment of a Cabinet-approved national intervention team consisting of representatives from several departments led by the DBE. It was their task to work with provincial counterparts to get systems back in place. However, the provincial authority mounted a successful legal challenge to the authority of the national department in the province, reaffirming a more limited role of the national team in addressing the crisis there. Thus, the tragedy of the Eastern Cape continues. At the time of writing, the South African Democratic Teachers' Union (SADTU) was threatening strike action during matric exams to effect removal of the Basic Education Superintendent-General in the province (see reports on the Eastern Cape to the Parliamentary Portfolio Committee, 23 March 2011; *Daily Dispatch* 15.09.11; *Daily Dispatch Online* 05.11.11).

The national department has vested considerable energy in seeking alignment and national co-ordination of provincial initiatives so that they focus more equitably on the key priority of improving teaching and learning in the classroom. The main instrument for this has been the ANAs. Through the Council of Education Ministers and Heads of Education Departments, a methodology has been developed to assist all provincial and district officials and schools to analyse the results and to develop plans and strategies to address them. Leading by example, the national minister and deputy minister have visited poorly performing schools and districts across the provinces, checking scripts, providing feedback to schools on difficulties experienced by learners in the tests, meeting with regional-level principal and district bodies, motivating them to turn their schools around by setting realistic improvement targets and providing concrete suggestions for the kinds of improvement strategies to be adopted. In this way, the message is going out that the expectations are higher than the outcomes that are being delivered, and that turning education around requires concrete plans and action from everyone at all levels in the system.

Curriculum

Other national-level initiatives to support teaching and learning have included a continued focus on the strengthening of early childhood education curricula and teacher education, the streamlining of the national curriculum and assessment framework, new developments in teacher recruitment, education and development, the introduction of a national catalogue of textbooks and the development of 24 million Grade 1–6 workbooks for learners in 18 854 public primary schools. Successful curriculum implementation requires not only clear and accessible curricula, but also motivated, knowledgeable and well-qualified teachers, adequate teaching and learning support materials, appropriate district support and guidance and realistic implementation time frames. In line with the recommendations of a review committee (DBE 2009; see also *Curriculum News* 2010, 2011), the Curriculum and Assessment Policy Statements (CAPS) combine previously disparate documents and provide more detailed guidance to teachers on what is to be taught and assessed on a term-by-term basis. Implementation will be gradual and incremental, starting with the Foundation Phase in 2012. Provinces will continue to develop plans for the improvement of teaching home languages and the first additional language from Grade 1 and up.

Teacher recruitment, education, development and deployment

Improvements in teacher recruitment, education, development and deployment are critical to better teaching and learning. This is a function that is split between the DBE and the Department of Higher Education and Training (DHET). The DBE manages the recruitment of students intending to enter teaching, and provides in-service training to already-serving teachers, whereas the DHET manages the provision of teacher education. In order to address shortages, the Funza Lushaka

bursary scheme was introduced in 2005. These bursaries specifically target students intending to become language, mathematics and science teachers, as well as those who intend to teach in the Foundation Phase. Bursaries are provided at all 23 institutions providing teacher training. The number of awards has risen from 5 447 in 2008 to 8 532 in 2011. The average value of a bursary is R52 700. Additional bursary opportunities are provided through provinces and the Education, Training and Development Practices Sector Education and Training Authority (ETDP SETA). More than 65 per cent of Funza Lushaka graduates are teaching in schools that serve poorer communities.

Despite teachers graduating in increasing numbers, the profession is still not attracting enough new teachers; consequently, the allocation to the Funza Lushaka fund for 2012 and 2013 has been increased by R220 million. In order to retain bursaried teachers in the system, the contractual obligations attached to the bursary have been increased and require that newly qualified teachers provide a minimum of four years of service. Should they default, they have to repay the bursary with interest. In addition, incentives are in place for teachers who teach in rural areas and hard-to-reach schools.

In 1994, 65 per cent of teachers had a matric plus a three-year qualification; 95 per cent of teachers are now so qualified (DBE 2011a). Teacher development is being provided at some 140 district teacher development centres. However, despite the improvement in qualifications and a long history of in-service teacher development, there seems to be little relationship to learning outcomes. Questions are raised, therefore, about the quality of teacher education and development programmes. A National Institute for Curriculum and Professional Development is being established to ensure, among other things, that content-rich, pedagogically sound short courses are in place that are aligned to the content frameworks of particular subjects and phases or specialist areas. Successful learning on these courses must enable teachers to improve their teaching practice.

In order to ensure that teacher education and development are oriented towards providing the knowledge and skills that teachers require to do their jobs well, the DHET has developed a policy on minimum requirements for teacher education qualifications. This is in accordance with the Strategic Planning Framework for Teacher Education (2011) developed by the department and teacher unions. The DBE, together with the Treasury, is also finalising a protocol in terms of which teacher unions will be able to provide for teacher development. Departmental training initiatives in 2011 focused on the redesign of roles and responsibilities of district officials to support the curriculum, as well as preparation of training frameworks for provinces to use in the implementation of the Curriculum and Assessment Policy Statements. A Mathematics and Science Strategy focuses specific attention on how to increase the numbers and improve the quality of teachers teaching mathematics and science.

> In a context where only 45 per cent of children in South African schools have sole use of a textbook, cheaply-produced yet attractive workbooks can play a supplementary role in boosting literacy and numeracy practices in schools.

Inefficiencies in the appointment and deployment of teachers that result in mismatches are a major focus of attention for the short to medium term.

Resources

Good resources are vital in all contexts, but are more so in schools and classrooms surrounded by poverty. Decentralised systems of textbook procurement introduced in the post-apartheid dispensation have not had equitable consequences, and have been expensive for the state. Each child still does not have a textbook and other necessary resources for each subject. In order to ensure that every learner has a text for every subject, the department has sought to improve equity and efficiency in the system. In line with the recommendations of the Curriculum Review Committee (DBE 2009), it developed a national catalogue for books to be used in Grades 1–3 in 2012. This catalogue recommends eight books in each subject (languages, mathematics and life skills) from which schools can choose. The intention of the catalogue is also to control pricing. The rapid introduction of the new approach led to considerable anxiety on the part of publishers and tensions between publishers and the department. After consultation with publishers, the system is being introduced more gradually for other grades. Such consultation and dialogue is ongoing and considers various aspects of the process.

Another controversial new development in 2011 was the department's initiative to provide learner workbooks to children in the poorest quintiles. In a context where only 45 per cent of children in South African schools have sole use of a textbook (IIEP 2010), cheaply-produced yet attractive workbooks can play a supplementary role in boosting literacy and numeracy practices in schools. The intention, accordingly, was to provide something where there is nothing and/or augment resources where they are limited. Although the principle of state development and distribution of learner workbooks has been welcomed, critics have had difficulties with the underlying conceptualisation of literacy acquisition, the perceived threat to the professionalism and autonomy of teachers embodied in the provision of texts to teachers, and the inefficiency in the delivery of the books to schools. The latter was due to gaps in information systems. This is another area where national and provincial alignment is being sought, as there is great variation in the quality of the learner and school information-gathering systems in provinces.

There is a long way to go in the development, use and dis-tribution of workbooks. Workbooks on their own are unlikely to result in major learning improvements. They need to be supported by more extensive and linked teaching resources and broader reading, writing and numeracy practices that cut across home, community and school. Still, they are a small start that can make a difference alongside other small changes contributing towards a bigger reorientation in schools to focus on teaching, learning and providing better resources. Already, the department is responding to difficulties picked up in information systems and delivery, and in improving the content and presentation. The intended evaluation of the workbooks will no doubt generate important suggestions on how to improve their development, distribution and use.

Intended furniture and infrastructure improvements are now not only part of a national departmental initiative running alongside additional provincial infrastructure budgets, they are also a priority for the government as a whole, as Finance Minister Pravin Gordhan spelt out in his medium-term budget policy statement in October 2011. The backlogs are enormous and hugely varied, and the process requires careful planning for effective delivery. The Development Bank of Southern Africa has been appointed to improve existing structures, while the implementing agents for basic services are the Mvula Trust, the Independent Development Trust and Eskom. Their work should result in infrastructure maintenance and upgrades to schools, including windows, water, electricity, libraries and laboratories, as well as the replacement of mud structures and the building of new schools to keep pace with demand.

Accountability

Accountability in the system is being improved through a refocus on teaching and learning in the classroom and through the institutionalisation of performance contracts with managers across the system. In order to ensure that principals are indeed the instructional leaders they should be, new appointment procedures are in the process of being developed. The NPC plan proposes that only qualified people are appointed in school (and that there is no undue political or union interference), more teachers are trained and better trained, and test scores are used as accountability measures (Manuel 2011). Since 2010, principals and teachers have no longer been permitted to hold political office. The emphasis is firmly on ensuring that principals and teachers commit to their core task of instruc-tional leadership. A bill for the formal establishment of the National Education and Evaluation Development Unit as a statutory body is scheduled for tabling in Parliament soon.

Conclusion

The achievements of the post-apartheid government in education are largely obliterated by persistently vast socio-economic inequalities, as well as inequalities in learning outcomes and the exceptionally weak literacy and numeracy results of learners in poor communities. The approach in basic education is informed, on the one hand, by the view that schools can make a difference in poor communities if they function as schools should, with all the essentials of good leadership, management, teaching, resourcing and support in place, and, on the other hand, by the performance and outcomes-oriented approach of the government as a whole. National targets have been set for improving learner performance, broken down at provincial and then individual school level, assessments have been conducted to identify weaknesses and areas for intervention, and strategies and activities have been designed with appropriate monitoring and evaluation processes to check progress.

Target-setting and performance-monitoring are common international tools, best known in the UNESCO Education For All (EFA) and Millennium Development Goals (MDGs) initiatives. These have had both strengths and limitations as strategies for intervention: while few analysts question the good that targets can do, there is now considerable knowledge about why and how they are not always achieved. In South Africa, many risks (including those relating to capacity, participation, agency and accountability) confront the implementation of all new activities.

Nonetheless, one of the greatest achievements in the last few years has been the mobilisation and rallying of significant sectors in society to a recognition of the depth and breadth of the challenge. The government, as one of these sectors, has acknowledged that there is a problem and has made a concerted effort to focus the work of everyone in the sector on improving literacy and numeracy. There is a plan that is being implemented and assessed. Pitfalls, weaknesses and unintended consequences there certainly are, but at least the building blocks are in place and there seems to be broad agreement on the overall direction being taken.

OPINION | Do uniform targets help to improve schooling outcomes?

BALANCED CRITERIA SHOULD REPLACE PERVERSE PASS-RATE INCENTIVES

Nick Taylor [1]

Indicators of any activity always serve a dual purpose. On the one hand, they are measures of performance; on the other, they set targets to aim for. The problem with indicators is that they are generally achievable in one of two ways: by improving performance or by taking a short cut. A good example of the latter approach is given by the twin brothers who each ran half the Comrades Marathon and were caught out only when a sharp-eyed official noticed that in one video sequence the runner was wearing his watch on the left arm and in a later sequence the runner with same number had his watch on the right arm.

Indicators of school quality are particularly problematic because schooling is such a complex activity and its quality, consequently, difficult to measure. A simplistic set of indicators is easier to manipulate than a well-designed set. At the same time, increasing the consequences of any set of indicators tends to increase pressure towards manipulation. For example, reports of schools and even whole districts in the United States cheating in the tests used to measure progress on the No Child Left Behind accountability system are increasing, while in South Africa system-wide manipulation of the National Senior Certificate (NSC) examinations is known to have occurred in the years 1999–2003.

Pass rate

The main measure of learning achievement in South Africa is the pass rate in the NSC examination at the end of Grade 12. However, this is an unreliable indicator of quality, which is strongly correlated with the number of candidates writing the examination, with the pass rate increasing when the number of candidates decreases and *vice versa*, as is clearly shown in Figure 3.2.1.

It makes sense that the smaller the numbers in Grade 12 classes the more individual attention teachers can provide and the higher the likelihood that students will pass; this will be particularly apparent if weaker candidates are excluded from progressing to Grade 12 and from writing the exam. One way of manipulating pass rates, therefore, is to screen learners at the end of Grade 11. There is evidence that this is happening on a large scale, with a fall-off in school enrolment between Grades 11 and 12 of around one-third across the country. Take, for example, the cohort of students who entered Grade 10 in 2008 and wrote the NSC in 2010: of the one million Grade 10 students in 2008, only 54 per cent survived to Grade 12, and of the cohort who started Grade 10 in 2009, only 52 per cent made it to Grade 12 two years later (see Table 3.2.1).

Opportunity

A far more appropriate indicator of improvement in NSC results than the ubiquitously quoted pass rate would be the number of passes in absolute terms in relation to the population of 18-year-olds. There has been a steady increase in the number of learners passing in the last decade, growing from 249 831 to 364 513 (an increase of 46 per cent) over the period 1999–2010. The number passing matric as a proportion of 18-year-olds between 1990 and 2008 varies between 25 per cent and 35 per cent, a very low figure by international standards. However, the good news is that this proportion has been increasing steadily since 1999, a fact that cannot be explained by an increase in population, as population growth has remained essentially flat over this period.

Quality

Given the chronic underperformance of the South African system in comparison with many of our poorer neighbours, the highest priority should be given to improving educational quality. The quality of school outcomes depends essentially on learners' ability to analyse, describe and reason in natural and mathematical languages, in verbal and written forms. From this perspective, much obviously stands on how well the learner can speak, read and write in the language used as medium of instruction. On this issue, the majority of South African learners suffer their greatest educational disadvantage, having to learn all their subjects in English, which for them is a second or even third language. It follows that one of the most important mechanisms for improving the quality of schooling for the greatest number would be to raise the standard of the language curricula and to improve the teaching and learning of all languages, especially the language of instruction. In this regard, the provisions in the new curriculum to be implemented in Grades 1–3 in 2012, which give greater weight to the learning of English as a subject from the very first year of schooling, are to be welcomed. At the high-school level, the fact that those who do not speak English as a home language are schooled in what is known as English First Additional Language (EFAL) is a major disadvantage. EFAL is pitched in a lower academic register than English Home Language (EHL) and, therefore, EFAL learners do not acquire as easily the linguistic resources needed to sustain sophisticated arguments in subjects such as history, biology and chemistry. Perhaps we should strive to move more schools and greater numbers of children onto the EHL curriculum and set the ratio of EHL to EFAL passes as one indicator of matric quality. Given the emotional nature of the language debate, this is likely to be a controversial proposal but, if we are serious about improving quality, one that the country needs to face.

Another indicator of quality is generally taken to be the number of students qualifying to register for a bachelor's degree at university, the highest grade of NSC pass. The number of candidates obtaining a bachelor's pass has shown a marked increase in the last three years, rising from 15 per cent of the cohort in 2007 to over 23 per cent in 2010 (see Table 3.2.2).

However, universities have expressed concern over the quality of bachelor-level passes since the introduction of the new NSC curriculum in 2008. These concerns are supported by the fact that there has been a significant fall-off in numbers taking the 'difficult' subjects of mathematics, science and accounting in the last two years (see Table 3.2.3).

Since all students are required to take either mathematics or mathematics literacy, an important quality indicator for the system would be the ratio of mathematics to mathematics literacy passes. Nearly 36 000 fewer candidates registered to write mathematics in 2010 compared with 2008, and nearly 9 000 fewer passed. Over the last three years, the proportion of students taking mathematics has declined from 56 per cent of the cohort to 49 per cent (see Table 3.2.4). This indicates that principals are directing students away from mathematics towards mathematics literacy, a practice that narrows student options for further study. This is a trick for making it easier to pass and, thereby, to increase the pass rate, but it is a cynical step that disadvantages both the student and the country.

It seems that while the numbers of students qualifying to enter university are increasing, the quality of these passes is declining, certainly in terms of numbers of candidates for

Figure 3.2.1: Enrolment, passes and pass rate, Senior Certificate, 1994–2010

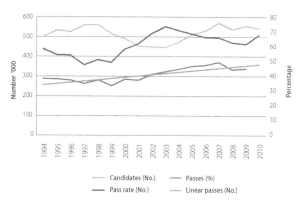

Source: DBE (2011a)

Table 3.2.1: Survival rates, Grades 10–12, 2008–2011						
Year	Enrolment			Fall-off Grade 10–12	Per-centage lost	Per-centage survival
	Grade 10	Grade 11	Grade 12			
2008	1 076 527	902 752	595 216			
2009	1 017 341	881 661	602 278			
2010	1 039 762	841 815	579 384	497 143	46	54
2011	1 094 189	847 738	530 000	487 341	48	52

Source: Constructed from DBE (2010), DBE (2011a) and DBE (2011c)

Note: These figures do not take account of the many students who spend more than one year in any grade, and, therefore, give only a crude idea of survival rates.

Table 3.2.2: Bachelor-level NSC passes, 2003–2010		
Year	Bachelor's pass	Bachelor's pass (%)
2003	82 010	18.6
2004	85 117	18.2
2005	86 531	17.0
2006	85 830	16.2
2007	85 454	15.1
2008	107 274	20.1
2009	109 697	19.9
2010	126 371	23.5

Source: DBE (2011a)

courses in mathematics, engineering, basic science, commerce and economics. This does not auger well for the government's plan to increase university enrolment sharply in the next five years. Not only should we be tracking numbers taking and passing mathematics in the NSC as a key systemic indicator, but we should also begin to measure the number of candidates who write the third mathematics paper, which deals with the tougher aspects of the subject and which is presently optional. Here, the universities should take the lead: for example, faculties of mathematics, statistics and engineering could set Paper 3 first as a 'recommendation for entry', and later as a requirement. In parallel, the DBE should measure and annually report on the proportion of students taking Paper 3.

Equity

An analysis of the examination results by race shows that, while Africans constitute nearly 83 per cent of NSC candidates, their low pass rate ensures that they make up only 77 per cent of passes. Furthermore, while two out of every three white children qualify for bachelor's entry, only one in five African children does. Of course, race remains strongly overlain by poverty, and the underlying problem of the figures shown in Table 3.2.5 is that it is poor children who continue to receive inferior schooling.

The same patterns are apparent in enrolments and passes in mathematics (Table 3.2.6). While the proportion of African candidates taking mathematics is surpassed only by Indian candidates, the pass rate in mathematics for Africans is less than half of that for Indians. Again, the underlying problem is poverty and the poor quality of schooling offered to children from poor homes.

The country does a lot better with respect to gender equity, a fact that places us well in advance of all developing countries on this indicator. Nevertheless, there remains room for improvement in increasing female participation and success in mathematics and science. Girl students are more numerous than boys at the top end of high school, because boys fail more frequently. However, although the participation rates of boys and girls in mathematics are comparable, female candidates do not perform as well as their male counterparts (see Table 3.2.7). While 50 per cent of male candidates passed mathematics with an aggregate of 30 per cent or more in 2009, this was the case for only about 42 per cent of females. Similarly, 33 per cent of boys passed at the 40 per cent mark, while only 26 per cent of girls did so.

Table 3.2.3: Candidates taking mathematics, physical science and accountancy, 2009–2010

Subject	Candidates		Difference	Percentage decrease
	2009	2010		
Mathematics	290 630	263 034	-27 596	9.5
Physical science	221 103	205 364	-15 739	7.1
Accounting	174 420	160 991	-13 429	7.7
Total	552 073	537 543	-14 530	2.6

Source: Reply to parliamentary question by Minister of Education, issued by Parliament, 11 May 2011

Table 3.2.4: Students taking mathematics in the NSC, 2008–2010

Year	Total NSC candidates	Mathematics candidates	Mathematics as percentage of total
2008	533 561	298 821	56.0
2009	552 073	290 407	52.6
2010	537 543	263 034	48.9

Source: DBE (2011a)

Table 3.2.5: NSC entry and passes by race

Race	Candidates as percentage of total	Pass rate	Bachelor's pass rate
African	82.7	63.2	18.3
Coloured	7.1	78.4	24.2
Indian	2.6	100.0	57.6
White	7.6	100.0	67.0

Source: DBE (2011a)

One of the most important mechanisms for improving the quality of schooling for the greatest number would be to raise the standard of the language curricula and to improve the teaching and learning of all languages, especially the language of instruction.

Conclusion

The progress of our school system towards providing quality education for all must be measured against a balanced set of indicators. Unfortunately, an exclusive focus on the pass rate provides perverse incentives for officials, principals and teachers to withhold opportunity by failing students in Grade 11 or insisting that they register as part-time candidates, and to compromise quality by moving them onto an easier subject set. We need to set ourselves more sophisticated indicators, in order to incentivise all actors in the system to improve the quality of teaching and learning, rather than to look for ways to play the system, at the expense of individual students and the country as a whole.

Opportunity should be measured by the proportion of 18-year-olds who gain a level-4 qualification. This need not necessarily be the NSC; as the country improves its FET college system and expands enrolment in that sector, the National Certificate (Vocational), which is equivalent to the matric obtained in schools, should grow and add to the proportion of young people with a level-4 qualification.

On the issue of quality, simply measuring the number of students who qualify to enter university can lead to a devaluation of this metric. A far more appropriate measure of quality is the proportion of matriculants with mathematics. More controversially, I would suggest that the proportion who take English at the Home Language level will serve as an even more important indicator of the standard of the NSC.

Regarding equity, we should move increasingly to tracking the performance of poor children in the system, the overwhelming majority of whom attend schools formerly reserved for Africans. As the country slowly deracialises its school system, poverty must replace race as the standard against which equity is measured.

Finally, the pass rate is an effective measure of efficiency, but only once indicators of opportunity, quality and equity have been computed.

Notes

1. This paper draws heavily on DBE (2011a) *Macro-indicator trends in schooling: Summary report 2011*.

Table 3.2.6: NSC entry and passes in mathematics by race

Race	Mathematics candidates as percentage of total candidates	Passed ≥ 30% (percentage)	Passed ≥ 40% (percentage)
African	50.3	41.0	24.0
Coloured	27.9	62.5	42.0
Indian	58.8	86.5	73.7
White	48.4	95.1	85.9

Source: DBE (2011a)

Table 3.2.7: Mathematics participation and success rates by gender, 2009

Gender	Mathematics participation (percentage)	Passed ≥ 30% (percentage)	Passed ≥ 40% (percentage)
Female	48.8	42.4	26.3
Male	49.1	50.2	33.0

Source: DBE (2011a)

BEWARE OF THE MISLEADING MEANS AND MEASURES

Russell Wildeman

Is the publication of public schools' performance data a desirable way to extract accountability from public institutions and promote choice in the selection of schools for our children? On the basis of available statistical evidence and the need to find fairer measures to judge schools' performance, it is argued here that school league tables provide misleading information about school quality to administrators and parents. Furthermore, it is suggested that in spite of strong external pressures to adopt performance measures in South African schools, the government would be far better served by focusing on other quality-enhancing approaches with higher international success rates.

This article firstly examines the case for the use of performance information, especially school league tables. School league tables rank schools on the basis of their learners' performance in routine examinations or, in some instances, on the results of standardised language and mathematics tests. Although different criteria can be used for ranking schools, usually a school's mean outcome on a subject is compared to its predicted outcome (controlling for a range of variables, of course) and the difference is viewed as an 'effect' of the school, hence the term 'school effects'.[1] Schools are then ranked according to the magnitude of their effects. Thereafter, the article reviews arguments and evidence against the use of school league tables as an accountability tool. The arguments for and against the publication of school league tables are then considered in the context of present debates in the education sector. Given the need for some information to gauge progress in schools, a compromise position is discussed, after which concluding thoughts are offered on the use of performance information in promoting school quality.

The case for performance information in schools

The call for comparative performance benchmarking has often been based on the perception that education standards are declining, do not exist or are variable across the schooling system. Inevitably, the incessant preoccupation with the way modern societies spend scarce government resources is related to the concern about educational standards. Proponents of public performance measures or school league tables argue that governments' resources agendas are removed from the reality of schooling, and that schools and education admini-stration are not given any incentives to preserve or better utilise financial and non-financial resources. The same argument holds that schools are given no concrete, minimum educational standards to achieve and that this organisational practice is outdated and contributes to negative social and economic outcomes in society. Measurement of performance is seen, therefore, as a viable way to tackle the performance gap in schools, designate role expectations for those who are responsible for results (teachers, principals and administrations), devise school improvement targets, monitor such targets and take action against schools that show no visible signs of improvement. In some parts of the developed world, where such practices still exist, institutional targets are based on student performance in standardised tests of verbal (language) and numerical (mathematics) reasoning. Although the performance of individual students is measured, such results are aggregated to the institutional level and then compared to schools that have a similar schooling profile (socio-economic characteristics and school resources).

In the United Kingdom (UK), these results are published, and parents are encouraged to study and use them to make sound decisions about future schools for their children. Administrators, in turn, would use such data to make decisions about so-called 'outlying' schools, which require dedicated support and turn-around strategies. At the start of the implementation of school league tables in the UK, raw scores of students, aggregated to the school level, were used as comparative performance measures. However, pressure from academic researchers, whose work indicated that differences in results were in the main due to different learner intakes, forced the government to adopt 'value-added' measures, in terms of which the predicting equation includes measures of prior academic achievement as well as other individual attributes that predict performance. In this way, comparisons can be made between learners with similar profiles, but who attend different schools. By calculating average learning gains over each school's learner populations, the ground is prepared for statements about the relative effectiveness of schools.

Generally speaking, the value-added school effects were regarded as better and fairer estimates of schools' contributions, but academic researchers still insisted that uncertainty intervals be published for all estimated school effects. These intervals would enable users of the data to make better

Using school league tables rewards affluent schools because of the clientele they are able to draw, and unfairly punishes poor schools because their learner populations are poor and educationally disadvantaged.

judgements about the relative precision of the school effects and whether school performance was sufficiently different to justify alternative choices. On the whole, most results reveal wide uncertainty intervals, which is indicative of the imprecision with which the effects (and hence overall quality) of schools are measured.

Those who oppose the publication and promotion of school league tables as an accountability and choice tool have put forward an impressive array of statistical evidence and appeals to notions of social equity and justice. The most notable counter-arguments are introduced and explained below.

The causal fallacy

Raudenbush (2004) makes the important point that one cannot establish school quality or claims of effective institutional practice merely by looking at the academic results of schools. In order to make such a claim, researchers must presume an intervention or treatment (managerial quality or teacher excellence) and assume that the effect of this treatment can be separated from other variables that are associated with academic outcomes. In survey research, the best that research-ers have been able to do thus far has been to identify those factors that most powerfully predict academic results. In this research, prior academic achievement has emerged as a strong predictive factor, whether it refers to individual learners' earlier cognitive achievements or to a context where learners with similar achievement levels are concentrated in certain schools (compositional effect). In fact, when this variable is controlled for, many of the differences in performance among schools in American and British samples disappear. This suggests that schools that do consistently well have access to the same quality intakes on an annual basis; as such, the results tell us more about their students (and their parents) than about the schools and their practices. In fact, there are complex effects operating in such schools, because, as some research has shown, teachers respond positively to such schooling contexts and learners, thus further implicating factors that are difficult to separate from each other. Theoretically, this process (or, actually, its inverse) operates in poor schools where learner and teacher expectations are lowered, leading to a mediocre academic climate, which, in turn, creates poor results. Using school league tables in such situations rewards affluent schools because of the clientele they are able to draw, and unfairly punishes poor schools because their learner populations are poor and educationally disadvantaged.

Imprecision of measured school effects and instability of school effects over time

This article has already referred to the wide uncertainty intervals that surround estimates of school effects, thus indicating the lack of precision with which school effects have been measured. The reasons are statistically simple to explain. Trying to extract a lot of information from typical sample sizes (class sizes) of about 30 will not add much precision to the measures; yet, this is all we will ever have in trying to make inferences about whether some schools are better than other schools, or whether a particular school's performance falls below the benchmark for schools with similar socio-economic profiles.

Apart from the statistical imprecision with which school effects are measured, research has found relatively low correlations between different cohorts' outcomes. In other words, if we were to compare the results of a group of students now with those of a group that wrote the same tests a few years ago, the trend would be one of weakened correlations between cohort results the further apart the tests of the various cohorts were. This suggests that schooling effects (or performance), controlled for prior academic achievement and other relevant factors, are variable over time. Therefore, when parents need to choose a school for their children, they are likely to rely on present performance data (or ranking in a league table), while the results that ought to matter are an assumed level of performance of schools somewhere in the future (see Goldstein & Leckie 2008; Leckie & Goldstein 2009). Given the low correlations between school effects in different cohorts, school league tables undoubtedly provide mislead-ing and questionable information to parents who base their choice of school on simple league tables.

This point is very vividly illustrated by research that examined school performance in the UK over a three-year period (Thomas et al.1997). The rather low correlation between cohorts who wrote the examinations only two years apart (1990 and 1992) was particularly notable, thus further questioning the useful-ness of school ranking tables in assisting parents with choosing the 'right' school for their children (see Table 3.3.1).

Longitudinal data and the introduction of fairer and non-punitive measures

In school effectiveness studies, consensus has emerged on the importance of longitudinal data in studying changes within and among schools. This has reduced the policy importance that is attached to results from cross-sectional surveys; yet, just about all the information that goes into school league table information is derived from one-shot, cross-sectional surveys. Arguably, the most interesting development from studies of change has been the focus placed on the *rate of learning* instead of mean achievement levels. In other words, when learners with similar academic profiles, but enrolled in different schools, are compared, what value does the school contribute to their academic achievement? Raudenbush (2004) calculated the correlations between two measures of school effectiveness, namely achievement levels and the rate of learning (value-added measure) from the same national survey. His strategy was to show how these two measures give different results and how high-poverty and low-poverty schools would be affected by each of the measures. Table 3.3.2 shows the results for Grades 8 and 10 on the science and mathematics results.

For Grade 10 mathematics, for example, ranking schools on mean achievement levels and on the rate of learning produces discordant results, as is manifested in the rather low correlation of 0.46. The same pattern is observed for Grade 8 mathematics, and even the slightly higher correlations for science do not support the view that these two measures capture the same performance dimension. Although value-added measures are far from perfect, they at least ameliorate some of the difficulties associated with mean performance measures. As Raudenbush indicates, if mean performance measures are used, most high-poverty schools would be regarded as failing, but when value-added measures are used (measuring learning gains from one year to the next), rich and poor schools contribute equally to the learning gains of their respective learner populations. These results demolish the myth that more learning happens at affluent schools and support the view of teachers in poor schools that their efforts go unrecognised because of the severe educational and social disadvantages of their learners. How does one reconcile such results with the reality in which rich schools consistently produce better results than schools serving poor learners? Learners have different cognitive entry points, and, therefore, in spite of the gains made by poor learners during high school, these uneven entry levels have a significant bearing on the final, unequal academic outcomes.

Table 3.3.1: Correlations across cohorts in a UK three-year study, 1990–1992

Subject	1990 cohort vs. 1991 cohort	1990 cohort vs. 1992 cohort	1991 cohort vs. 1992 cohort
English	0.86	0.40	0.77
Mathematics	0.59	0.56	0.83
Science	0.52	0.41	0.59
History	0.92	0.71	0.83
English literature	0.84	0.38	0.71
French	0.48	0.38	0.57

Source: Adapted from Thomas et al. (1997: 190)

Table 3.3.2: Correlation between mean achievement levels and value-added measures for Grades 8 and 10 (USA national data)

Subject	Grade 8	Grade 10
Science	0.78	0.67
Mathematics	0.59	0.46

Source: Adapted from Raudenbush (2004: 26)

There are two points worth noting. By focusing on the actual learning that takes place, researchers have posited a fairer and more equitable way of judging what schools do. This also has the effect of portraying teachers at working-class schools for what they are – hard-working professionals in the main, but clearly not magicians. The latest research suggests that in spite of valiant efforts by teachers at poor schools, the results of these schools are consistently lower than those of their richer counterparts. The important lesson we need to learn here is that while schools cannot fix the ills of society, this should not lead us to dismiss their importance in countering the effects of poverty and inequality.

Reliability versus validity in school performance measures

The point has been made above that average achievement levels, as an indicator of school quality, are problematic because such results are greatly affected by the social and economic composition of the school. Yet, it is just such a measure that is used in school league tables. Some consider it a less valid measure of school effectiveness than learning rates because schools have arguably more control over the rate at which learners amass new knowledge (Von Hippel 2009). However, while learning rates are regarded as more valid measures than school achievement levels, the latter are more reliable because they are less variable from one year to the next. Von Hippel makes the point that the gains in reliability that achievement levels have over learning rates are not large enough to offset poor validity. Ultimately, we should be measuring the actual contributions of schools and not promoting measures that blend and confound socio-economic advantage and school practices.

Schools are differentially effective

It is often assumed that a school that does well in one subject should be doing well in all subjects. However, recent research has shown that schools are differentially effective in at least two ways (see Yang & Woodhouse 2001; Lauder et al. 2010):

» Firstly, it is not certain that performance in one subject (or measure) necessarily translates into the same performance in all the school subjects offered. Thus, one-shot measures suffer from bias and may provide an incomplete picture of the effectiveness of schools.
» Secondly, some schools achieve better results for learners who have particular social and economic profiles, and, hence, it becomes problematic to use an omnibus performance measure to judge the overall effectiveness of a school.

Perverse behaviour as a result of the pressures of school league tables

If schools are rewarded for good test results, then there is very little to stop schools from 'engineering' good results. We have already seen ample evidence of this practice in South Africa, where learners routinely are asked to enrol as private candidates, learners are encouraged to take softer subject options, and Grade 11 hopefuls (who are considered risky prospects) are not promoted to Grade 12. This results orientation makes schools less likely to deal with problem cases arising from socio-economic deprivation, thereby further sliding schools into the 'win and produce results at all costs' syndrome. In any society with large socio-economic inequalities, the school league table and testing approach is likely to accentuate performance rifts and produce inequitable schooling outcomes.

Given the arguments for and against school league tables, we need to ask whether the present educational situation in South Africa is ripe for the acceptance and promotion of these blunt instruments. There is, firstly, a growing consensus that our schooling system fails to produce sufficient quality, as demonstrated by our low scores in international standardised tests. Whatever problems one may have with these international and regional instruments, there is ample evidence to vindicate general concerns about the quality of our schooling system. Secondly, there is some appetite for school rankings, as manifested in the Sunday Times' Top 100 School Survey done in 2009 and academic research conducted shortly after the first democratic elections in 1994 (Crouch & Mabogoane 1998). While these attempts at ranking schools can be dismissed as lacking academic rigour, it is symptomatic of the growing clamour to measure and judge the overall perform-ance of schools. Thirdly, the Department of Basic Education (DBE) is under pressure to deliver an improving set of results at both the primary and high-school phases. This situation, coupled with forceful attacks by influential personalities on the perceived role of the South African Democratic Teachers' Union (SADTU) in the quality quagmire, means that the DBE will come under increasing pressure to provide performance information about individual schools. In short, the social and educational situation in the country makes the final push for the adoption of some performance measures in schools easier, and it is only a matter of time before the government enters this problematic and explosive arena. These developments are supported by the government's own attempts at develop-ing a system-wide monitoring and evaluation mechanism, and politicians' acceptance of an outcomes-based framework as per 'delivery agreements' with the president of the Republic of South Africa.

The consequences of adopting school league tables in South Africa are truly frightening. Already, we have significant competition for learners from advantaged backgrounds (academically and economically), and we know how this

> Public school league tables, which have funding and reputational consequences, could only result in a race to the bottom in an environment that is already too competitive and deeply unequal.

'creaming-off' process continues to devastate the talent pool at schools in poorer communities. If schools are under pressure to show incremental changes in annual assessments, this fighting over learners will become even more intense, with negative implications for poor schools. Furthermore, talented working-class learners will find it increasingly hard to enter schools that are focused on boosting their middle- and upper-middle-class clientele. None of these scenarios is far-fetched, because we know that South African schools eliminate learners with weaker potential to complete Grade 12, actively encourage risky learners to enter as private candidates, and practice an outdated concept of catchment areas to make sure 'undesirable' learners do not enter the system. Public school league tables, which have funding and reputational consequences, could only result in a race to the bottom in an environment that is already too competitive and deeply unequal.

While voices for quality, performance measurement and so-called accountability have become louder, other viewpoints that focus on equity and redress have been drowned out. If South Africa's unequal and entrenched socio-economic situation is predicted to remain the same in the next 20 years, then the Minister of Basic Education should ask the following questions. Are there examples of schools that consistently achieve high levels of academic performance *and* succeed in blunting or muting the relationship between socio-economic (dis)advantage and academic outcomes? How do we teach, manage, provide resources and create conditions that make this equity-realising scenario the focus of our education interventions in the next 20 years? By adopting these questions, the education authorities could shift the debate decisively away from the need to publish unfair and socially discriminatory school league tables to informing the nation on an annual basis how far we have come in producing greater equity in educational outcomes in our public schools. This strategy must not be promoted as optional; given the miserable recent history of the country, adopting a careful yet firm approach to the management of schooling quality, it should be a primary obligation. Instead of dividing constituencies, as is presently the nature of the discourse on quality, the education authorities should pull out all the stops to cement social cohesion among key role-players. However, they can only do so if they present a compelling vision of quality, equity and redress for the schooling system.

The question, nevertheless, remains whether any information about schools' performance should be provided to the public? We are, after all, at a moment in South Africa where the right of access to information is critical. It would be odd indeed if we were to marshal credible statistical and social justice arguments to block any positive information and feedback to schools. This article does not argue against providing information on the performance of schools, but it does suggest that misleading information – as is contained in school league tables – is just as bad as no information. However, it is entirely defensible to provide performance information to the relevant role-players (school management, parents, teachers and learners) and allow schooling communities and education authorities to develop acceptable improvement plans. Also, it must be understood, as Leckie and Goldstein (2009) argue, that information about how well one school does relative to other schools is but one piece of information, which should not be privileged above other equally valid pieces of information. The authors argue that if comparative school performance information is used with other accountability tools, then the circumscribed use of such information could be quite productive and empowering to schooling stakeholders. Hence, instead of promoting further socio-economic inequality, we should be encouraging improved functioning of school governance structures and better working relationships between district officials and local school governance structures. In instances where local school governance is weak, community stakeholders need to think beyond the confines of one school and adopt effective structures with a wider area/regional import.

What then is the way forward in forging a better connection between providing relevant performance information and affecting academic outcomes in a positive way? In my view, there are four things that the education authorities need to prioritise:

» The government should invest resources in strengthening the existing Education Management Information System (EMIS) and align the data-collection process with the targets agreed between the president, the premiers and their respective education ministers. EMIS units are understaffed, still do not attract professionals with the right skills, and do not understand their role in the quest for better-quality education. Ideally, a senior official should be appointed to head the EMIS unit, with this person reporting directly to the head of the department.

» The DBE should invest in high-quality education panel data or longitudinal studies. These data are critical for establishing the annual gains schools make, determining how the rate of learning is affected by school composition factors, identifying those factors that explain differential learning rates within and between schools, and identifying schools that consistently achieve high academic outcomes (large intercepts) while moderating the relationship between (dis)advantage and outcomes (flatter slopes). The data should be made available to researchers in academia and civil society to stimulate healthy debate about school effectiveness and to develop context-specific benchmarks that could be used by schools and education authorities.

» The DBE should develop a policy that specifies minimum norms and standards around the kind of information that ought to be published on an annual basis. The purpose of such a document should be to promote access to quality education indicators and to empower all stakeholders to have an informed debate about the state of our public schools.

» Provincial education departments should be encouraged to develop reasonable estimates of schools' effects by using longitudinal data and tracking the average rates of learning over time. These authorities should also use cross-sectional data on average achievement levels and combine this with the longitudinal data estimates. Such comparative school information should be made available to stakeholders, but the education authorities must make it clear that the release of data to stakeholders is intended to inform school improvement plans. Both the DBE and provincial education authorities must analyse and monitor school improvement plans and results, and publish findings in their annual reports. The auditor-general must be requested to do a proper performance audit and to report to Parliament on whether our schools are making progress towards more quality and equitable outcomes.

What this debate shows is that in an attempt to right a wrong (fixing poor-quality education), advocates for quality education could act punitively against high-poverty schools and reward low-poverty schools, on the basis of school rankings in league tables. In doing so, they would make no contribution to solving real equity and educational problems, and merely reinforce an ingrained anti-poor attitude so pervasive in South Africa.

Notes

1. This way of calculating school effects is actually outmoded and relies on what methodologists call the means-on-means regression approach. Today, the standard way of calculating school effects is to take the average of the residuals of all learners in a school and pre-multiply this school residual by a shrinkage factor. The sample size of the school is critical in this calculation – the smaller the sample size, the more the calculation of the school effect relies on the population average (intercept) because the sample contains so little information. In these situations, the raw mean school residual is shrunk to the value of the population average. Conversely, the larger the school sample size, the smaller the shrinkage of the raw mean residual to the population average, which means that the raw mean residual and the calculated school effect would be almost identical.

Poverty and Inequality

> In real terms, those who find themselves in lower income categories have not seen an increase in their earnings in the post-apartheid years. Relative to those in higher income categories, earnings have actually dropped.

Chapter 4

Poverty and Inequality at a Glance

South Africa's apartheid legacy remains most visible in the country's systemic and high levels of poverty and inequality. Since 1994, great progress has been made in the reduction of access and income poverty, through broadened access to basic services and an exponential growth in the extension of social grants and pensions to the most vulnerable citizens. Longer-term expenditure at current levels on both, but particularly the latter, will be difficult to sustain. Levels of inequality within the broader society, but also within the country's historically defined population groups, have continued to increase. This will be difficult to address in the absence of higher levels of job creation.

SOUTH AFRICA IN A GLOBAL PERSPECTIVE: LIFE EXPECTANCY AT BIRTH

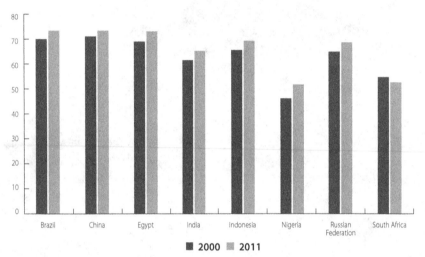

■ 2000 ■ 2011

Source: Life expectancy at birth: UNDESA (2011)

52.8
Average life
expectancy of
a South African

Per capita income Gini coefficient					
	Aggregate	Black African	Coloured	Indian	White
1993	0.67	0.55	0.43	0.46	0.42
2000	0.67	0.61	0.53	0.50	0.47
2005	0.72	0.62	0.60	0.58	0.51
2008	0.70	0.62	0.54	0.61	0.50

Source: PSLSD (1993), IES (2000, 2005) and NIDS (2008): Calculations by Leibbrandt, M. et al.

INCOME POVERTY IN SOUTH AFRICA

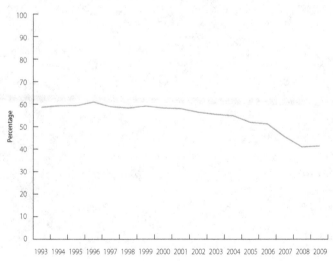

Source: All Media Products Survey (poverty line used: R3 864 per capita per annum, 2 000 prices)

Note: This is the official poverty line proposed by Murray Leibbrandt and Ingrid Woolard, and has been commonly used in recent literature. It stands for the amount required to spend on food and essential non-food items.

TOTAL NUMBER OF GRANT AND PENSION RECIPIENTS (MILLION)

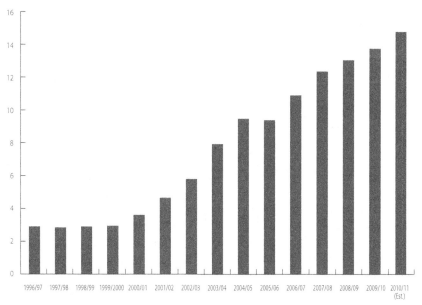

Source: National Treasury: Intergovernmental Fiscal Review, Editions 1999, 2003, 2005, 2007 and Medium-Term Budget
Policy Statement, 2010

14.8m
South Africans drawing grants and/ or pensions from government

LIVING STANDARDS: PROPORTION OF HOUSEHOLDS STAYING IN FORMAL DWELLINGS

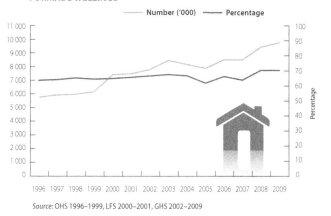

Source: OHS 1996–1999, LFS 2000–2001, GHS 2002–2009

HOUSEHOLDS WITH PIPED WATER IN DWELLING OR ON SITE

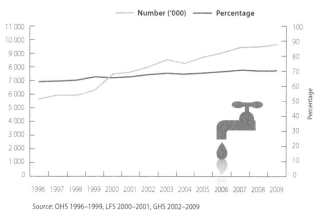

Source: OHS 1996–1999, LFS 2000–2001, GHS 2002–2009

HOUSEHOLDS WITH FLUSH OR CHEMICAL SANITATION FACILITY

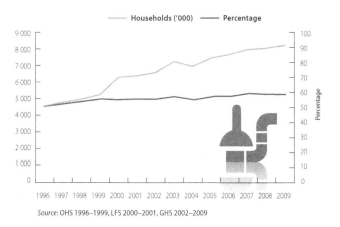

Source: OHS 1996–1999, LFS 2000–2001, GHS 2002–2009

HOUSEHOLDS USING ELECTRICITY OR SOLAR ENERGY AS FUEL SOURCE FOR COOKING

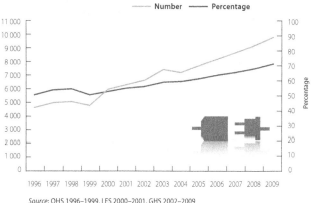

Source: OHS 1996–1999, LFS 2000–2001, GHS 2002–2009

REVIEW | Policies for reducing income inequality and poverty in South Africa

Arden Finn, Murray Leibbrandt & Eva Wegner

. . . .

Introduction

When viewed from a political perspective, the post-apartheid South African landscape looks markedly different from its apartheid predecessor. From a developmental vantage point, however, the legacy of apartheid is still there for everybody to see. Poverty and inequality continue to detract from what many have referred to as a 'miracle transition'. Highly skewed and entrenched patterns of distribution persist, reinforcing poverty and inequality.

Undoing them remains the major preoccupation of policy-makers in democratic South Africa. As such, proper data and analysis are critical, both to understand the scope of the challenge and to devise appropriate policy responses. Thus far, research into the phenomenon of inequality has focused largely on its measurement and proximate causes on the basis of inequality decompositions. Generally, the findings have shown that inequality levels have increased, but that their strongly racial character has diminished since the end of apartheid. Poverty, on the other hand, has decreased but still bears the enduring racial markers of apartheid.

Another strand of research has concentrated on fiscal redistribution, or the extent to which state revenues have been channelled successfully towards appropriate areas of need. Most findings suggest that the majority of social policies have been well targeted towards the poor. Social grants, in particular, have been instrumental in lifting millions out of poverty. What they have not succeed in, however, is to reverse inequality trends through the provision of equal opportunities to all South Africans.

This is an overview of major inequality and redistribution trends since South Africa's democratic transition in the 1990s. A comparative perspective is provided, and education policy is singled out as an area that has specific relevance to the question of income inequality.

At the outset, a summary is provided of key poverty and inequality trends in South Africa since the transition. The second section discusses redistributive policies since the end of apartheid, and a fiscal incidence analysis for 1993 and 2008 is performed. Education policy is then examined in more detail, beginning with a study of the relationship between education and income in 1993 and 2008, and ending with a discussion of a number of constraints behind the education policy choices of the post-apartheid government.

Post-apartheid inequality and poverty trends[1]

Inequality: a gap that is still growing

An analysis of census data that dates back as far as 1917 shows that the average real incomes of South Africans have been increasing steadily for all population groups (Leibbrandt, Van der Berg & Bhorat 2001). National household surveys from the past 15 years confirm that this trend has also been visible since the country's democratic transition.[2] However, income growth has not resulted in a decline in South Africa's historically high levels of inequality. On the contrary, levels of inequality have widened during the post-apartheid years. A comparison of aggregate Gini coefficients (the most widely used measure of inequality) for 1993, 2000, 2005 and 2008 illustrate this point (see Table 4.1.1). The trend stays the same, even when alternate datasets for different years are used (Leibbrandt, Woolard & Woolard 2009). Analyses of income deciles show that income has become increasingly concentrated in the top income deciles at the expense of all other deciles.

The make-up of our labour market keeps this skewed picture intact. Key statistics in this sector show that labour force participation rates are highest in the top income deciles, which also have the highest labour absorption rates. This means that employment rates in the top income deciles are higher than those in lower income groups. In fact, rates of unemployment have fallen in the upper categories since 1993, and especially after 2000. Yet, the reverse is true for those in the lower deciles, where the number of those without employment showed a sharp incline. As a result, overall unemployment rates have also increased by a significant margin. Without solving the labour market question, South Africa will not solve the inequality question. Labour market income was 'responsible for' 83 per cent of income inequality in 1993 and 85 per cent in 2008 (see Leibbrandt, Finn & Woolard 2010). There is no way around it.

These decompositions point to rising unemployment as a key driver of inequality, but they also emphasise the problem of rising inequality of earnings amongst the employed. In real terms, those who find themselves in lower income categories

Income growth has not resulted in a decline in South Africa's historically high levels of inequality. On the contrary, levels of inequality have widened during the post-apartheid years.

have not seen an increase in their earnings in the post-apartheid years. Relative to those in higher income categories, earnings have actually dropped. Sadly, therefore, employment does not necessarily provide a ticket out of poverty. This is especially so for unskilled workers, who are unlikely to move out of the lower income distribution deciles.

Given South Africa's history of racial discrimination, it is to be expected that these large and increasing income disparities bear a strong racial footprint. While it is true that inequality between the country's historically defined racial groups remains high, the importance of race as a factor that explains overall inequality has decreased quite significantly. As can be seen from the Gini coefficients for each racial group presented in Table 4.1.1, within-group inequality has increased markedly for all racial groups. By 2008, the most populous racial group, the African group, made up 80 per cent of the population and had the highest inequality of the four major racial groups.[3] The Gini coefficient for Africans was 0.12 points higher than the same measure for the white group. Thus, dynamics within racial groups have become more important, and those within the African group have become especially important, in driving aggregate changes in inequality.

Spatial dynamics must also feature prominently in our understanding of what shapes inequality in South Africa. Apartheid not only prioritised development in certain geographical areas at the expense of others, it also forcibly displaced and resettled millions to live in so-called rural 'homelands'. As such, the rural/urban dimensions of poverty cannot be ignored. 'Homelands' remained predominantly underdeveloped and poor. Those able to leave for urban areas did so; those who stayed behind continue to live in conditions of underdevelopment, low employment and limited infrastructure. Our research shows that such migration to cities and towns, in pursuit of better lives, has increased urban inequality since 1993, but has contributed to lower rural inequality over the same period (Leibbrandt, Finn & Woolard 2010). Of course, the latter is not as much the result of improved rural conditions as it is the consequence of the large influx of poorer people into areas where higher incomes are being earned.

The question of to what extent access to endowments, such as social services and education, can change current patterns of distribution is relevant to these geographic distinctions.[4] The South African data at our disposal suggest that increased access does indeed bring positive change, but it is not enough to alter the distribution of per capita income (Leibbrandt &

Levinsohn 2011). This sobering outcome seems to be the effect of two countervailing trends. On the plus side, there is increased support to children, which is driven by the implementation of a new child support grant. Counterbalancing this, however, is the low level of return on these endowments or deliverables. Nowhere is this more evident than in the returns to education in the labour market (Lam, Leibbrandt & Garlick 2010). It is this strangulation of skills that continues to underpin both unemployment and the inequality of labour market earnings, which drive household inequality.

Poverty: some gains, but are they sustainable?

Overall poverty levels declined between 1993 and 2008. In Table 4.1.2, findings are presented for two alternative poverty-line benchmarks, namely US$1.25 per day and a more conservative US$2.00 per day. The downward movement on both measurements is visible and corresponds with the findings of several others in this regard (see, for example, Bhorat & Van der Westhuizen 2009; Van der Berg et al. 2008). This decline in poverty is even more pronounced if other measures of poverty, such as the poverty gap ratio, which is sensitive to the depth of poverty, are used (see Leibbrandt, Woolard, McEwen & Koep 2010; Leibbrandt, Woolard, Finn & Argent 2010). Not everybody agrees about when poverty levels started to drop – some believe that it has only been a post-2000 phenomenon (Hoogeveen & Özler (2006) – but there is little disagreement about the longer-term trend. There is also little contention about the positive trajectory of poverty dimensions that are not measured purely in terms of income (non-money-metric well-being) (Bhorat, Naidoo & Van der Westhuizen 2006; Bhorat, Van der Westhuizen & Cassim 2009). In all analyses, access to services, formal dwellings and private assets are shown to improve in the period from 1996 to 2001, and then on through to 2008.

Because of the country's segregated past, poverty trends – as is the case with inequality trends – show development patterns that are distinct for the country's historically defined racial groups. Its incidence amongst black Africans remains the highest, followed by the coloured, Indian and white groups. Given the relative size of the black African section of the population, this group makes up more than 90 per cent of the country's poverty share. Coloured people make up the remaining share, with some nuances. In line with declining national poverty rates, black African poverty has decreased over time, but the incidence of poverty amongst coloured

South Africans has increased. In terms of the geographic distribution of poverty, and in line with the changes in urban/rural Gini coefficients, rural poverty has barely changed over the last 15 years, while urban poverty has shown an increase. Unemployment, particularly amongst young South Africans, serves to sustain these unacceptably high levels of poverty. Even in instances where people are employed, they are not fully protected from the scourge of poverty. This is especially true for one-worker households in the lower-income categories.

As is to be expected, poverty is most prevalent amongst people who have no post-school education. This underscores the lack of demand for low-skilled workers. Yet, despite the increased risk of unemployment for households in this category, they have not become poorer over time (see Leibbrandt, Woolard, Finn & Argent 2010). This points to an alternative source of income, namely social grants, of which there are now close to 15 million recipients. Unlike wealthy households, where employment accounts for the bulk of household income, poor South Africans derive most of the income that they need to sustain themselves from the government. This reliance on state assistance becomes increasingly evident the lower one moves down the income deciles, with the proportion of multiple-worker households decreasing and the number of no-worker households rising.

The effectiveness of such government assistance is particularly visible in the substantial decline in the incidence of poverty amongst the oldest age cohorts, who are no longer considered a part of the labour market. State old-age pensions have proven to be particularly effective in terms of poverty alleviation. The same can be said of the government's child grant programme. Proof of this, ironically, can be found in the higher incidence of poverty amongst childless households, as opposed to households with children that receive this grant. The poorest households are typically those that have no access to income, through either the labour market or government grants.

Despite their impact in terms of reduced poverty rates, state transfers have not managed to push down inequality levels. While they have been sufficient to move households out of the bottom two deciles, clustering transfer recipients nearer the middle of the income distribution, disproportionate growth at the higher end of the scale has neutralised any real move towards greater equality.

Redistributive policies

The trends highlighted thus far suggest that much still needs to be done to realise the promise of greater material dignity

Table 4.1.1: Gini coefficients of per capita income, aggregate and by race

Year	Aggregate	African	Coloured	Indian	White
1993	0.67	0.55	0.43	0.46	0.42
2000	0.67	0.61	0.53	0.50	0.47
2005	0.72	0.62	0.60	0.58	0.51
2008	0.70	0.62	0.54	0.61	0.50
1993–2008, % change	4.50	12.70	25.60	32.60	19.10

Source: Project for Statistics on Living Standards and Development (PSLSD) (1993); Income and Expenditure of Households (IES) (2000, 2005); National Income Dynamics Study (NIDS) (2008)

Table 4.1.2: Poverty headcount ratios

Year	Total population	$1.25 per day	$2 per day
1993	40 002 316	20.70	33.90
2000	45 134 247	18.20	30.80
2005	46 971 312	16.70	31.20
2008	48 687 036	17.70	30.00
1993–2008, % change	21.70	-14.50	-11.50

Source: PSLSD (1993); IES (2000, 2005); NIDS (2008)

Table 4.1.3: Gini coefficients for market and disposable income, 1993 and 2008

Year	Market Gini	Disposable Gini	Difference
1993	0.75	0.69	-8.65%
2008	0.77	0.70	-10.24%

Source: PSLSD (1993); NIDS (2008). Authors' calculations.

for the majority of South Africans. In our evaluation of the government's performance in this regard, it is worthwhile to keep in mind that 18 years of democratic government is a short time in comparison to centuries of colonial and apartheid marginalistion, during which skewed patterns of distribution were entrenched. We should not have unrealistic expectations. Nevertheless, almost two decades into this new dispensation, it is necessary to critically evaluate the efficiency of policies that have been introduced with the aim of altering historic patterns of distribution.

This article concentrates specifically on levels and trends in fiscal redistribution in South Africa since the end of apartheid. In other words, how have state revenues been employed to promote a more equitable society? South Africa has a progressive income tax system, a number of direct transfers, of which the old-age pension and the child support grant are the most notable, as well as public healthcare and education. These represent significant developmental achievements but, in the interests of resource efficiency, we constantly need to ask about the extent to which they are being productively leveraged.

In the sections below, the article will look first at South African fiscal redistribution in a comparative perspective. As the available cross-national data are on taxes and direct transfers, the analysis is initially restricted to these items. Subsequently, the trends and nature of different types of social policy since the 1990s, including healthcare and education, are interrogated.

Fiscal redistribution in comparative perspective

Redistribution through taxes and transfers is less common in developing countries than in so-called developed states. In Latin American countries, for example, the redistributive impact of taxes and transfers on the market income Gini coefficient is negligible (Goñi, Lopez & Serven 2008). In South Africa, Van der Berg (2005, 2009) has carried out several fiscal incidence analyses that consider the complete set of social policies, including healthcare and education. For the purpose of comparative analysis of international data here, however, we exclude the latter and examine only the redistributive effects of direct taxes and social grants.

In order to gain a clearer understanding of how the state's redistributive effectiveness has changed over the years, we compare the measured level of household per capita income inequality for market income and disposable income (see Goñi et al. 2008).[5] The former consists of household income, before taxes are deducted and government grants are added, while the latter simply represents household income, after direct taxes have been deducted and government grants received. Comparison of the difference in the level of inequality between the two measures allows us to gauge how effective the redistributive regime is in reducing inequality. As mentioned above, we are measuring the redistributive effects of direct taxation and government grants, and not the redistributive consequences of indirect taxation, such as value added tax,

which is generally regressive in nature. We also do not take into account broader welfare measures, such as the extent to which poor households gain increasing access to state-supplied healthcare facilities and schools over time.

The data for this study come from the 1993 PSLSD and the first wave of the NIDS from 2008. Given that the scale of government spending on social assistance and the level of efficient tax collection increased significantly over the period in question (Ajam & Aron 2009), we are able to assess the changing impact of these factors on inequality reduction over time.

Table 4.1.3 summarises the findings for market versus disposable income for the years 1993 and 2008, and shows that market income inequality and disposable income inequality increased in the period under study. The difference between the two increased from 8.65 percentage points in 1993 to 10.24 percentage points in 2008. This indicates increased effectiveness of state redistributive actions, despite the continued rise in overall inequality. It is also significantly higher than in Latin America, where the average was a decrease of 2 percentage points for Argentina, Brazil, Chile, Columbia and Mexico (Goñi et al. 2008). In Europe, where state redistribution has traditionally been high, the difference between the two Gini measures is close to 20 per cent (Goñi et al. 2008).

Progressivity of social policies

Besides taxation, redistributive policies consist of, on the one hand, direct social transfers (such as pensions) and, on the other, social services provision (such as education). Direct transfers include both social insurance and social assistance. The South African social insurance pillar (essentially unemployment insurance), is restricted in both its reach and duration. In 2009, it covered only around 10 per cent of the unemployed.[6] The maximum claim period is 238 days. The social assistance pillar is far more developed, providing basic resources to those who are unable to work either because of their age (old-age pension and child-support grant) or because of disabilities (disability grant). Between 1997 and 2009, the number of beneficiaries increased for all grants, most dramatically for those receiving the child-support grant (see Table 4.1.4). In this period, the number of beneficiaries for the most important social grants rose from fewer than 3 million to more than 12.5 million – almost a quarter of South Africans. At the same time, while government spending on social assistance increased, it remained stable as a percentage of GDP. This figure stood at 3.2 per cent in 1995, and the comparative figure for 2009 was 3.1 per cent (Van der Berg & Siebrits 2010). Not only have these grants played an important role in lifting people out of poverty, they also have affected other outcomes such as school enrolment (Leibbrandt, Woolard, Finn & Argent 2010).

Table 4.1.5 presents the concentration ratios for different types of social spending in 1995, 2000 and 2006. A concentration ratio is a measure of how a given income stream is distributed across the income spectrum. A value of 1 is fully regressive, of -1 fully progressive. This analysis shows that government grants have concentration ratios that are closest to -1 and, therefore, are seen to be the most progressive social policies in South Africa. This is to be expected, as these grants are means tested. Concerning trends, it is noteworthy that the degree of progressivity for social grants has not increased since 1995.

The second type of social policy that has an impact on redistribution concerns the provision of social services, of which healthcare and education are the most notable. In view of the highly unequal access to healthcare and education at the end of apartheid, these two policies have been considered critical for post-transition transformation. As a percentage of GDP, spending on healthcare has remained stable since 1995 at slightly above 3.0 per cent; spending on education decreased from 7.0 per cent to around 5.5 per cent of GDP between 1995 and 2007 (Van der Berg & Siebrits 2010). With the exception of tertiary education and housing, spending on social services has been progressive in the 2000s. The real decline in tertiary education spending is to be expected as higher income groups typically attend universities at higher rates than the poor. Health spending appears generally more progressive than education spending, most importantly in the category of public hospitals. This finding is probably not unrelated to the fact that more affluent groups have opted out of public health-care into private health insurance.

In summary, direct taxation and social policies in post-apartheid South Africa have contributed to a decrease in inequality levels. For taxes and direct social transfers, progressivity has been on the increase since 1993. Similarly, overall social spending has become more progressive since 1995. However, the contribution of taxes and transfers to a decrease of the market Gini coefficient is only slightly above Latin American levels and substantially below European levels. Moreover, for some items of social spending progressivity has stagnated or decreased.

Education provision in post-apartheid South Africa: policy and policy constraints

This section considers education policy in post-apartheid South Africa. Needless to say, education plays a critical role in determining an individual's position on the income distribution scale and, therefore, represents one of the most important policy tools that can potentially address inequality. Here, we examine the changing relationship between education levels and inequality between 1993 and 2008. We describe the patterns of education spending since the end of apartheid, as well as the educational attainment of South African students, and then conclude with a discussion of several factors that have guided the choices in education policy since 1994.

Education and inequality
Education is the key variable in determining, firstly, whether an individual finds employment and, secondly, the nature of that

Table 4.1.4: Numbers of beneficiaries of social grants in 1997 and 2009

	1997	2009
Old-age grant	1 737 602	2 414 192
Disability grant	737 322	1 281 556
Child-support grant	362 631	8 825 824
Total	2 837 635	12 521 563

Source: Based on Van der Berg and Siebrits (2010)

Table 4.1.5: Concentration ratios for social spending

Spending category	1995*	2000*	2000**	2006**
Social grants	-0.434	-0.431	-0.371	-0.359
Child support			-0.247	-0.318
Disability			-0.291	-0.288
Old age pension			-0.412	-0.436
Education				
School	-0.016	-0.104	-0.121	-0.128
Tertiary	0.235	0.497	0.528	0.641
Health	-0.045	-0.082	-0.118	-0.137
Public clinics	-0.103	-0.132	-0.177	-0.257
Public hospitals	-0.014	-0.057	-0.105	-0.103
Housing	-0.018	0.007	0.16	0.07
Total across services	-0.057	-0.12	-0.112	-0.152

Source: * Based on Van der Berg (2005); ** Based on Van der Berg (2009)

employment and its remuneration. The section above focused on changing measures of inequality at the household per capita income level. We now move on to a deeper analysis in order to explore the changing relationship between educational attainment and inequality.

The data for this undertaking come, once again, from the PSLSD (1993) and the first wave of the NIDS (2008), with household income per capita serving as the unit of comparison, and with 8 663 and 7 168 households forming the respective comparison groups. Three different types of analysis are used: a) a comparison of the unconditional income distributions by education between 1993 and 2008; b) a comparison of the conditional distributions of income by education between 1993 and 2008; and c) unconditional versus conditional distributions within each year.

The unconditional distributions are constructed by dividing up household per capita income into quintiles and then assessing the probability that an individual with education level x falls into income quintile y. Because we are investigating inequality as measured by household income per capita, we use the household head's level of education as the unit of analysis.[7]

The conditional distributions are the end product of an ordered probit model that was run with the five income quintiles as the dependent variable. The right-hand side of the regression equation included controls for household size, province, geo type (urban, rural), a dummy for whether at least one household member was employed, and the household head's age, race, gender and level of education. All ordered probit regressions are weighted using census-raised weights (1993) and post-stratification weights (2008), and all standard errors are robust.

Since the initial results of the ordered probit model are somewhat cumbersome to interpret, we move on to an analysis of the probability of a household being in a particular income quintile, given the level of education of the household head and the full range of controls. For this, we have constructed a measure of the probability of being in each income quintile by the head of a household's education.

Let us start with a comparison of the unconditional 1993 situation versus the unconditional 2008 situation as reflected in Table 4.1.6 and Table 4.1.7. A feature of this comparison in both benchmark years is the high level of predictability when a household is headed by someone with tertiary education. The same cannot be said for matric-headed households. Between 1993 and 2008 there was a marked decline in the probability of a matric-headed household being in the top quintile. Correspondingly, there was a significant increase in the likelihood that people in this category would fall into income quintiles 1 or 2. Not surprisingly, households headed

Table 4.1.6: Unconditional probabilities, 1993

	Quintile 1	Quintile 2	Quintile 3	Quintile 4	Quintile 5	Percent-age
No education	37.49	30.76	18.46	9.08	4.21	22.01
Primary	26.05	26.53	22.50	18.35	6.58	29.99
Incomplete secondary	12.20	15.59	25.63	29.45	17.13	28.23
Matric	3.60	4.63	13.11	26.28	52.39	10.21
Tertiary	2.10	0.79	4.89	16.54	75.67	9.56

Source: PSLSD (1993). Number of households = 8 663. Authors' calculations.

Table 4.1.7: Unconditional probabilities, 2008

	Quintile 1	Quintile 2	Quintile 3	Quintile 4	Quintile 5	Percent-age
No education	31.58	34.75	24.19	7.81	1.67	13.82
Primary	28.53	29.95	24.08	13.24	4.20	23.44
Incomplete secondary	21.07	17.69	23.91	24.77	12.57	31.65
Matric	9.02	11.34	14.67	29.73	35.24	20.60
Tertiary	2.50	1.61	4.71	17.31	73.86	10.50

Source: NIDS (2008). Number of households = 7 168. Authors' calculations.

Education is the key variable in determining, firstly, whether an individual finds employment and, secondly, the nature of that employment and its remuneration.

by an individual with incomplete secondary education have become increasingly concentrated in the lower quintiles.

With this unconditional comparison as the benchmark, we now compare the conditional situation in 1993 with that of 2008 (see Tables 4.1.8 and 4.1.9). By far the most striking feature of this comparison is the change in probabilities for households headed by an individual with tertiary education. There was huge 'probability migration' from quintiles 1 to 4 into 5 between 1993 and 2008 for this group. People with a tertiary education in 2008 were far more likely to come from high-income households than they were in 1993. In fact, the probability of a tertiary-headed household being in the richest quintile jumped from 17.51 per cent to 40.59 per cent. Conversely, the chances of people with little or no schooling finding themselves in this category declined considerably. The general trend was towards greater concentration in the lower quintiles. For matric-headed households, the middle and the top quintiles were stable, while the probability of being in quintile 1 or 2 increased.

With Table 4.1.6 and Table 4.1.8 we compare the unconditional and conditional situations in 1993. For no education and primary education-headed households, there is a greater concentration in the middle of the income distribution, once other factors are controlled for. The same goes for households headed by somebody with an incomplete secondary education, where those at the top of the unconditional distribution have shifted downwards in the conditional distribution. For tertiary-headed households, there was a very large movement out of the highest quintile from the unconditional distribution (76 per cent) to the conditional distribution (18 per cent).

Finally, Table 4.1.7 and Table 4.1.9 report on the same unconditional versus conditional comparison for 2008. Here, less movement occurred between unconditional and conditional distributions in 1993 and 2008. In 2008, there was much less movement within no education and primary education-headed households than in 1993, and the distributions are relatively stable. There have been significant shifts in both directions for households headed by an individual with an incomplete secondary education. Matric households saw shifts out of the top quintile and into the 3rd and 4th quintiles. Tertiary-headed households, once again, saw a drop in the conditional likelihood of being in the top quintile, but the drop was much less than in the 1993 data (33 per cent versus 58 per cent).

The most significant trend to emerge from these analyses is that it has become far more likely for households headed by tertiary graduates to fall into the top income quintile. There-

Table 4.1.8: Conditional probabilities from ordered probit, 1993

	Quintile 1	Quintile 2	Quintile 3	Quintile 4	Quintile 5
No education	14.51	34.65	34.36	14.95	1.53
Primary	10.39	30.79	36.84	19.48	2.5
Incomplete secondary	6.22	24.63	38.14	26.39	4.62
Matric	1.86	12.91	33.21	39.23	12.79
Tertiary	1.11	9.47	29.43	42.48	17.51

Source: PSLSD (1993). Authors' calculations.

Table 4.1.9: Conditional probabilities from ordered probit, 2008

	Quintile 1	Quintile 2	Quintile 3	Quintile 4	Quintile 5
No education	21.46	32.53	29.38	14.41	2.22
Primary	20.59	32.20	29.82	15.01	2.38
Incomplete secondary	14.84	29.10	32.37	19.75	3.93
Matric	5.27	18.04	32.27	32.57	11.86
Tertiary	0.52	4.20	16.36	38.34	40.59

Source: NIDS (2008). Authors' calculations.

fore, higher education was even more likely to 'pay off' in 2008 than in 1993. The situation of all other education groups looks less promising. For them, the likelihood of being in one of the lower income quintiles increased in the period between 1993 and 2008, with matric-headed households experiencing a particularly sharp decline in terms of their position on the income continuum. Even after controlling for a wide range of individual and household characteristics, the same strong patterns emerge.

Education spending and outcomes [8]

Education spending has increased greatly since 1995, from R31.1 billion to R165 billion in 2010/11. Real growth in this sector from 1994 to 2005 totalled 49 per cent, and with an annual average of 5.5 per cent of GDP, South Africa's education expenditure can be described as respectable for a middle-income country.

Despite this, there is wide recognition, also by the South African government, that the quality of education outputs does not render the expected returns on the budgetary investment (DBE 2010). Students perform dismally in international tests, such as the Trends in International Mathematics and Science Study (TIMSS) and the Progress in International Reading Literacy Study (PIRLS) (DE 2008). While greater access in terms of available infrastructure has contributed to an increase in enrolment figures in primary and secondary education, the quality of education has remained an obstacle to providing the economy with the skills it requires.

The progressivity of public spending on schooling can be examined in three ways. It can be measured, as indicated earlier, through the use of concentration ratios. According to Van der Berg (2009), the concentration ratio for school education was -0.016 in 1995, -0.121 in 2000 and -0.128 in 2006, suggesting that not only is spending on school education progressive, but also that it has become more so over time. However, this measure does not reflect the quality of the school attended, which is likely to be worse for the poor. Indeed, much larger proportions of African students experience very basic problems of education provision, such as lack of text books and low quality school facilities (DE 2006). [9]

A second yardstick that has been used for progressivity is the extent to which spending has become more equitable across provinces. This has definitely been the case over the past 15 years. Whereas rich provinces (Gauteng, Western Cape, Northern Cape) were spending per capita almost 50 per cent more on education than the national average in 1995, the figure decreased to less than 20 per cent by 2003. Poor provinces (Eastern Cape, KwaZulu-Natal, Mpumalanga and Limpopo) have almost caught up with the national average in the same time period (Wildeman 2008).

A third means of assessment is to look at funding for different types of schools within the same province. Fiske and Ladd (2005) analyse public education spending in the Western Cape by grouping schools in terms of the former education department under which they fell during apartheid, because they generally capture the formula of allocation that occurred in this era. These departments included the African (DET), coloured (HOR), Indian (HOD) and white (HOA), with most resources being allocated to the HOA and least to the DET schools. [10] The authors find that in 2001, former HOA schools (both primary and secondary) received not only the largest amount of publicly provided resources per learner, but generally also received larger amounts of public funds than former DET schools. Only one programme, titled 'Norms and Standards', which directly targeted poor schools, could be described as progressive. A similar analysis of education spending in Gauteng shows a slightly more complicated picture, with 'winners' and 'losers' in all school categories. Yet, overall, state per capita expenditure was still higher in former HOA schools in 2002. A key difference, however, was that in Gauteng this was followed by DET schools, while former HOD and HOR schools were worst off (see Motala 2006).

Inequality in educational achievement is remarkably high in South Africa. Learners' performance in maths and science, as reflected in the TIMSS, conveys a very unequal and highly skewed picture. A comparison of DET and DOA TIMSS data for the years 1999 and 2003 shows not only a pronounced difference in maths and science command, but also that this gap in performance has widened. Out of a maximum of 800 points, students from former DET schools achieved an average score of 227 in mathematics in 2003, compared to 468 for students of former HOA schools. [11] For former DET schools, this represented a decline from the 238 average in 1999, while the result for former HOA schools marked an increase from the 442 it achieved in that year. HOA schools almost reached the international average of 488 in 2003 (see Reddy 2006). In a similar vein, Servaas van der Berg (2007) observes important differences in the senior certificate pass rates of 'racially homogenous' schools, with an average of 97.3 per cent for white schools and 43.3 per cent for black schools. [12] Evaluations performed by the DE (now the DBE) also show large differences in the performance of the respective provinces, with the Eastern Cape and Limpopo consistently below the national average (DE 2005). The same applies to senior certificate pass rates.

In summary, the evidence at our disposal suggests that the objective of broadened access to quality education has not been achieved, despite high levels of resource mobilisation. In some instances, the performance of formerly disadvantaged schools has declined, and the gap between their performance and that of HOA schools has actually increased. Despite the stated intent, spending across provinces has also not been equalised. Moreover, within relatively well-resourced provinces, such as the Western Cape and Gauteng, formerly privileged schools continue to receive more state funding than their historically marginalised counterparts. Not surprisingly, therefore, education outcomes, as measured in the performance of students, are still highly unequal.

> There has been some success with reducing poverty levels since 1993, but none with decreasing inequality, which has increased since South Africa's transition to democracy.

Discussion

This section asks why the government's education spending has not favoured schools in disadvantaged communities more explicitly.[13] We consider a number of factors that have worked as constraints on education spending and its transformation into education quality.

Firstly, the apartheid legacy has been especially hard to address within the education sector. In the previous political dispensation, policy prioritised the education of white learners over that of learners from other groups. Education infrastructure for learners in the latter groups was generally inferior and teachers, on average, were less qualified. The extreme differences in educational infrastructure and human resource allocation constituted a huge burden on a new government that committed itself to equalising conditions in education provision. Education, of course, was not the only sector that needed redress and other social transfers and policies have weighed heavily in the budget.

Secondly, the context and nature of South Africa's negotiated transition to democracy constrained the ways in which education policy could be designed and implemented. One key limitation that the transition settlement imposed was a considerable degree of institutional decentralisation, which allowed significant room for discretionary spending and implementation in provinces. Lack of control over provincial spending implies, among other things, that provincial governments can decide which share of their budget to allocate for education. Indeed, the National Treasury has expressed its 'concern' regarding the decline in share of education expenditure in provincial budgets, from 44.7 per cent in 2005/06 to 40.8 per cent in 2008/09 (National Treasury 2009).

The implementation of education policy has also been mismanaged in some provinces, because of corruption or maladministration, due to a lack of qualified personnel to implement the sophisticated education policies that have been designed at the national level. The scope for more control over spending and implementation is limited: the constitution prohibits centralisation and it would be a politically very sensitive step, bound to be interpreted as the ANC's reneging on the transition agreements.

Another constraint arising from the context of South Africa's transition has been the ANC's aim to keep the white population inside the public school system so that they would support education spending. In practice, this meant that extensive autonomy was given to so-called Section 21 schools regarding the raising of school fees and the remuneration of teachers (Fiske & Ladd 2005; OECD 2008; Rensburg 2001). Consensus-oriented policies towards the white population also implied that targets had to be set for the upgrading of African schooling, rather than to take funding away from schools serving the white population. Arguably, the net result has been the entrenchment of inequality in educational outcomes.

Finally, the salary component of the education budget has become a contentious issue. Teachers were an important part of the anti-apartheid struggle and, hence, an important component of the ANC's potential constituency. The equalisation of salaries took on a distinctly political character: consequently, teacher salaries accounted for more than 90 per cent of education expenditure during the early years of transition (declining to below 80 per cent in 2006/07), leaving little space for polices targeted at the poor (Fiske & Ladd 2005; OECD 2008).

Thus, the constraints on education spending have been considerable. That said, a critical inspection of the figures and spending choices raises two questions. The first is to what extent education has, in fact, been a top priority. As several reports point out, although education spending is considerable, it is below the United Nations Educational, Scientific and Cultural Organisation (UNESCO) target of 6 per cent of GDP and, given the backlog due to apartheid policies, it could be considered insufficient (OECD 2008; Fiske & Ladd 2005). Moreover, while expenditure on education has increased considerably, it has declined as a share of government expenditure, from 19.2 per cent in 1996 to 18 per cent in 2007, and as a share of GDP from 5.7 per cent to 5.4 per cent in the same period (OECD 2008). Education also has the slowest growth rate compared to other social expenditures (OECD 2008).

The second question is whether redistribution – to the extent that it would bridge the gap between schools serving poor students and those serving richer ones – has received the attention that it deserves. Indeed, 'affirmative action' has been largely absent in education spending. Equity of spending across provinces has yet to be reached, but it seems attainable even if it is not clear to what extent this is actually a policy goal.[14] The degree of inequality in education provision at the end of apartheid, however, would require disproportionate amounts of funding for poorer schools in order to provide their students with opportunities similar to those of the better-equipped schools. There are some components of current education policy that promote equality, such as the no-fee schools and the 'Norms and Standards' programme, but funding for these appears too small to bridge the gap. Additionally, the pattern of education spending within provinces, observed by Fiske and Ladd (2005) in the Western Cape, and Motala

(2006) in Gauteng, where disproportionate amounts of education funding go to privileged schools, shows that spending equity across provinces will not necessarily improve schools serving disadvantaged students.

Conclusion

Reducing inequality and poverty levels inherited from apartheid was always going to be a formidable challenge for post-transition governments. There has been some success with reducing poverty levels since 1993, but none with decreasing inequality, which has increased since South Africa's transition to democracy.

A possible reason for this is that tackling inequality is more complicated and politically contentious than tackling poverty, as the former implies a 'rearrangement' of the positions of the poor *and* the rich in the income distribution, whereas the latter involves only the socio-economic conditions of the poor. Redistribution levels are a highly political issue in any country, and are even more so in the context of a negotiated transition to democracy where former elites need to be accommodated. Indeed, as discussed above, while fiscal redistribution is progressive in South Africa, its levels are relatively low. Similarly, while present, the progressive impact of social policies (i.e. the extent to which policies address entrenched inequality) has increased only slightly since 1995.

Education policy is a good area for a focus on reducing 'poverty' rather than 'inequality'. Education spending has concentrated on improving the situation of poor provinces, and to some extent poor schools, while keeping relatively high levels of funding for the formerly privileged schools. Given the high inequality between these schools at the moment of the transition, such policies that are directed only at the poor will take a long time to bridge the gap between schools. The same might be true for inequality in general.

Notes

1. In the main, this section is drawn from: Leibbrandt, Woolard, McEwen and Koep (2010); Leibbrandt, Woolard, Finn and Argent (2010); and Leibbrandt, Finn and Woolard (2010).

2. See Leibbrandt, Woolard, Finn and Argent (2010), as well as Bhorat and van der Westhuizen (2009). Van der Berg, Louw and Yu (2008) provide further backing with work carried out on national accounts data and an annual marketing survey.

3. Leibbrandt et al. (2009) provide standard errors and inequality dominance analysis to show that the increases in inequality in aggregate and within all racial groups are robust and are not sensitive to choice of the Gini coefficient as the index of inequality.

4. Endowments include: public assets, in the form of basic government deliverables; private assets, such as houses, cars and appliances; and also individual assets, such as health and education.

5. Goñi et al. (2008) compare the redistributive effects of taxes and government grants for a set of Latin American countries versus a set of European countries. They find that the effectiveness of fiscal redistribution on overall inequality is far stronger in Europe than in Latin America. Their study uses total household income as the basis of inequality measurement, while in this paper we use total household income per capita in order to take household size effects into account.

6. This summary of social policies draws on Leibbrandt, Woolard, McEwen and Koep (2010).

7. As a robustness check of our findings we ran both the unconditional and conditional analyses using 'highest level of educational attainment for anyone in the household' and compared this to the case when 'household head's level of education' is used. The patterns that emerge using both measures are very similar (particularly for 1993), and are especially stable for matric and tertiary levels of education.

8. This section focuses mainly on school education, which accounts for around 65 per cent of the education budget; higher education absorbs around 12.5 per cent (National Treasury 2009).

9. In the Western Cape, schools serving poorer students also have less-qualified teachers (Fiske & Ladd 2005).

10. This is still correlated with the level of affluence of the enrolled students (Fiske & Ladd 2005).

11. The scores for former HOR (coloured) and HOD (Indian) schools lie in-between these two, with HOR closer to DET, and HOD closer to the performance of DET.

12. Van der Berg (2007) classifies a school as belonging to a certain 'race-type' if more than 70 per cent of its students are of that race.

13. Whether the observed differences in educational outcomes are directly attributable to differences in spending patterns is a debated question, which we do not seek to address here.

14. There is no official policy document that defines such convergence as a goal (Wildeman 2008).

OPINION | Is it time to adopt a new developmental model?

. . . .

PLANNING THE STATUS QUO? A SUSTAINABLE DEVELOPMENT MODEL NEEDS NEW THINKING

Patrick Bond

. . . .

The move by the world's bottom 99 per cent to challenge the top 1 per cent's economic and ecological destructiveness is why, over the next decade, the hope for the continent will jump from Tunisia and Egypt to the main cities and even *dorpies* of South Africa.

More than ever since the country's transition from racial apartheid, the neoliberal developmental model – understood as 'class apartheid' – will come under fire. After all, no other major country is more unequal.

Over the past decade, only China seems to have had as many protests per person, according to available police statistics. In no other country is the word 'nationalisation' bandied about so regularly, and this will continue even without the hyperbole of the now-banished leader of the African National Congress Youth League (ANCYL), Julius Malema. No major society has such a strong trade union movement, winning not only above-inflation wage increases thanks to regular strikes but also expressing visions that transcend the proletariat's needs, to support what is being termed the 'precariat' (precarious informal-sector workers and the unemployed).

Although currently losing its battles against labour brokers and the pro-corporate state-subsidised lowering of the minimum wage for younger workers, the Congress of South African Trade Unions (COSATU) remains this society's single largest coherent citizens' power bloc.

Moreover, unions and the independent left have come together more than in any period since 1994, with the world climate summit in Durban featuring a joint march for 'system change, not climate change'. Equally encouraging is the One Million Climate Jobs campaign, launched in early 2011. The campaign suggests ways for activists to co-operate towards a 'just transition' out of South Africa's fossil fuel addiction, which manifests itself in the country's status as one of the world's highest carbon dioxide emitters.

Tracing the money

After predicting a 'Tunisia Day' for South Africa in 2020, former president Thabo Mbeki's younger brother, Moeletsi, remarked recently, 'Big companies taking their capital out of South Africa are a bigger threat to economic freedom than Malema'.[1] We could argue that he did not do the argument full justice, asserting that 'Capital flight means there is no capital for entrepreneurs in South Africa'. That is probably not true, for local financial markets are as speculative and liquid as ever, especially now that the real estate bubble is gradually deflating. More pervasive problems that prevent both entrepreneurship and job creation include constrained consumer buying power, the market dominance of monopoly capital in most industries, and excessive trade liberalisation.

Consumption is stagnant, due largely to over-indebtedness; the banks' 'impaired credit' list now has 8.5 million victims, representing nearly half of all South African borrowers. That would include many of the 1.3 million who lost and did not regain their jobs as a result of the recession. There is very little scope for local entrepreneurs to open up manufacturing facilities, which President Jacob Zuma unhappily observed in August were virtually all in white hands. Waves of East Asian goods continue to descend on South Africa because of the still-overvalued rand, as many more local industries will understand once Walmart begins with cheap imports in earnest. Asked about the entrance of that US retailing behemoth, Mbeki was correct to ridicule the neoliberal agenda that his brother's government so decisively implemented from 1994: 'In South Africa we think we will just open the doors and everything will be hunky dory. Of course it won't.'

The doors swung open not only to East Asian imports but also the other way – for rich South Africans and our biggest companies to exit with apartheid's ill-gotten gains. In 1995, they lobbied hard for the abolition of the 'financial rand' dual exchange rate and for permission to relocate financial headquarters from Johannesburg and Cape Town. Mbeki complains that there was never 'an explanation for why companies like Anglo American and Old Mutual had been allowed to list in London. On what basis did they allow them to go, to move their primary listing from South Africa to London? Why did they approve it? What did they get out of it?'

These are tough questions, especially because the outflow of profits, dividends and interest payments to Anglo, De Beers, Old Mutual, SAB Miller, Mondi, Liberty Life and BHP Billiton is the main cause of South Africa's dangerous current account deficit (far worse than the trade deficit) and, in turn, our soaring foreign debt. Answers will not necessarily be found in the implied backhanders of corruption. We need to look much deeper, for ideology is now at stake.

Ideology in flux

This was made abundantly clear in a report released in August 2011 by the International Monetary Fund (IMF 2011). Every year, the IMF provides South Africa with an 'Article IV Consultation' and, even in mid-2011, it became evident that last-century orthodox ideology prevails. In its meetings with Treasury officials, the IMF recorded how 'Discussions centered on the timing and strength of the required exit from supportive policies', which translates into cutting the budget deficit. 'Staff recommended stronger fiscal consolidation beyond the current fiscal year than currently being considered'. Orthodox ideology typically blames workers, and the IMF (as could be expected) advocated policies to moderate any real growth in wages.

As for capital flight, the IMF Article IV report noted that 'Relatively low public and external debts, mainly denominated in domestic currency, and adequate international reserve coverage offset risks from currency overvaluation and current account deficits funded by portfolio flows' (IMF 2011). Relatively low? South Africa's US$100+ billion foreign debt is, in reality, a very high proportion of GDP, which financial sector economists have observed now approaches mid-1980s crisis levels. The increase in foreign reserves from US$40 billion to US$50 billion over the last 18 months offsets only half of the rise in foreign debt over the same period.

Recent experience raises questions about the IMF's judgment on debt crises. Orthodox thinking left the institution utterly unprepared in 2008 for the world's worst financial crisis since 1929. Neither have ideologies shifted much in Pretoria under President Zuma. Despite replacing Mbeki with Zuma, Trevor Manuel with Pravin Gordhan, and Tito Mboweni with Gill Marcus, the country's labour movement failed to replace neoliberalism with a genuinely social democratic ('Keynesian') ideology.

Deregulatory tendencies continue, as witnessed by our extremely volatile currency, which has experienced more crashes since apartheid ended than any other except, possibly, the Zimbabwean dollar. The relaxation of exchange controls on nearly 30 separate occasions since 1994 is the main reason, and Gordhan is hastening the trend. True to form, the IMF is oblivious to this, and its Article IV report praises the Reserve Bank's 'prudent' policies, 'together with a flexible exchange rate', which allegedly 'helped dampen the adverse effects of those global cycles'. The opposite is true: South Africa's vulnerability has been amplified by capital control relaxation.

In an equally puzzling utterance, the IMF observed: 'Although the government's borrowing requirements remained large, they were easily met through the issuance of rand denominated bonds and bills at low interest rates against the backdrop of large capital inflows'. This statement ignores a recent Reserve Bank admission that of 50 major countries, only Greece has higher nominal rates.

The implications of IMF logic are now clear; when it comes to the exchange controls, we need to heed Moeletsi Mbeki's concerns. If even a 'small tax on inflows to try to curtail inflows or at least change their composition' is suggested, IMF staff point out 'significant drawbacks', so as to dissuade Pretoria bureaucrats. According to the IMF Article IV consultation, even mild-mannered exchange controls 'likely would raise the government's financing costs'. Not surprisingly, the financial institution also reiterates its call for 'wage restraint', in order to 'enhance competitiveness.'

The rebuttal is easy. Impose exchange controls on outflows of capital, to address capital flight, and then systematically lower interest rates and manage the appropriate decline in the rand's value, to the point at which workers can return to at least the wage/profit share they had won by the end of apartheid – 54/46 (compared to just 43/57 today).

The status quo is untenable, and more crises loom. As South Africa again barely broke into the World Economic Forum's top 50 countries in business competitiveness in July, the prevailing neoliberal ideology is clearly both ineffectual and inhumane. Control of capital flight is the first step away from this perpetual crisis, and is gaining pace across the world as more than a dozen countries have put 'speed bump' controls of various sorts on hot money inflows. The search is intensifying for ways to properly regulate financial capital, with even the November 2011 G20 meeting in Cannes witnessing 'financial transactions tax' advocacy led by France's Nicholas Sarkozy and supported by Zuma. However, with Italy joining Greece in the latest system-threatening debt crisis, we have

Control of capital flight is the first step away from this perpetual crisis, and is gaining pace across the world as more than a dozen countries have put 'speed bump' controls of various sorts on hot money inflows.

> To claim that 'South Africa today has much to celebrate on the economy and infrastructure' would mean pretending that debilitating bubbles – such as the JSE and middle-class consumption based on excessive consumer debt – are actually strengths.

to continue subjecting economic policy rhetoric to much more careful critique.

World trends in SA

Recall the context. The 2008/09 financial meltdown was supposedly solved by throwing money at bankers in Wall Street, the City of London, Frankfurt, Paris and Tokyo. It did not work, though, and on BBC's Newsnight in October 2011, Robert Shapiro of the Georgetown University Business School blew the whistle on the European debt crisis.[2] 'If they cannot address it in a credible way I believe within perhaps two to three weeks we will have a meltdown in sovereign debt which will produce a meltdown across the European banking system,' warned Shapiro. He cautioned that not even the largest banks in Germany and France would be immune to this, and that the United Kingdom and the rest of the world should prepare itself for contagion.[3] As if to respond to Shapiro, the European Union's leaders cut a deal with banks to whittle down Greek debt in the hope that this would pacify society.

The banks didn't crash on Shapiro's schedule, although many expect them to do just that when more countries cannot make their debt repayments. Reflecting the inexorable tensions between bankers' and people's interests, George Papandreou's government fell in early November 2011, after promising – and then withdrawing – a democratic option for voters to approve the austerity plan. A few days later, Italy's Silvio Berlusconi was also compelled to resign as financial pressure and rule by IMF and EU technocrats replaced his profligate corruption.

Replacing venal politicians with Washington/Brussels bankers is no solution, of course. South Africans should pay attention, because in early October 2011 Finance Minister Pravin Gordhan offered their tax monies as an emergency R2 billion bailout loan from Pretoria via the IMF. This came on the heels of his R2.4 billion bailout offered to Swazi dictator King Mswati, in spite of widespread opposition by civil society in Swaziland and South Africa.

What Gordhan explained to SAfm listeners about the European emergency credits was chilling. The radio station's Alec Hogg asked Gordhan: 'Even if it is only a small amount, relatively speaking, that we are putting in, many African countries went through hell in the seventies and eighties because of conditionality according to these loans. Are you going to try and insist that there is similar conditionality now that the boot is on the other foot, as it were?'

'Absolutely,' replied Gordhan, 'The IMF must be as proactive

in developed countries as it is in developing countries. The days of this unequal treatment and the nasty treatment, if you like, for developing countries and politeness for developed countries must pass.'[4] Gordhan's call for more proactive nastiness by the IMF and its Brussels allies against the Italian, Greek, Spanish, Portuguese and Irish poor and working people throws ANC traditions of international solidarity into disrepute.

These sentiments were also the subject of political wit amidst the World Cup hoopla of a year and a half ago, when one of the greatest losers, team Argentina, was consoled by a Buenos Aires magazine, which congratulated the victors, Spain, thus: 'Crisis, unemployment, poverty, the end of welfare, submission to the International Monetary Fund and sporting success: the poor countries of the world salute the Spanish – *Welcome to the Third World!*' Rodrigo Nunes (2011) of the magazine *Turbulence* notes that 'Apart from being a brilliant joke, the headline made an excellent point: why is it that what is crystal clear for people in the global North when talking about the global South seems so difficult to process when it happens "at home"?'.

Continued Nunes, 'Ask any relatively well-informed British citizen about violence in Brazil, and they are likely to tell you something about unequal wealth distribution, lack of opportunities... how the police make matters worse by being widely perceived as corrupt and prejudiced, and how the political system mostly reproduces this situation'. In England, too, the productive economy wallowed in recession following the country's biggest-ever bank bail-outs and accompanying state fiscal crisis, with bankers receiving massive bonuses and inequality soaring. Top police officials in league with Rupert Murdoch's phone-tapping 'journalists' resigned in disgrace and the Tory-Liberal government took the axe to social programmes, raising tuition fees at nearly 40 per cent of universities to £9 000 per year. Why was anyone surprised at the logical consequences: an anarchic insurrection of multiracial, working-class, supremely alienated youth from Tottenham to Birmingham?

Establishment reality check: a national plan?

That scream from the margins, at the time Standard & Poors was downgrading the US credit rating, with a subsequent loss of $5 trillion of paper wealth in the world's stock markets in the first week of August alone, shocked establishment observers. Except for one: a man nicknamed 'Dr Doom' because of his prescient warnings about the financial meltdown of 2008, Nouriel Roubini. The *Wall Street Journal* asked the New York

University business professor, 'What can government and what can businesses do to get the economy going again or is it just sit and wait and gut it out?'

'Businesses are not doing anything,' replied Roubini, referring to the US, Europe and Japan, but also South Africa. 'They claim they're doing cutbacks because there's excess capacity and not adding workers because there's not enough final demand, but there's a paradox, a Catch-22. If you're not hiring workers, there's not enough labour income, enough consumer confidence, enough consumption, not enough final demand.'

According to Roubini, 'In the last two or three years, we've actually had a worsening because we've had a massive redistribution of income from labor to capital, from wages to profits, and the inequality of income has increased. And the marginal propensity to spend of a household is greater than the marginal propensity of a firm because they have a greater propensity to save, that is firms compared to households. So the redistribution of income and wealth makes the problem of inadequate aggregate demand even worse.'[5] Add to this that the supposed prosperity of the middle class was ultimately a fiction based on consumer debt.

Are South African elites paying attention to these underlying economic dynamics? They are not, judging by this year's long-range response from the talented technical, political, civil society and business thinkers of the National Planning Commission (NPC). Its fascinating diagnostic analysis of why South Africa is beginning to slide off the rails is negated by the screaming silences on economic management. To be sure, the NPC's main revelation was striking: 'State agencies tasked with fighting corruption are of the view that corruption is at a very high level. Weak accountability and damaged societal ethics make corruption at lower levels in government almost pervasive. Corruption in infrastructure procurement has led to rising prices and poorer quality.' NPC (2011a)

This is an easy critique, however. The NPC diplomatically deferred from analysing the deeper corruption of the economy, the wasting of productive capacity in favour of what is now regularly termed 'financialisation'. Perhaps such a diagnosis would have implicated the minister in charge of the NPC, Trevor Manuel, who was finance minister from 1996 until 2009. Thus, in the NPC's diagnosis, capital is incorrectly said to be 'scarce' when, in reality, we have the opposite problem of excess liquidity in ultra-speculative markets. South African real estate was the world's biggest bubble by far before the price crash began in 2008. The NPC actually applauds some of the most misguided features of economic management. To claim that 'South Africa today has much to celebrate on the economy and infrastructure' would mean pretending that debilitating bubbles – such as the JSE and middle-class consumption based on excessive consumer debt – are actually strengths.

The JSE is attracting speculative financial funding that simply is not being turned into brick-and-mortar investments

and machinery. South Africa's corporate fixed investment rates remain very low by historical standards, especially in manufacturing, and levels of consumer debt are at an untenable level. With house prices *still* falling (after a brief uptick in 2010), the inability to liquidate those assets has turned consumer credit opportunities into debt slavery for millions more South Africans. Amazingly, the NPC did not notice the ongoing job massacre, with its claim that 'Unemployment levels are decreasing since 2002'.

Upon launching the NPC in June, Manuel remarked, 'When you can't locate where you are, your ability to reach your destination will be constrained. Last week the centenary of the Titanic was marked. If there are going to be icebergs on the route then you'd better know.' NPC members did not want to see the world financial iceberg looming immediately ahead. Had they wished to, there was an old navigator they could have turned to. At the end of the Wall Street Journal interview, Roubini reminded us: 'Karl Marx had it right. At some point, capitalism can destroy itself. You cannot keep on shifting income from labour to capital without having an excess capacity and a lack of aggregate demand. That's what has happened. We thought that markets worked. They're not working.'

Instead, democratic planning will be needed, and the seeds of this are found outside the NPC's November report, in the struggles of ordinary people for a better life.

Planning the status quo?

The NPC's inability to diagnose economic problems is matched by its disjointed approach to broader socio-environmental decay. On the one hand, the NPC lists atop its infrastructure priority plan two objectives: 'The upgrading of informal settlements' and 'Public transport infrastructure and systems' but, on the other hand, inveighs that 'users must pay the bulk of the costs, with due protection for poor households'. How can this contradiction be reconciled, when the vast bulk of state investments in commuter rail are being made in luxury Johannesburg-Pretoria train lines that are affordable only to a tiny fraction of the public, and when the e-tolling system is so onerous for ordinary people that COSATU and its allies have forced a rethink on the matter?

Likewise, in supplying electricity, the source of so many service delivery protests, Eskom's huge price increases – 127 per cent between 2008 and 2011 already, with many more years of 25 per cent annual rises still to come – apply to poor households but not to BHP Billiton and the Anglo American Corporation. These two were recipients of special pricing agreements made with apartheid officials two decades ago (two such officials, Finance Minister Derek Keys and Eskom Treasurer Mick Davis, promptly joined BHP Billiton after apartheid). The agreements will be valid for another two decades, supplying power to smelters (transforming imported bauxite into aluminium that is priced too high for local consumption) at R0.12 per kilowatt hour, around a tenth of what poor households pay via self-disconnecting pre-payment meters. The NPC report is silent on such contradictions.

Its third and fourth infrastructure priorities are also contradiction ridden: the 'development of the Durban-Gauteng freight corridor, including the development of a new dug-out port on the site of the old Durban airport' (part of a R250 billion 'back of ports' strategy to expand the notorious petrochemical industry) and the 'construction of a new coal line to unlock coal deposits in the Waterberg' and 'extension of existing coal lines in the central basin', in spite of the vast damage (not acknowledged) done by coal to local and global ecologies.

Ironically, though, the very next paragraph begins, 'South Africa needs to move away from the unsustainable use of natural resources', but optimistically asserts that 'South Africa can manage the transition to a low-carbon economy at a pace consistent with government's public pledges, without harming jobs and competitiveness'. What the NPC report demonstrates, in reality, is that we are locked so deeply into the minerals-energy complex tyranny that no change to status quo climate-destroying politics is on the cards. The new climate white paper also fails to grapple with the fact that South Africa ranks 20 times worse than even the United States when our energy-related CO_2 is corrected for per capita GDP growth. Our economy is diabolically coal-addicted with no real prospect of changing. As the NPC argues, as its top priority for economic growth, we must 'Raise exports, focusing on those areas where South Africa has the endowments and comparative advantage, such as mining', even though this status quo strategy has been utterly destructive to economy, society, polity and ecology (see NPC 2011b).

Pressure from below and above?

Given that Durban hosted the 17th Conference of the Parties (COP17) to the United Nations Framework Convention on Climate Change in December, these are the contradictions that Pretoria could have set out to resolve in the interests of the planet and the people. This could have been a moment to reject the Kyoto Protocol strategy of emissions markets – a 'privatisation of the air' scheme to allow Northerners to continue polluting – to address humanity's most crucial survival challenge, at a time when financiers are indisputably wrecking the world economy. The carbon markets were, after all, still crashing from a high of more than €30 per ton of carbon to around €8 per ton as the COP17 began, with the UBS bank in Switzerland predicting a further fall to €3 per ton in coming months. Yet, even the vast Green Climate Fund, co-chaired by Manuel, ultimately gave credence to the idea that markets would save the day.

Instead of saving the planet, profit prevailed above all else, especially for carbon traders and huge mining conglomerates, the latter linked to the ANC not only through murky campaign contributions and black economic empowerment (BEE) deals, but also via Eskom. The ANC, in turn, will look forward to the pay-off of its 25 per cent share in the local arm of the Hitachi corporation, which will be supplying multi-billion rand boilers to the new Medupi and Kusile coal-fired plants. The electricity from these plants will be used overwhelmingly by big business, in view of the inability of poor people to afford the perpetual 25 per cent annual price increases.

Such highly questionable relationships, associated with the economy's reliance upon coal-based energy and mining, are nothing new. The role of actors such as former Environmental Affairs Minister Valli Moosa (a carbon trader whose conduct as Eskom Chairperson prior to 2010 was deemed 'improper' by the Public Protector, when he failed to recuse himself during the process that saw Hitachi win the tender) continues to entrench neo-apartheid's deep power relations. Behaviour such as this will leave the masses powerless due to excessive price increases, while the world's two biggest mining and metals houses will continue to benefit from the world's cheapest electricity. The rising rage of protesters, who cannot get access to electricity, will never be understood, much less resolved, given the prevailing power relations.

This state of affairs is untenable, however. Regardless of formula or calculation, South Africa's developmental data remain dismal. Current policy continues to perpetuate this in the face of crisis. In Tunisia and Egypt, the Ben Ali and Mubarak regimes could not forever operate with the Bretton Woods Institutions, the US government and local capital in exploiting their societies. Justice can, and will, be done – and hopefully well before Moeletsi Mbeki's 2020 predicted dead-line. What remains to be seen is whether, from below, the activists of leading trade unions, community groups, women's organisations and environmental lobbies are going to guide this revolution, or whether right-wing populist currents will prevail. This is the struggle of the period ahead, making Mangaung manoeuvres pale in political comparison.

Notes

1. *The New Age*, 5 September 2011. Available at: http://thenewage. co.za/27987-1007-53-Capital_flight_a_threat_to_economic_ freedom_Moeletsi_Mbeki.

2. BBC Newsnight interview, 2011. Available at: www.youtube.com/ watch?v=6UGDTtqkISo.

3. *Business Insider*, 6 October 2011. Available at: http://articles.business-insider.com/2011-10-06/markets/30250050_1_british-banks-significant-bank-largest-banks.

4. *Moneyweb*, 29 September 2011. Available at: http://www.moneyweb. co.za/mw/view/mw/en/page295799?oid=553257&sn=2009+Detail& pid=299360.

5. *Wall Street Journal*, 15 August 2011, republished by Global Research, 15 August 2011. Available at: http://www.globalresearch.ca/PrintArticle. php?articleId=26031

SOCIAL AND ECONOMIC INCLUSION IN POST-APARTHEID SOUTH AFRICA

Vusi Gumede

Introduction

South Africa's democracy is founded on one of the noblest constitutions in the world. Forged against the backdrop of struggle and dispossession, it not only enshrines political freedom, but also sets itself apart in terms of the provision that it makes for the material dignity of the country's people. The state is obliged to 'respect, protect, promote and fulfil the rights' of everyone in the country (Constitution of South Africa 1996: Section 7(2)). This is as true of economic freedom as it is for political liberty. Yet, the former has been more challenging to achieve than the latter.

Since the country's political transition, much of the state's efforts, and those of other social partners, have been devoted to devising policies and programmes that seek to bring to life the ideals of human dignity, non-racialism and non-sexism, universal adult suffrage and a prosperous nation. Development, in a nutshell, has been the *raison d'être* of the post-apartheid state. The public polices and legislative interventions that have been implemented since 1994 can be said to have been deliberate attempts to broaden the concept of liberty to include human development and socio-economic justice.[1]

However, as protests in democratic and non-democratic countries alike over the past year have shown, states are increasingly challenged by their citizens if their founding objectives become deferred to the point that ordinary people lose faith in the likelihood of them being realised. For this reason, among others, it remains fundamentally important to track change and to be transparent about progress or lack thereof. In the absence of critical assessment that reflects reality, people lose faith because their plight comes to be perceived as unacknowledged and unimportant.

This article explores South Africa's progress in advancing human development, especially for the previously disadvantaged and those groups that often bear the brunt of poor performance by the government, the economy and society broadly. The analysis also reflects, given what the data suggests, on the much-debated issue of whether South Africa is a developmental state or not. The article uses the latest available developmental statistics to tell the story. The statistics presented and discussed below are unambiguous in showing that despite significant progress on certain scores, socio-economic development in South Africa is highly unequal. It benefits those that have always been at a structural advantage, and condemns the majority of the historically marginalised to lives that are still far removed from the promise of material dignity contained in the Constitution. Essentially, poverty remains very high and, along with underdevelopment, largely biased towards the country's black population group.

The various indicators and indices presented confirm that race, gender and spatiality have not been sufficiently redressed. Indeed, as observed by Bhorat and Van der Westhuisen (2010), little progress has been made in South Africa as far as eradicating household poverty is concerned. For example, the black population group is still, on average, worse off in all the measures of human development, and in relation to human poverty. Women bear a disproportionate load. Rural areas continue to have lower Human Development Index (HDI) scores and higher Human Poverty Index (HPI-1) scores. Also, the findings imply that the government has not yet succeeded in ensuring a more egalitarian society. In essence, the conclusion reached is that remnants of South Africa's unfortunate political history are still prevalent in the country's poverty and human development dynamics.

Methodology

These findings and the discussion below are based largely on the National Income Dynamics Study (NIDS), which is a nationally representative household survey that was conducted in 2008.[2] The NIDS is intended to become a longitudinal dataset with revisits to the sampled households every two years – the households visited in 2008/9 were visited again in 2010/11. The NIDS, importantly, allows for the calculation of various significant estimates that other datasets do not readily allow for. For instance, for the first time ever, South Africa would have HDIs by income quintiles. The NIDS dataset also permits an estimation of comparative human development and poverty across subgroups, as well as the calculation of relative human development at different points in the income distribution – something that has not been done in South Africa before. However, like most datasets, there are caveats. In particular, the Indian subsample is relatively small and likely to be imprecise for any inference specifically focused on this population group; hence, the focus of this analysis is largely on the black and white population groups.

This article focuses on two primary indicators to state its case. Besides the standard measures of poverty, human development is measured through the HDI, which is calculated by first creating an index of all three dimensions (life expectancy, education and income). The second indicator is the HPI, which was introduced in 1997 in an attempt to build a composite index from the different features of deprivation in quality of life to arrive at an aggregate judgment on the extent of poverty in a community. The HPI is calculated separately for developing and developed countries to better reflect socio-economic differences. For developing states, the annotation HPI-1 is used to distinguish the poverty measurements from those of the developed states that are measured in terms of HPI-2. South Africa falls in the former category.

Human development indicators

The HDI has three components: longevity, knowledge and income (Haq 1995, in Fukuda-Parr & Kumar 2003). In essence, it is a synopsis of a country's human development, and combines statistics on life expectancy, education and income. With regard to the HPI-1, Anand and Sen (1994: 229, in Fukuda-Parr & Kumar 2003) indicate that 'both [the HDI and the HPI] have to use the rich categories of information that are associated with human development: characteristics of human lives and the quality of living that go much beyond what income information can provide'.

In summary, therefore, human development is the process of enlarging people's choices and raising their levels of well-being. Sen (1993: 35) describes well-being as a 'person's being seen from the perspective of her own personal welfare'. The pursuit of human development in South Africa, therefore, is about seeking improvement in the quality of life of the people of this country. The human development measures are better placed to capture the desired improvement in quality of life. There is ongoing work to improve human development and human poverty measures, because the HDI and gross domestic product (GDP), in particular, have been recognised as falling short in comprehensively quantifying 'human progress'.[3] That said, the HDI and HPI-1 remain useful measures of human development. Unlike conventional poverty indicators that focus narrowly on household income or consumption data, the various components of the HDI and HPI-1 indicate progress in the various social and economic indicators.

The major thrust that underpins HDI and HPI-1 calculations is life expectancy. The estimated life expectancy rates and probabilities of South Africans living to the ages of 3, 40 and 60 years are reported in Table 4.3.1. The estimates show that, on average, South Africans live up to the age of 50 years. Women live, on average, three years longer than men do and have an average life expectancy of 51 years compared to 48 years for men. There may be various reasons for this. It could be ascribed to the fact that women generally live much healthier lifestyles than men. Women are, for example, less likely to engage in life-threatening behaviour (smoking, crime, car racing, etc.) than are men. The data further suggest that

Table 4.3.1: Estimates of life expectancy – national, gender-, race- and province-specific estimates

	Life expectancy (years)	Prob. (not 3) (%)	Prob. (not 40) (%)	Prob. (not 60) (%)	N
Total	**49.5**	**7.9**	**38.8**	**65.8**	**28 845**
Male	47.8	10.3	37.1	69.1	13 311
Female	51.1	5.6	40.2	63.3	15 534
Black	45.2	9.0	44.7	73.4	22 318
Coloured	62.4	1.6	14.6	44.7	4 519
Indian	76.5	0.0	0.0	28.6	495
White	74.1	0.0	14.5	16.7	1 513
Western Cape	59.1	2.4	20.7	41.9	3 680
Eastern Cape	50.1	2.9	31.7	69.4	3 711
Northern Cape	53.0	2.6	38.7	61.7	1 972
Free State	38.8	17.8	53.7	75.9	1 694
KwaZulu-Natal	37.2	9.1	69.1	88.8	8 155
North West	51.2	11.9	36.3	60.7	2 374
Gauteng	62.5	5.6	14.5	49.4	2 638
Mpuma-langa	45.1	16.0	58.2	65.3	1 915
Limpopo	52.9	8.0	26.2	54.4	2 706
Poorest 20%	39.6	7.7	57.2	84.2	5 652
20–40% poorest	45.8	5.4	51.87	74.5	5 650
40–60% poorest	44.5	7.0	46.25	77.8	5 653
20–40% richest	51.2	12.6	29.33	60.4	5 653
20% richest	64.9	11.1	24.05	39.9	5 647

Source: Author's calculations, based on NIDS 2008

males are also almost twice as likely to die within the first year of their lives than are their female counterparts.

Given the inequalities in South African society, the country's developmental story cannot be told without referring to the differential development of its constituent groups that historically have been categorised by race and geographic location.

In this context, black people have the lowest life expectancy rate of all population groups. On average, black people live for 45 years, while coloured and white people live for 62 and 74 years, respectively. The estimate for Indians is imprecise for the reasons given above. The urbanised provinces of Gauteng and the Western Cape have higher life expectancies; Gauteng with 63 years followed by the Western Cape with 59 years. There is substantial variation among the other provinces, such as KwaZulu-Natal and the Free State, with the lowest life expectancies at 37 and 39 years, respectively. The highest child mortality rate – children not living beyond the age of 3 years – occurs in the Free State (18 per cent), followed by Mpumalanga (16 per cent). KwaZulu-Natal has relatively lower child mortality rates, but 70 per cent of the population do not live beyond the age of 40 years. The mortality patterns in KwaZulu-Natal and the Free State have been ascribed largely to a significantly higher incidence of HIV/AIDS in these provinces.

Progress in education is measured by two statistics: adult literacy rates and gross school enrolment (for primary, secondary and tertiary education). As Table 4.3.2 shows, almost 10 per cent of adult South Africans cannot read. Illiteracy amongst women is 2 percentage points higher than amongst men, and is more prevalent in the black group than the other population groups. Limpopo and KwaZulu-Natal have the highest illiteracy rates, followed by the Eastern Cape, the Northern Cape and the North West. Gauteng (3.5 per cent) and the Western Cape (4.3 per cent) find themselves at the other end of the spectrum. Another striking feature of this data, of course, is the concentration of illiteracy amongst the poorest South Africans.

In addition to education, measurement of the access component of poverty includes basic amenities such as clean drinking water and the weight of children. Again, similar patterns reveal themselves. As Table 4.3.3 indicates, about 7 per cent of all South Africans rely on springs, streams, pools or dams for household water. Black people are by far the most likely to lack access to improved water sources. The backlog is most severe in the Eastern Cape, where 23 per cent of South Africans live without an improved water source, and KwaZulu-Natal (14 per cent). With regard to the weight

Table 4.3.2: Estimated literacy and illiteracy rates for all adults

	Adult literacy rates (%)	Adult illiteracy rates (%)	N
Total	**90.6**	**9.4**	**18 630**
Male	91.9	8.1	8 124
Female	89.4	10.6	10 506
Black	88.8	11.2	13 988
Coloured	92.6	7.4	3 048
Indian	93.8	6.2	366
White	99.7	0.3	1 228
Western Cape	95.7	4.3	2 657
Eastern Cape	87.1	12.9	2 287
Northern Cape	87.6	12.4	1 317
Free State	93.4	6.6	1 141
KwaZulu-Natal	85.6	14.4	4 861
North West	87.3	12.7	1 556
Gauteng	96.5	3.5	1 928
Mpumalanga	90.9	9.1	1 234
Limpopo	85.5	14.5	1 649
Poorest 20%	86.9	13.1	3 273
20–40% poorest	86.0	14.0	4 059
40–60% poorest	87.6	12.4	4 310
20–40% richest	91.2	8.8	4 073
20% richest	98. 5	1.5	2 915

Source: Author's calculations, based on NIDS 2008

of children, Body Mass Index (BMI) results show that under-nourishment amongst children aged 5 years and younger is a particular problem for the coloured group (14 per cent). Black and white children, with 8 per cent and 7 per cent, respectively, measured to be underweight, are less at risk. Girls are more than twice as likely to be underweight than boys. The Northern Cape and Mpumalanga have the highest rate of underweight children, while KwaZulu-Natal has the lowest rate, at just 5 per cent.

Human development and poverty

Calculations based on NIDS give an aggregate national HDI of 0.69 for 2008. Again, it makes more sense to break down the aggregate figures into constitutive groups. While there is little gender distinction in terms of HDI scores for women and men, there is a distinct racial pattern. Black South Africans recorded the lowest HDI score at 0.63, compared to that of the white group at 0.91. As such, the human development of black South Africans is more or less on a par with aggregate scores of countries like Bhutan. White South Africans, conversely, enjoy development standards that are comparable to the levels of Cyprus and Portugal. Table 4.3.4 shows estimates of the HDI and the HPI-1.

Gauteng, the most industrialised of the country's nine provinces, has the highest average HDI and KwaZulu-Natal the lowest. At 0.81, Gauteng can be compared to countries like Turkey and Mauritius, while KwaZulu-Natal with 0.60 would rank next to Congo.

There is a finding that requires further reflection: income poverty, the data implies, is not the only cause of human poverty. As Table 4.3.4 indicates, the HPI-1 is higher on average in KwaZulu-Natal than the average for the poorest 20 per cent of households, which suggests that households in KwaZulu-Natal experience lower human development on average than can be expected from provinces with a comparable income status. The HDI of the white group (and of Indians) is better than the average for the richest 20 per cent of all South Africans, which suggests that there are factors in addition to household income that determine inter-racial differences in human development and which are probably captured in much lower life expectancy rates for black South Africans. In this context, it is a persuasive argument that the legacy of apartheid remains profound and/or that the government (perhaps understandably) has not succeeded in redressing racial inequalities.

Table 4.3.3: Access to safe drinking water and child nutritional status		
	Share of population lacking access to clean drinking water (%)	Share of under-5s who are underweight (BMI) (%)
Total	**6.7**	**8.2**
Male	6.3	4.7
Female	7.1	11.5
Black	8.4	7.7
Coloured	0.7	13.5
Indian	0.0	10.0
White	0.0	6.7
Western Cape	0.2	8.8
Eastern Cape	23.1	9.4
Northern Cape	0.2	12.6
Free State	0.0	6.8
KwaZulu-Natal	13.7	4.9
North West	0.3	9.4
Gauteng	0.0	9.0
Mpumalanga	0.4	12.5
Limpopo	6.0	8.5
Poorest 20%	14.0	9.3
20–40% poorest	11.9	9.1
40–60% poorest	4.4	7.1
20–40% richest	2.3	8.3
20% richest	0.9	5.2

Source: Author's calculations, based on NIDS 2008

State capacity and organisation are arguably the primary constraints to South Africa becoming a fully fledged developmental state.

South Africa as a developmental state

Given the ongoing debates about South Africa as a developmental state, this subsection presents preliminary conclusions drawing from the aforementioned findings. An analysis of the extent to which the South African state is indeed developmental has significance, because it has on numerous occasions indicated that it is pursuing such a model.[4] It is useful to examine the notion of a developmental state comparatively, hence some reference to India, Brazil, Botswana and Mauritius – countries that are broadly viewed as (emerging) developmental states.

This article defines a developmental state in terms of its institutional attributes, objectives and capacity to deliver on economic growth and human development. The working definition used here is that a developmental state 'is active in pursuing its agenda, working with social partners, has the capacity and is appropriately organized for its predetermined developmental objectives' (Gumede 2011: 180). Examining the various aspects of a developmental state encapsulated in this definition, South Africa is not yet a developmental state.

State capacity and organisation are arguably the primary constraints to South Africa becoming a fully fledged developmental state. The slow progress towards effectively reducing poverty and expanding human capabilities may be attributed largely to poor state capacity. State capacity can be conceptualised on four dimensions: ideational, political, technical and implementational (Cummings & Nørgaard 2004). Ideational capacity refers to the degree to which the state (its actors, role and policies) is legitimated and embedded in state institutions. Political capacity refers to the effectiveness of state institutions. Technical capacity involves an understanding of the policy context and the ability to devise policy options for a particular policy challenge. Implementational capacity entails the technical know-how for a particular policy action that has to be undertaken to implement a programme. Mkandawire (2001), on the other hand, emphasises the importance of the 'ideology-structure nexus' for a state to be considered developmental. He differentiates between two core components of such states: the ideological and the structural. It is a matter of debate whether the South African government is appropriately organised/structured for its predetermined developmental objectives.

As presented above, findings on human development and human poverty suggest that South Africa has made some headway in terms of improving its HDI score, peaking at 0.69 in 2008. There has been a downward slide, however, and the country recorded a far lower 0.61 in 2011.[5] The country's performance, therefore, has been inconsistent and is vulnerable to external shocks. It is against the background of this vulnerability that South Africa, arguably, should be classified as a 'developmental state in the making'. In other words, although the country still has some way to go in this regard, it has some key attributes of such a state, which, if strengthened, could see it emerge fully as one.

Table 4.3.4: Estimates of the Human Development Index and the Human Poverty Index

	HDI	HPI-1
Total	0.691	17.1
Male	0.693	25.8
Female	0.689	28.2
Black	0.630	31.2
Coloured	0.752	10.9
Indian	0.886	5.0
White	0.914	10.1
Western Cape	0.760	14.4
Eastern Cape	0.646	23.4
Northern Cape	0.695	27.2
Free State	0.630	37.3
KwaZulu-Natal	0.599	48.1
North West	0.677	25.5
Gauteng	0.806	10.2
Mpumalanga	0.676	40.4
Limpopo	0.677	19.3
Poorest 20%	0.488	40.0
20–40% poorest	0.563	36.3
40–60% poorest	0.586	32.9
20–40% richest	0.675	22.2
20% richest	0.868	17.3

Source: Author's calculations, based on NIDS 2008

At this stage, however, the country needs to make more gains, faster. In a broad, comparative context, South Africa is lagging behind its peers. HDI scores in the *2011 Human Development Report* show that the country, with its score of 0.61, trails other modern or emerging developmental states, such as Brazil (0.71), Botswana (0.63) and Mauritius (0.72). Although the HDI score for India, another of South Africa's developmental peers, is even lower at 0.54 in 2011, this represents a significant 21 per cent gain on the 0.387 it recorded in 1999 (UNDP 2011). One possible explanation for South Africa's lagging behind its peers is that the country's economy has not expanded to the same degree as those of Brazil, India, Mauritius and Botswana. Another important feature of these economies has been that they have managed to reduce income poverty and income inequality at a much faster rate. Both scenarios relate to the monopolised structure of the South African economy, with its strong dependence on the resource-export and financial sectors and its exceptionally high levels of unemployment. The transformation of the South African economy has been slow and, consequently, it has failed to create a sufficient number of jobs. Obviously, context-specific policies in particular countries account for some of the differences in economic and developmental outcomes, but it is possible to implement such policies more easily in environments where there is greater cohesion between major policy stakeholders.

Concluding remarks

South Africans today enjoy not only the benefits of political freedom but, on average, a better standard of living. However, statistics can be misleading if not properly interrogated. Deeper analysis reveals the discomforting truth that improvement generally only holds true for South Africa in aggregate terms. As demonstrated above, the immense structural socio-economic inequalities of the apartheid era are still very much alive today.

The findings presented above suggest that – almost two decades into a politically liberated South Africa – it is important to revisit the strategies that have informed our developmental trajectory. If anything, the data appear to demonstrate that the current path is unsustainable. Although some progress has been made in addressing human development and poverty, the pace has been slow and, in both the quantitative and qualitative sense, it has been insufficient. Poverty and inequality remain at intolerable levels.

The analysis underscores two fundamental points, namely that the black population group has the lowest HDI, and that inter-racial differences in HDI continue to be significant. It shows that economic transformation (and consequent social and economic inclusion) has been slow. It is in this context that we cannot yet refer to South Africa as a fully fledged developmental state. For it to be one, state capacity and systems have to be strengthened to the extent that the country's

developmental trajectory becomes less vulnerable to economic fluctuations. Until such time as it consolidates its position on both counts, South Africa will remain a developmental state in the making.

Notes

1. For instance, since 1994, a multitude of legislative and policy instruments have been introduced to improve the situation of targeted groups. These include the Promotion of Equality and Prevention of Unfair Discrimination Act 4 of 2000, the National Policy Framework for Women's Empowerment and Gender Equality of 2000, the Children's Act 38 2005 (amended in 2008), the National Policy for the Advancement and Co-ordination of Children's Rights in South Africa of 2003, the National Empowerment Fund Act 105 1998, the Integrated National Disability Strategy White Paper of 2000, the National Youth Development Agency Act 54 of 2008, the National Youth Policy 2009–2014 and the Integrated Strategy for the Treatment of HIV and Aids (which has been updated for the period 2008–2012).

2. The NIDS dataset contains information on more than 28 000 individuals in 7 305 households across South Africa, and has detailed information on expenditure, income, employment, schooling, health, social cohesion, etc. (see http://www.nids.uct.ac.za/home).

3. Stiglitz, Sen and Fitoussi (2010) contend, for instance, that new and more inclusive parameters for measuring economic growth are critical if countries are to achieve the overall goal of improving the quality of life.

4. The 'declaration' that South Africa wants to be a developmental state is succinctly captured in the revised 2007 Strategy and Tactics document of the ruling party, the African National Congress (see http://www.anc.org.za/docs/pdf).

5. It should be noted that the 2008 HDI is not directly comparable with the 2011 HDI, because of the two different sources of data from which the two indices are calculated. That said, it would seem that the various components of the HDI are declining.

Perceptions of Well-being

The lesson of 2011 should be that the citizenry, especially when under material strain, will have no patience with those who offer timid responses or abuse their trust.

ECONOMIC SECURITY IN A TIME OF UNCERTAINTY:
A SOUTH AFRICAN PUBLIC OPINION PERSPECTIVE

Jan Hofmeyr & Lucía Tiscornia

98

Chapter 5

Public Opinion on Economic Security

The ultimate objective of economic transformation is an improved sense of well-being and dignity amongst citizens. Macro-economic data give us an impression of outcomes in terms of targets, but they do not necessarily provide insight into the real impact on people's lives. Data from the SA Reconciliation Barometer Survey show that when prompted to single out the most stubborn obstacle to national unity, most South Africans point to income inequality.[1] Findings like these have particular relevance for the understanding of our social dynamics in a challenging economic period, such as the present.

MOST IMPORTANT SOURCES OF SOCIAL DIVISION

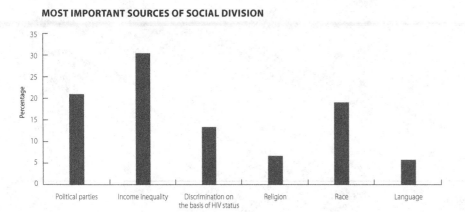

Source: IJR (2011) *SA Reconciliation Barometer Survey*

32%
of South Africans regard inequality as the most important source of social division

HOW DO YOU THINK SAs ECONOMIC SITUATION WILL CHANGE IN THE NEXT 12 MONTHS?

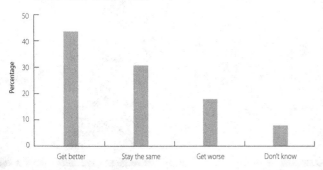

Source: IJR (2011) *SA Reconciliation Barometer Survey*

HOW DOES YOUR FINANCIAL SITUATION COMPARE TO WHAT IT WAS 12 MONTHS AGO?

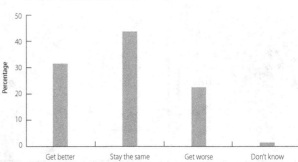

Source: IJR (2011) *SA Reconciliation Barometer Survey*

34%
of South Africans feel that their chances of finding employment have worsened

HOW DO YOUR CHANCES OF FINDING A JOB COMPARE TO WHAT THEY WERE 12 MONTHS AGO?

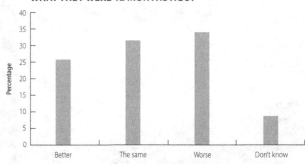

Source: IJR (2011) *SA Reconciliation Barometer Survey*

NATIONAL LEADERS ARE NOT CONCERNED ABOUT PEOPLE LIKE ME

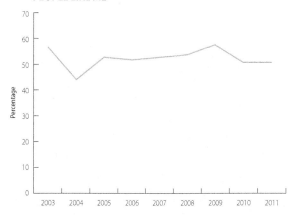

Source: IJR (2011) *SA Reconciliation Barometer Survey*

THERE IS NO WAY TO MAKE PUBLIC OFFICIALS LISTEN TO MY CONCERNS

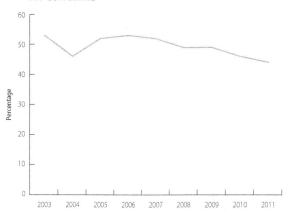

Source: IJR (2011) *SA Reconciliation Barometer Survey*

Comparative perceptions of change in corruption, 2008–2010			
Country	Decreased	Stayed same	Increased
China	25%	29%	46%
India	10%	16%	74%
Indonesia	27%	30%	43%
Brazil	9%	27%	64%
Mexico	7%	18%	75%
Russia	8%	39%	53%
Nigeria	17%	10%	73%
South Africa	24%	14%	62%

Source: Transparency International: Global Corruption Report 2010

CONFIDENCE IN NATIONAL GOVERNMENT

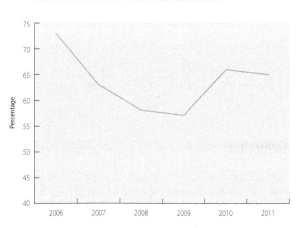

Source: IJR (2011) *SA Reconciliation Barometer Survey*

CONFIDENCE IN LOCAL GOVERNMENT

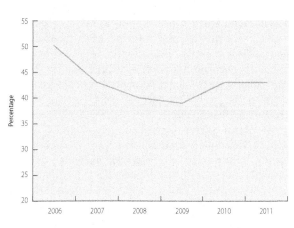

Source: IJR (2011) *SA Reconciliation Barometer Survey*

CONFIDENCE IN PROVINCIAL GOVERNMENT

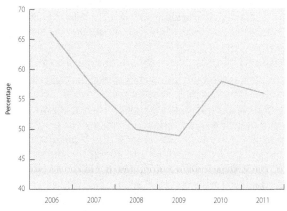

Source: IJR (2011) *SA Reconciliation Barometer Survey*

Economic security in a time of uncertainty: A South African public opinion perspective

Jan Hofmeyr & Lucía Tiscornia

. . . .

Introduction

Popular revolts around the world in 2011 underscored the fact that the legitimacy of states, in whatever form they exist, rests on their ability to pursue the common good of all citizens. Inclusive development – the most basic principle under-pinning the existence of the modern state – still matters, citizens reminded their governments in no uncertain terms.

What made this wave of protest so significant was that it swept across authoritarian and democratic states alike, and thus challenged the notion that political freedom alone is enough to make citizens content. The most fundamental of all human needs is to live in conditions of material and physical security. In both contexts, growing insecurity, resulting from a flailing global economy, and governments' perceived timidity in addressing inequitable (and often unlawful) elite accumulation, drove people to the streets.

As the revolts gained momentum across North Africa in early 2011, Western governments were quick to embrace the term 'Arab Spring', reminiscent of the 'Prague Spring' of 1968, as a catchphrase to capture what they branded as a rejection of undemocratic forms of government. When youths ransacked upmarket boroughs and districts of cities across England in August, UK Prime Minister David Cameron initially failed to see the parallels between what was happening in the streets of London and Cairo. At first, he dismissed the behaviour of the English youths as hooliganism, but later had to concede that it was rooted in a system that, despite the rights and opportunities that it extends in theory, marginalises people at the bottom of society and offers them little in the way of future prospects.

This same sense of alienation was obvious in skirmishes against government austerity in the streets of Athens, sit-ins on Spain's city squares to draw attention to poor economic management, protests in Israel against the cost of living, and marches by thousands across India in support of anti-corruption campaigner, Anna Hazare. *Financial Times* columnist, Gideon Rachmann (2001) cautions against simple generalisations, given the diverse contexts from which these protests had arisen, but notes they all do 'pit an internationally-connected elite against ordinary citizens who feel excluded from the benefits of economic growth, and angered by corruption'.

Responding to Azare's arrest in an editorial titled 'Corrupt, repressive, and stupid', the Indian daily, *The Hindu* did not hold back in articulating the degree of indignation referred to by Rachmann.

In South Africa, protests against poor 'public service delivery' – a catch-all that encompasses much more than the term implies – continued unabated as an increasingly pervasive form of political expression. Given their frequency, these protests have become less of an event to our media and, as a result, have received less coverage in recent years. It would have stayed that way, were it not for two significant incidents in the course of 2011. The first was the nationally broadcasted killing of Andries Tatane, a protester from Ficksburg, allegedly at the hands of riot police. The second, which should be read together with the first, is the fact that toilets became a key campaign issue of the local government elections in May, after it came to light that certain local governments had failed to enclose those that were provided to poor communities. It was a sad indictment on South African society that its most marginalised could get arrested, or even killed, for insisting on access to the most basic forms of dignity.

Incidents like these have called for introspection. Various contributions to consecutive editions of this publication have argued for a new vision and political will to accelerate inclusive growth. Over the years, its scorecards have pointed to important achievements with regard to GDP growth, and how it has been employed to alleviate poverty and provide broadened access to government services. However, they also have alluded to the slow progress in education, its devastating impact on the labour market, and its cumulative result of growing inequality.

What the case of Mr Tatane and the thousands of protests (here and abroad) over the past year have underscored is that development policy cannot rely only on report cards and compliance with monitoring and evaluation objectives. They also need to take proper cognisance of people's own sense of security and the extent to which progress on paper translates into experienced well-being. Progress and social justice are as much questions of perception as they are of hard statistics (OECD 2011). GDP and per capita income growth mean little if they are not perceived as affecting a critical mass of people.

In addition to the macro trends described in the preceding

In South Africa, protests against poor 'public service delivery' – a catch-all that encompasses much more than the term implies – continued unabated as an increasingly pervasive form of political expression.

Table 5.1: Main divisive elements in South Africa

	2003	2004	2005	2006	2007	2008	2009	2010	2011
Political parties	22%	28%	18%	19%	12%	22%	23%	25%	22%
Income inequality	30%	24%	31%	30%	31%	29%	27%	25%	32%
Discrimination on the basis of HIV status	14%	16%	21%	18%	21%	17%	19%	16%	14%
Religion	7%	7%	6%	7%	7%	7%	7%	7%	7%
Race	20%	20%	17%	20%	21%	19%	19%	21%	20%
Language	6%	5%	6%	6%	7%	6%	6%	6%	6%

sections of this Transformation Audit, this chapter presents a brief overview of South Africans' sense of their own material security. It draws on data obtained from the IJR's annual SA Reconciliation Barometer Survey, which is conducted nationally with a representative sample of South Africans. It focuses specifically on respondents' sense of their own economic situation, expectations around employment, and general impressions of their own living conditions and how these compare with others around them.

Inequality matters

Since first conducted in 2003, the survey has asked South Africans what they regard as the main source of division in South Africa. Although the issue of race features prominently in all rounds of the survey to date, the 'gap between rich and poor' – or income inequality – has been identified consistently as the country's major fault line. This was no different in 2011, with 32 per cent of respondents pointing to its divisiveness (see Table 5.1). This finding has to be read within the context of the strong overlap of race and poverty, which has also been alluded to in several editions of this publication. While the two cannot be separated completely, it nevertheless remains significant that when offered the opportunity, more South Africans would point to the predominance of class dimensions than they would to race dimensions.

The fact that inequality is an issue for South Africans is important. They observe it in their relationship to other South Africans and, significantly, regard it as a critical obstacle to creating a more inclusive society.

The economic situation: South Africans feeling the strain

South Africa's dip into recession in 2009 was brief, but its impact disproportionately severe. Employment was haemorrhaged at the time, and has not returned to levels prior to the downturn. Although not an entirely reliable indicator of financial distress, the total number of liquidations in 2010 was 21 per cent higher than in 2008 (Stats SA 2011), and in mid-2011, 46 per cent of the country's 18.6 million credit-active consumers had impaired credit records (Moodley-Isaacs 2011). In sum, recovery thus far has been fragile, uneven and much slower than initially anticipated. During his Medium-Term Budget Policy Statement speech in October, Finance Minister Pravin Gordhan acknowledged that the Treasury has underestimated the severity of the key factors that hold back global growth (National Treasury 2011).

To what extent has this impacted on South Africans' perception of the country's economic prospects, and on their own financial fortunes in the coming year? In this section, we report on respondents' opinions regarding these questions.

Table 5.2 summarises the trends in public perception of the country's economic prospects for the 12 months that follow the survey. The data show that since 2003 most South Africans have felt (at variable levels) that the country's economic prospects have been improving. In 2006, at the height of the pre-recession growth cycle, respondents recorded the highest level of optimism at 56 per cent. This, however, changed markedly in 2008 as economic activity slowed down and then slipped into recession in 2009. Optimism dropped by close to

13 percentage points in these two years. In 2010, as the economy returned to growth, it increased again by 10 points, only to slump back by 5 per cent to 46.3 per cent in 2011. Predictions about worsening conditions showed an inverse pattern, reaching their lowest point in 2006, then doubling during the years prior to and during the recession, followed by a decline to levels that remain somewhat higher than they were before the recession. It is more difficult to draw conclusions about responses indicating that the situation will 'remain the same'. Given that these responses reached their lowest levels during the recession (where the 'worse' category doubled and the 'get better' category declined significantly), we have to assume that sentiment generally worsened. An increase in the 'remain the same' scores after the recession, therefore, may also signify a sense that this situation is likely to continue.

Table 5.3 shows that South Africans generally have been less upbeat about their personal financial situation than they have been about the general economic prospects for the country.

In 2006, at the apex of the growth cycle, 44.3 per cent of respondents felt that their situation would improve in the subsequent year. Following several years of increased employment and growth, almost 40 per cent felt that similar circumstances would prevail and only 14.3 per cent sensed that it would become worse. Within two years, this situation turned around completely with more respondents feeling that their financial situation would worsen rather than improve in the 2008 and 2009 rounds of the survey. In 2010 and 2011, levels of optimism increased somewhat, while there was a decline in the percentage of those who felt that their situation would worsen. However, levels of optimism have not regained their pre-recession highs. A steady growth in 'the same' assessments suggests a stabilisation in sentiment, probably an acceptance that although the situation will not improve much in the immediate wake of the recession, it will also not get any worse.

Employment: finding it is a tough job

As the review article in Chapter 4 indicates, high unemployment lies at the core of South Africa's entrenched levels of poverty and inequality. In September 2011, a quarter of working-age South African job-seekers were unable to find employment. When the broader definition, which includes discouraged work-seekers, is used, this percentage increases to over one-third of the labour force. With only one in three able-bodied South Africans working, this implies, firstly, a greater immediate burden on the fiscus and, secondly, longer-term social repercussions associated with a growing number of disillusioned (mostly young) people, frustrated by their lack of agency in determining their own destinies.

While major stakeholders have recognised the critical proportions and risks of unemployment, the dilemma of how to solve them remains one of the most contested policy issues.

In this section, we look at respondents' perceptions of their chances of finding a job. We then proceed to report on sentiments regarding job security, looking finally at whether it is better to have a low-paid job or to have to fend for yourself, which raises the question of lowering the minimum wage one of the biggest sticking points in current labour debates.

The responses in Table 5.4 speak volumes about the depressing situation in the labour market. Apart from in 2006, South Africans have felt that their chances of obtaining employment or new employment within the job market have decreased. In 2009, the recession year (and in the year prior to it), negative responses peaked at around 40 per cent and declined again to 34 per cent in 2011. While positive sentiment in 2011 grew slightly by just over three percentage points from its recession low, the proportion of those indicating that things would 'stay the same' under these adverse circumstances has grown steadily, suggesting that close to two-thirds ('the same' and 'worse' responses combined) are distinctly pessimistic about opportunities within the labour market.

Given the responses reported in Table 5.4, those in Table 5.5 should not come as a surprise. Since 2006, close to 40 per cent of South Africans responded that they were likely to be unemployed in the year to follow. This comes close to the number of unemployed in terms of the expanded definition of unemployment. A combination of the 'agree', 'uncertain' and 'don't know' categories suggests that close to three-quarters of respondents consistently experienced a sense of job insecurity.

Turning to the question of whether it is better to have a low-paying job than no job at all, the majority of respondents have agreed consistently that this is indeed the case (see Table 5.6). The figure has decreased from its highest mark of 60.7 per cent in 2005 to 48.2 per cent in 2011. However, the decline has not boosted the 'disagree' responses, but rather has increased the 'don't know' and 'uncertain' responses. In sum, while the trend seems to be downwards, most South Africans still seem to agree that when in dire straits they would accept a low wage rather than having to fend for themselves.

Access to government services

The South African government's achievement in providing its people with access to basic services has been widely acknowledged. The statistics provided at the outset of Chapter 4 graphically depict the great strides that have been made in terms of the provision of formal housing. Furthermore, the state has been able to extend social welfare, in the form of a pension or social grant, to around 15 million of its neediest citizens (National Treasury 2011). Figure 5.1 shows the exponential growth in grant recipients over a fairly short period. This rate of expansion is without doubt unsustainable, but it does signify a considerable and commendable response in addressing immediate need.

Despite the great strides that have been made in terms of the provision of services and grants, population growth has

Table 5.2: How do you think the economic situation in South Africa will change in the next 12 months?

	2003	2004	2005	2006	2007	2008	2009	2010	2011
Get better	46.0%	54.0%	48.4%	56.3%	51.3%	38.9%	38.9%	48.3%	43.6%
Stay the same	25.5%	24.6%	26.0%	24.6%	25.1%	23.4%	23.6%	26.1%	30.7%
Get worse	21.4%	14.6%	18.3%	10.7%	15.5%	30.8%	31.7%	19.2%	17.9%
Don't know	7.2%	6.9%	7.2%	8.3%	8.1%	7.0%	5.8%	6.3%	7.8%

Source: IJR (2011) *SA Reconciliation Barometer Survey*

Table 5.3: How does your financial situation compare to what it was like 12 months ago?

	2004	2005	2006	2007	2008	2009	2010	2011
Better	40.8%	38.0%	44.3%	35.0%	28.1%	27.95	32.1%	32.0%
The same	37.1%	37.2%	39.6%	42.7%	37.3%	36.7%	41.5%	43.8%
Worse	19.5%	23.0%	14.3%	20.6%	33.1%	34.3%	24.6%	22.5%
Don't know	2.6%	1.8%	1.7%	1.7%	1.4%	1.1%	1.7%	1.7%

Source: IJR (2011) *SA Reconciliation Barometer Survey*

Table 5.4: How do the chances of you finding a job compare to what they were like 12 months ago?

	2004	2005	2006	2007	2008	2009	2010	2011
Better	29.8%	27.4%	32.1%	25.7%	23.4%	22.4%	26.1%	25.8%
The same	25.6%	24.2%	27.4%	27.5%	27.7%	26.7%	28.6%	31.5%
Worse	30.2%	37.0%	27.5%	34.9%	39.1%	40.6%	34.6%	34.0%
Don't know	13.2%	10.5%	12.2%	11.5%	9.9%	10.2%	10.5%	8.7%

Source: IJR (2011) *SA Reconciliation Barometer Survey*

Table 5.5: It is highly likely that I will be unemployed at some stage during the next year

	2004	2005	2006	2007	2008	2009	2010	2011
Agree	33.0%	39.9%	37.9%	40.2%	42.8%	43.5%	40.7%	37.8%
Uncertain	20.3%	19.2%	19.5%	17.7%	20.2%	19.1%	17.9%	21.5%
Disagree	28.7%	26.4%	24.6%	25.8%	24.7%	22.7%	25.8%	25.2%
Don't know	15.2%	14.5%	16.6%	15.0%	12.3%	14.5%	15.3%	15.2%

Source: IJR (2011) *SA Reconciliation Barometer Survey*

Table 5.6: It is better to have a low-paying full-time job than it is to have to make your own living

	2004	2005	2006	2007	2008	2009	2010	2011
Agree	53.0%	60.7%	60.6%	57.2%	50.2%	51.1%	51.8%	48.2%
Uncertain	18.5%	12.6%	13.5%	13.8%	18.0%	16.0%	15.4%	19.6%
Disagree	24.5%	24.4%	22.9%	24.5%	28.4%	29.1%	29.4%	26.6%
Don't know	4.0%	2.2%	2.9%	4.6%	3.4%	3.8%	3.5%	5.7%

Source: IJR (2011) *SA Reconciliation Barometer Survey*

dictated that pure numbers only tell part of the story. Figure 5.2 shows that while close to four million households gained access to formal dwellings between 1996 and 2009, it represents only a 7 per cent increase from 63.7 per cent to 70.7 per cent for this period. Close to one third of the population, therefore, did not live in formal dwellings in 2009.

Figures relating to the provision of other basic services, like sanitation and running water, provide similar pictures. Despite progress, the challenges remain as big as ever and, in a context of scarce resources and great demand, the frequency of public protests about delayed delivery should not be surprising.

Given South Africa's history of unequal development along racial lines, as well as its current challenges in providing services to communities that remain largely separated along these same lines, it is necessary to ask whether citizens perceive access to public services to be more equitable than in the past. As suggested by the OECD (2011), it is important to gauge perception on this issue, because it provides clues to patterns of cohesion and conflict in society.

In the figure and tables below, we look at the extent to which South Africans still perceive race to be significant in terms of their access to services. In essence, the survey question asked respondents whether they perceived their chances as better, the same, or worse, given the historically defined racial group that they belong to.[2] Figure 5.3 provides the overall national response for all South Africans, while Tables 5.7 and 5.8 summarise respondents' perceptions in terms of their historically defined racial categories, and their Living Standards Measurement (LSM) categories, respectively.[3]

Figure 5.3 shows that just less than a third of South Africans (29 per cent) feel that they are getting equal treatment when it comes to accessing the services of the post-apartheid state. The same proportion feel that they have better access than other groups, but a majority of respondents indicated that their racial category puts them at a disadvantage in this regard. Six per cent are unsure whether this was the case.

Table 5.7 provides an overview how South Africans from historically defined racial categories responded to this question.

About a third of white and Indian South Africans (32.3% and 33.7% respectively) indicated that their racial background did not influence the extent to which they have access to public services. The figures for black and coloured South Africans were only slightly lower at 28.9 and 29.0 per cent, respectively.

The more telling feedback is within the 'better' and 'worse' response categories, where different groups recorded more divergent sentiments. Majorities in all groups, with the exception of respondents in the black category, suggested that they were being disadvantaged by their 'racial background'. Even within the black group, only a fraction of a percentage separated the 'worse' category from being the majority response. At least as far as public services are concerned, many across South African society seem to view themselves as a victim of

Figure 5.1: Total number of grant and pension recipients ('000s)

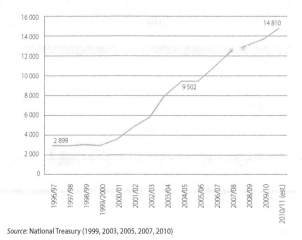

Source: National Treasury (1999, 2003, 2005, 2007, 2010)

Figure 5.2: Access to formal dwellings in numbers and as proportion of population

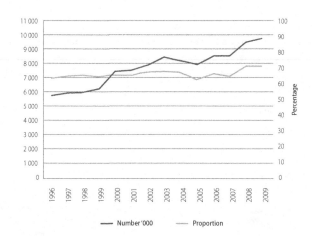

Source: Stats SA (1996–1999, 2000–2001, 2002–2009)

their racial heritage. Coloured and white respondents were most likely to agree with this. The percentage recorded for coloured respondents was 46.9 per cent, while the comparative percentage for white respondents stood at 45.0 per cent. Responses for Indian South Africans came in somewhat lower at 37.3 per cent, while black respondents (at 32.1 per cent) were the least likely to believe that their skin colour puts them at a disadvantage when it comes to accessing services.

The black group was also the most likely to agree that their racial category puts them at an advantage. Responses for the three minority groups on this option again clustered together around the 20 per cent mark, with the white group (at 17.7 per cent) the least convinced that their skin colour provides them with any advantage.

In conclusion, Table 5.8 reports on the same question in terms of respondents' living standards measurement categories (LSM).

An interesting feature that emerges here is that respondents who found themselves in the upper-middle categories of LSM 5–7 seemed most content about their access to services. Sixty-six per cent of those in LSM 6 felt that their group gets either the same or better treatment than other groups. For LSM 5, this figure was about 63 per cent and for LSM 7, 62 per cent. The most negative sentiments were to be found in the lowest three categories (55.0, 42.5 and 43.5 per cent for LSMs 1, 2 and 3 in turn) and the top two categories (37.7 and 43.5 per cent for LSM 9 and 10, respectively). From an access inequality point of view, this finding that South Africans at the top and bottom of society perceive their racial background as a disadvantage in accessing the state is important to note. Given the country's income distribution patterns, we have to assume that a strong racial overlap is likely in terms of responses. This raises issues for further research, such as the question of whether this sense of being disadvantaged at either end of the income spectrum makes South Africans at these extremes more receptive to direct or subtle forms of racial political mobilisation. Conversely, it must be asked what the more positive responses in the middle LSM categories can tell us about creating greater cohesion across groups in terms of their relationship to the state.

Living conditions: 'struggling, but getting by'

In the final section of this chapter, we present data that show how South Africans feel about their own living conditions in general (the sum total of several factors, including these that have been discussed above) and, importantly also, how they perceive their position to be in comparison to those around them.

Table 5.9 summarises South Africans' perceptions about their personal living conditions. In terms of the general national response, close to a quarter of respondents described their living conditions as being either 'very well off' or 'living comfortably'. White South Africans were the most likely to respond in this way, with 46 per cent agreeing that this is

Figure 5.3: Perceptions of whether respondents' racial category affects their chances of access to public services in 2011

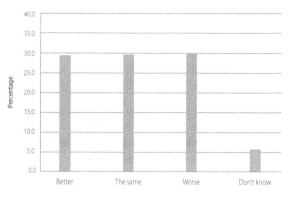

Source: IJR (2011) *SA Reconciliation Barometer Survey*

Table 5.7: Are your chances of accessing public services...than other people in 2011?

	Total	White	Asian/Indian	Coloured	Black
Better	29.4%	17.7%	20.4%	21.2%	32.7%
The same	29.5%	32.3%	33.7%	29.0%	28.9%
Worse	35.2%	45.0%	37.3%	46.9%	32.1%
Don't know	5.9%	5.0%	8.6%	2.9%	4.9%

Table 5.8: Are your chances of accessing public services...than other people in 2011? (LSM)

	Living Standards Measurement									
	1	2	3	4	5	6	7	8	9	10
Better	14.6%	19.2%	22.4%	26.6%	33.5%	36.4%	37.6%	31.8%	21.1%	17.8%
The same	27.4%	30.1%	24.1%	31.1%	29.1%	29.4%	24.8%	30.4%	36.2%	36.7%
Worse	55.0%	42.5%	43.5%	36.8%	31.1%	28.7%	32.7%	34.4%	37.7%	43.5%
Don't know	3.0%	8.3%	10.0%	5.5%	6.3%	5.5%	4.9%	3.5%	5.0%	2.0%

the case (almost 10 per cent indicated that they were very well off). Indian South Africans followed at 34.3 per cent, with the coloured group at 28.1 per cent and the black group at 20.1 per cent in third and fourth place.

Nationally, and within each of the population groups, most respondents indicated that they were 'struggling, but getting by'. The overall national figure stood at 53.8 per cent, and there was little variation in the responses of each of the country's historically defined population groups. A difference of only seven percentage points separated the highest affirmative response, by black South Africans at 54.7 per cent, and white South Africans at 47.7 per cent.

Close to 20 per cent of South Africans regarded themselves as very poor. The difference is quite stark here between the 2.8 per cent of white respondents and the 23 per cent of black South Africans who answered in the affirmative to this category. Virtually the same proportion of coloured and Indian South Africans (12.1% and 12.2%, respectively) regarded themselves as very poor.

Of course, such perceptions, more often than not, differ in varying degrees from the realities that macro statistics might present, but they do provide an indication of the level of existential pressure faced by ordinary people. Therefore, they should be seen as indicators of the material insecurity that South Africans experience.

From here we proceed to report on the findings of South Africans' perceptions of their own material circumstances in relation to other people in the community where they live. Given that most South Africans continue to live in residential areas that are largely racially homogenous, we recognise that the term 'community' may be interpreted by some as a proxy for people from the same historically defined racial group.

Table 5.10 shows that on average most South Africans feel that they are living in communities that are struggling to get by. Responses amongst black, coloured and Indian South Africans clustered together in the lower fifties, with 54.7 per cent of black respondents feeling that this is the case, followed by 53.9 per cent of coloured respondents, and 51.3 per cent of Indian South Africans. There is a significant gap between responses from these groups and those of white respondents, amongst which a much lower 31.0 per cent felt that people in their communities were struggling to get by. Predictably, therefore, the white group's responses to the three remaining categories also diverge strongly from those of respondents in other categories. While only 5.7 per cent of white South Africans sensed poverty in their community, close to a quarter of black South Africans, or 24.9 per cent, suggested that it was prevalent where they live.

Following on perceptions of community well-being, we report in Table 5.11 on how respondents perceived their own living conditions in relation to other South Africans. Here respondents were asked whether they regarded their living conditions as 'better', 'the same' as, or 'worse' than those of most other South Africans.

Table 5.9: How would you describe your own living conditions in 2011?

	Total	White	Asian/Indian	Coloured	Black
Very well off	4.6%	9.20%	2.20%	3.50%	4.00%
Living comfortably	19.9%	36.80%	32.10%	24.60%	16.10%
Struggling but getting by	53.8%	47.70%	52.50%	55.90%	54.70%
Very poor	19.2%	2.80%	12.10%	12.20%	23.00%
Don't know	2.5%	3.50%	1.10%	3.80%	2.20%

Table 5.10: How would you describe the living conditions of most people in the community where you live in 2011?

	Total	White	Asian/Indian	Coloured	Black
Very well off	4.1%	12.4%	3.0%	1.2%	3.1%
Living comfortably	18.8%	42.8%	28.7%	17.8%	14.5%
Struggling but getting by	51.5%	31.0%	51.3%	53.9%	54.7%
Very poor	22.1%	5.7%	14.5%	23.7%	24.9%
Don't know	3.5%	8.1%	2.5%	3.3%	2.8%

An interesting result here is that nationally, and within each of the historically defined racial groups, people regard their situation as being the same as that of most South Africans. Almost 30 per cent regard themselves as being better off, and close to 23 per cent as being worse off. South Africans of Indian origin, on average, regard themselves as being better off than most other citizens, followed by white, coloured and black respondents, in that order. Almost a quarter of coloured and black respondents, with 24.5 per cent and 24.9 per cent, respectively, indicated that they were worse off than other South Africans.

Of particular interest is the fact that almost half of white South Africans (46.6 per cent) regarded their material conditions as being the same as those of other South Africans, and 11.4 per cent within this group felt that they were worse off than other South Africans. Developmental statistics, of course, show that for the average white South African these perceptions do not hold true at all. Although we must assume that when answering the question, respondents did not compare themselves with other racial groups, but with what they regard the living conditions of the average South African to be, this finding still seems to reflect a view that is divorced from reality. Whether this is an indication of the extent to which white South Africans' relative affluence insulates them from the experiences of the majority of their countrymen and women is a question that deserves further analysis and research attention.

In Table 5.12, we report on the extent to which citizens have sensed year-on-year improve-ments in their living conditions.

In 2006, a very large proportion of South Africans, 45.3 per cent, indicated that their living conditions were better than they had been in the previous year. This finding is not entirely surprising, given that in that year the country attained its highest level of GDP growth since the advent of democracy. The economy was steaming ahead, and unemployment, although still high in internationally comparative terms, was at its lowest in years. The picture looked decidedly different in 2008 when the South African economy, in response to the recession in the United States and several large European countries, slowed down significantly. While the country only dipped into recession during 2009, much of the damage to the economy had already been done in 2008. Although positive sentiment increased again and stood at 31 per cent in 2011, nearly 50 per cent of South Africans felt that not much had changed in terms of their material circumstances. In 2011, 18.3 per cent of South Africans – the second highest percentage for the reported measurement years after 2008 – sensed that their living conditions had worsened.

For all the measured years, black South Africans were the most likely to report an improvement – and the least likely to report deterioration in their living conditions – when measured against the previous year. Given that they constitute the single largest historically marginalised group, this can be regarded as a positive evaluation of government efforts to improve the

Table 5.11: Comparing your living conditions to those of most other South Africans in 2011, do you feel you are...?

	Total	White	Asian/Indian	Coloured	Black
Better	29.5%	37.6%	42.8%	29.8%	27.7%
The same	44.8%	46.6%	40.8%	42.2%	45.0%
Worse	22.8%	11.4%	15.3%	24.5%	24.9%
Don't know	2.8%	4.5%	1.1%	3.4%	2.4%

Table 5.12: How do your living conditions compare to what they were like 12 months ago?

	2004	2006	2008	2010	2011
National					
Better	39.8%	45.3%	28.9%	34.5%	31.4%
The same	45.6%	42.4%	43.3%	47.0%	48.3%
Worse	12.8%	10.6%	25.7%	16.9%	18.3%
White					
Better	25.6%	37.3%	16.8%	22.3%	28.2%
The same	55.8%	48.3%	39.6%	51.1%	52.5%
Worse	17.8%	12.7%	41.2%	25.8%	17.3%
Asian/Indian					
Better	43.0%	55.6%	15.6%	30.7%	26.0%
The same	41.1%	36.1%	57.8%	53.5%	57.1%
Worse	13.9%	7.6%	25.7%	14.2%	14.9%
Coloured					
Better	37.7%	50.3%	25.8%	30.2%	24.8%
The same	48.2%	41.7%	41.1%	46.3%	51.5%
Worse	13.9%	7.6%	25.7%	14.2%	14.9%
Black					
Better	46.7%	45.9%	31.8%	37.1%	33.2%
The same	40.7%	41.6%	43.6%	46.2%	46.7%
Worse	4.9%	4.5%	10.4%	7.2%	8.4%

> Over the past 17 years major gains have been made in addressing the immediate needs of society's most vulnerable, but given the scale of the challenge, the question remains whether it is enough.

livelihoods of those who bore the brunt of apartheid. However, the level of positive evaluation has subsided substantially from the high of 46.7 per cent in 2004 to 33.2 per cent in 2011. Conversely, reports of deterioration in living conditions have almost doubled from 4.9 per cent to 8.4 per cent. These changes have been relatively small, but nevertheless do communicate a message.

In 2011, lower percentages of respondents within each of the population groups were able to report an improvement in their living conditions, when measured against the previous year. While positive sentiment is still much higher than three years ago, the 2011 scores remain significantly lower than they were at the height of economic expansion in 2006. Given the prevailing gloom around the global economy at the end of 2011, it seems highly likely that a further deterioration in these personal evaluations will be evident in the results of the 2012 survey.

Political implications: leaders, pay attention

Against the backdrop of profound discontent and impatience with political leadership around the world, it must be asked how this country's steady, but slow, pace of developmental gains have translated into South Africans' views on their political leadership's commitment to accelerate change.

One option is to look at general election results. At first glance, observers may point to overwhelming consecutive victories of the African National Congress (ANC) as a resounding endorsement of government action. Deeper analysis of these figures, however, shows that in 2009 only 60 per cent of South Africans of voting age (not to be confused with registered voters) turned out at the polls. This has a number of implications. The most obvious of these is that 40 per cent of the South African voting-age population did not vote (see Schultz-Herzenberg 2009). Importantly, it also means that an absolute ANC electoral majority of 65.9 per cent of registered voters is reduced to a simple majority of only around 39 per cent of the voting age population. This, obviously, has similar implications for all other political parties. The question, therefore, arises as to whether the current party configuration offers voters enough choice to express their preferences. Moreover, it needs to be asked what the longer-term consequences of the status quo would be for the ways in which citizens express their existential preferences and anxieties.

Since 2006, the SA Reconciliation Barometer Survey has been measuring confidence in the institutions of national, provincial and local government, as well as public opinion on key aspects of leadership. Table 5.13 reports on these findings for the three spheres of government.

In 2011, confidence levels for the national government stood at a respectable 65 per cent; the comparable figure for provincial government was nine percentage points lower at 56 per cent. Local government, the sphere closest to ordinary people, managed to attract only 43 per cent. Approval rates for this sphere have been consistently low since measurement started in 2006, reflecting much of the discontent that has been voiced by both communities and national policy-makers. It is also noticeable that after the confidence slump that coincided with the ANC's damaging succession battle between Thabo Mbeki and Jacob Zuma, none of the three spheres of government has been able to regain the confidence levels of 2006.

Table 5.14 reports on responses to three leadership-related statements, which have been put to respondents in consecutive rounds of the survey since 2003. The first posits that the country's 'leaders are not concerned about people like me'. With the exception of the survey's second round in 2004, agreement with the statement has varied within the 50 and 60 per cent band. In 2004, close to 70 per cent of respondents agreed with the statement, 'I can trust national leaders to do what is right'. Seven years later in 2011, this figure has dropped significantly to just above 50 per cent. The only indicator where responses have signified an improvement is in relation to the statement: 'If public officials are not interested in hearing what people like me think, there is no way to make them listen'. Agreement with this statement has dropped by almost 10 percentage points from 2006 to the 44 per cent of today. It is nevertheless not insignificant that almost half of respondents have continued to agree about the intransigence of public servants.

These findings suggest, firstly, that there is a backdrop of disillusionment behind lower voter turnout. Secondly, they point to a definite degree of disaffection with processes and the mechanisms that are aimed at bringing about change. Thirdly, the findings raise questions about leadership at a time where low growth is likely to translate into existential anxiety amongst millions of South Africans.

Conclusion

This chapter has provided an overview of public opinion on South Africans' sense of economic security at a time when slow and low growth is having a debilitating effect on the cause of creating a more inclusive economy.

The findings of the SA Reconciliation Barometer Survey show that a large percentage of South Africans are taking strain as a result of these conditions. They are less upbeat about the general prospects for the economy, but also about

Table 5.13: How much confidence do you have in...?

	2006	2007	2008	2009	2010	2011
National government	73%	63%	58%	57%	66%	65%
Provincial government	66%	57%	50%	49%	58%	56%
Local government	50%	43%	40%	39%	43%	43%

Note: The percentages here reflect the combined total of the 'a great deal' and 'quite a lot' responses.

Table 5.14: Trust in leadership (agree with statement)

	2003	2004	2005	2006	2007	2008	2009	2010	2011
Leaders are not concerned about people like me	57%	44%	53%	52%	53%	54%	58%	51%	51%
There is no way to make public officials listen	53%	46%	52%	53%	52%	49%	49%	46%	44%
Trust leaders to do what is right	55%	68%	61%	65%	57%	49%	50%	58%	51%

their own financial circumstances and living conditions. While policy-makers are scratching their heads about how to boost employment, two-thirds of respondents indicated that their prospects of getting a job would either get worse or stay the same. Thirty-eight per cent predicted that it was 'highly likely' that they would be unemployed next year, and a further 22 per cent were uncertain about their fate in this regard.

In these trying times, more South Africans will resort to the state for assistance. Over the past 17 years major gains have been made in addressing the immediate needs of society's most vulnerable, but given the scale of the challenge, the question remains whether it is enough. Resources alone may not be sufficient. A plan and leadership are also required to steer the country through these troubled waters. The data at our disposal suggest that a large section of South Africans believe that the country is not seeing sufficient direction and leadership. Again, these responses have to be read within the current context of material deprivation; in exceptional circumstances like these, most states would be stretched to respond comprehensively. Yet, when leaders live large at the expense of citizens, or fail to halt maladministration, there must be swift and decisive action. The lesson of 2011 should be that the citizenry, especially when under material strain, will have no patience with those who offer timid responses or abuse their trust.

Notes

1. IJR (Institute for Justice and Reconciliation) (2011) *SA Reconciliation Barometer Survey: 2011 Report*, Cape Town: Institute for Justice and Reconciliation.

2. The question posed in the 2011 SA Reconciliation Barometer Survey was: 'Now I would like you to think about whether a person's race affects their chances in certain situations. What about people like you? In these situations, are your chances a great deal better, better, about the same, worse, or a great deal worse than other people?'

3. The LSM is a composite variable, based on survey items relating to access to and ownership of a variety of items and services that provide an indication of an individual's living standard. It divides the population into 10 LSM groups, with 10 being the highest and 1 the lowest.

References

....

CHAPTER 1

Ahmed F, Arzeki R & Funke N (2007) The composition of capital flows to South Africa. *Journal of International Development* 19(2): 275–294.

ANCYL (2011) A clarion call to economic freedom fighters: Programme of action for economic freedom in our lifetime. Available at: http://www.ancyl.org.za/docs/discus/2011/economicu.pdf.

DTI (Department of Trade and Industry) (2011) *Industrial policy action plan 2011/12-2013/14*. Pretoria: DTI.

GBR (Global Business Reports) (2011) Brazil mining. *Engineering & Mining Journal* January/February.

IMM (Indian Ministry of Mines) (1993) National mineral policy. Available at: http://mines.nic.in/nmp.html [Accessed 14 November 2011].

Manuel T (2011) Address by Minister Trevor Manuel to the Sunday Times Top 100 Companies Awards, Johannesburg. Available at: http://www.thepresidency.gov.za/pebble.asp?relid=5126.

Mohamed S (2010) The state of the South African economy. In Daniel J, Naidoo P, Pillay D & Southall R (eds) *New South African Review 2010: Development or decline?* Johannesburg. Wits University Press.

Presidency (2009) *Development indicators*. Pretoria: The Presidency.

PwC (PricewaterhouseCoopers) (2011) *Mine 2011. The game has changed: Review of global trends in the mining industry*. Available at: http://www.pwc.com/en_GX/gx/mining/pdf/mine-2011-game-has-changed.pdf [accessed 14 November 2011].

SARB (South African Reserve Bank) (2011) Online statistical queries. Data for gross fixed capital formation by type of organisation and for GDP. Available at: www.resbank.co.za [accessed October 2011].

Stats SA (Statistics South Africa) (1996) October Household Survey. Database on CD-ROM. Pretoria.

Stats SA (2002) *Labour Force Survey*, September 2002. Available at: www.statssa.gov.za [accessed March 2011].

Stats SA (2006) *Income and Expenditure Survey* 2005/6. Electronic database. Available at: www.statssa.gov.za [accessed October 2011].

Stats SA (2010a) *General Household Survey* 2009. Electronic database. Available at: www.statssa.gov.za [accessed October 2011].

Stats SA (2010b) *Millennium development goals: Country report 2010*. Pretoria: Stats SA.

Stats SA (2010c) *Quarterly Labour Force Survey*, fourth quarter 2010. Electronic database. available at: www.statssa.gov.za [accessed March 2011].

Stats SA (2011a) *General Household Survey* 2010. Electronic database. Available at: www.statssa.gov.za [accessed October 2011].

Stats SA (2011b) *Quarterly Labour Force Survey*, second quarter 2011.

Electronic database. Available at: www.statssa.gov.za [accessed October 2011].

Stats SA (2011c) Data on the GDP to 2nd Quarter 2011. Data in excel format Available at: www.statssa.gov.za [accessed October 2011].

World Bank (2011) *World development indicators*. Electronic database. World dataBank. Available at: http://databank.worldbank.org [accessed October 2011].

CHAPTER 2

Benjamin P & Bhorat H (2011) Five key labour market challenges and the labour bills' response. Presentation to the UBS Bank, February.

Bhorat, H & Van der Westhuizen, C (2010) Poverty, inequality and the nature of economic growth in South Africa. In Misra-Dexter, N & February J *Testing democracy: Which way is South Africa going?* Cape Town: IDASA.

Buhlungu S (2010a) *A paradox of victory: COSATU and the democratic transformation in South Africa*. Pietermaritzburg: University of KwaZulu-Natal Press.

Buhlungu S (2010b) Political influence without organisational power: COSATU'S contested future. In Hofmeyer J (ed.) *Recession and recovery: 2009 Transformation audit*. Cape Town: IJR.

Burger R & Von Fintel D (2009) Determining the causes of the rising South African unemployment rate: An age, period and generational analysis. Working Papers 24/2009, Stellenbosch University, Department of Economics.

COSATU (Congress of South African Trade Unions) (2010) *A growth path towards full employment* Braamfontein: COSATU.

COSATU (2010a) *A growth path towards full employment*. Available at: http://www.cosatu.org.za/list.php?type=Discussion.

COSATU (2010b) *The alliance at the crossroads: A political discussion paper*. Available at: http://www.cosatu.org.za/docs/discussion/2010/dis0903.pdf.

COSATU (2011) Resolutions of the 4th Central Committee. Available at: http://www.cosatu.org.za/docs/resolutions/2011/resolutions4.pdf.

COSATU (2011) *NALEDI research paper on living wage*. COSATU 5th Central Committee. Available at: http://www.cosatu.org.za/docs/reports/2011/naledi_research_paper.pdf.

Cottle E (2011) Scoring an own goal? The construction workers' 2010 World Cup strike. In Cottle E (ed.) *South Africa's World Cup: A legacy for whom?* Durban: University of KwaZulu-Natal Press.

Dawes N (2011) The great carve up. *Mail & Guardian*. Available at: http://mg.co.za/article/2011-07-22-the-great-carveup.

DED (Department of Economic Development) (2010) *The new growth path*. Available at: http://www.polity.org.za/article/new-growth-path-the-framework-november -2010-2010-11-23.

DoL (Department of Labour) (2011) *Annual Industrial Action Report 2010*. Pretoria: DoL.

Freidman S (2011) The other view: COSATU should stop playing at insider politics. *The New Age*. Available at: http://www.thenewage.co.za/blogdetail.aspx?mid=186&blog_id=1507.

Hausmann R (2008) *Final recommendations of the international panel on ASGISA*. CID Working Paper 161. Centre for International Development, Harvard University.

Lehohla P (2011) *Labour market dynamics in South Africa 2010*. Pretoria: Stats SA.

LRS (Labour Research Service) (2011) *Bargaining Monitor* (The Bargaining Indicators Edition) 25(176).

Magruder J (2010) *High unemployment yet few small firms: The role of centralized bargaining in South Africa*. Economic Research Africa, Policy Paper No. 16. University of California, Berkeley.

National Treasury (2011) Confronting youth unemployment: Policy options for South Africa. Discussion paper. Available at: www.treasury.gov.za/.../Confronting%20youth%20unemployment%20-%20Policy%20options.pdf [accessed 28 October 2011].

National Treasury (2011) *Medium-term budget policy statement (2011)*. Pretoria: National Treasury.

NPC (National Planning Commission) (2011) *National development plan: Vision for 2030*. Pretoria: NPC.

NPC (n.d.) *Economy diagnostic*. Available at: http://www.npc.gov.za/MediaLib/Downloads/Home/Tabs/Diagnostic/Diagnostic_Economy.pdf.

OECD (Organisation for Economic Co-operation and Development) (2010) *OECD Economic Surveys: South Africa, July 2010*. Available at: http://www.info.gov.za/view/DownloadFileAction?id=128402.

Owen L (2011) Strikes: A global perspective. Available at: www.owenaden.co.za/2010/10/19/strikes-a-global-perspective/ [accessed 28 August 2011].

Patel S (2011) Why no numbers for domestic workers? Presentation to the Domestic Workers Summit, 28 August. Available at: www.lrs.org.za.

Saville A (2011) Productivity is our best currency. *Mail & Guardian Online*. Available at: www.mg.co.za/article/2010-09-10-productivity-is-our-best-currency [accessed 28 October 2011].

Seekings J & Nattrass N (2006) *Class, race and inequality in South Africa*. Scottsville: University of KwaZulu-Natal Press:

Stats SA (Statistics South Africa) (2011) *Gross domestic product, November*. Pretoria: Stats SA.

Stats SA (Statistics South Africa) (2011) *Quarterly labour force survey, July*. Pretoria: Stats SA.

Webster E & Von Holdt K (ed.) (2005) *Beyond the apartheid workplace: Studies in transition*. Scottsville: University of KwaZulu-Natal Press.

Vavi Z (2009) Speech to a gala dinner in honour of trade union stalwarts, East London, 30 April. Available at: http://www.cosatu.org.za/show.php?ID=3261.

CHAPTER 3

Bloch C et al. (2011) Learning and language: Home, school and community. *HSRC Review* 9(3): 34–41.

Bloch G (2009) *The toxic mix: What's wrong with South African schools and how to fix it*. Cape Town: Tafelberg.

Carnoy M, Chisholm L & Chilisa B (forthcoming) *The low achievement trap: Comparing schools in Botswana and South Africa*. Cape Town: HSRC Press.

Casale D & Posel D (2010) Mind your language: The benefits of English proficiency in the labour market. In Hofmeyr J (ed.) *2010 Transformation Audit: Vision or vacuum? Governing the South African Economy*. Cape Town: IJR.

CREATE (Consortium for Research on Education, Access, Transitions and Equity) (n.d.) General findings. Available at: http://www.create-rpc.org/research/findings.

Crouch L & Mabogoane T (1998) When the residuals matter more than the coefficients: An educational perspective. *Journal of Studies in Economics and Econometrics* 22(2): 1–13.

Curriculum News (2010, 2011) Available at: http://www.education.gov.za/Curriculum/CurriculumNews/tabid/348/Default.asp

DBE (Department of Basic Education) (2009) *Report of the Task Team for the Review of the Implementation of the National Curriculum Statement. Final Report*. Pretoria: DBE. Pretoria.

DBE (2010) *Education realities 2010*. Pretoria: DBE.

DBE (2011a) *Macro-indicator trends in schooling: Summary report 2011*. Pretoria: DBE.

DBE (2011b) Annual National Assessments. Report to Basic Education Portfolio Committee. 16 August. Available at: http://www.pmg.org.za/report/20110816-department-basic-education-amendments-basic-laws-amendment-bill-b36d-.

DBE (2011c) *Education realities 2011*. Pretoria: DBE.

DBE (n.d.) *Hand in hand to improve education for all*. Available at: http://www.education.gov.za/Home/LaunchofAccordon-BasicEducation/tabid/676/Default.aspx.

Fataar A (forthcoming) *Schooling subjectivities across the post-apartheid city*. Stellenbosch: SUN Press.

Fleisch B (2008) *Primary education in crisis: Why South African schoolchildren underachieve in reading and mathematics*. Cape Town: Juta and Company.

Gilmour D & Soudien C (2009) Learning and equitable access in the Western Cape, South Africa. *Comparative Education* (Special Issue: Access to Education in Sub-Saharan Africa) 45(2).

Goldstein H & Leckie G (2008) School league tables: What can they really tell us? *Significance* 5: 67–69.

Howie SJ (2007) Reading literacy in South African schools. In Kennedy A, Mullis I, Martin M & Trong K (eds) *PIRLS 2006 Encyclopedia: A guide to reading education in the forty PIRLS 2006 countries*. Chestnut Hill MA: TIMSS & PIRLS International Study Center, Boston College.

Howie SJ & Plomp T (2008) Reading achievement: International perspectives from IEA's Progress in International Reading Literacy Studies (PIRLS). *Education Research and Evaluation* 14(6).

IIEP (International Institute for Educational Planning) (2010) In search of quality: What the data tell us. *IIEP Newsletter* XXVIII(3).

IIEP, UNESCO & SACMEQ (International Institute for Educational Planning, United Nations Educational, Scientific and Cultural Organisation & Southern and Eastern Africa Consortium for Monitoring Educational Quality) (2011) *Pupil achievement among*

SACMEQ school systems. Paris: IIEP/UNESCO/SACMEQ.

Jansen J (2011) *We need to talk.* Johannesburg: Pan Macmillan.

Kgobe P (2011) Mobilising communities. *HSRC Review* 9(3).

Lauder H, Kounali D, Robinson A & Goldstein H (2010) Pupil composition and accountability: An analysis in English primary schools. *International Journal of Educational Research*, 49: 49–68.

Leckie G & Goldstein H (2009) The limitations of using school league tables to inform school choice. *Journal of the Royal Statistical Society A* 172(4): 835–851.

Lewin K (2008) *Access, age and grade.* CREATE Policy Brief 2. Consortium for Research on Education, Access, Transitions and Equity, University of Sussex.

Lewin K (2009) Access to education in sub-Saharan Africa: Patterns, problems and possibilities. *Comparative Education* (Special Issue: Access to Education in Sub-Saharan Africa) 45(2).

Manuel T (2011) Two decades to make this the South Africa we want. *Sunday Times Review*, 13 November.

Meny-Gibert S & Russell B (2009) *Barriers to education.* Technical report of the National Household Survey. Johannesburg: Social Surveys Africa and Centre for Applied Legal Studies.

Motala S & Dieltiens V (2010) *Educational access in South Africa. Country research summary.* Consortium for Research on Educational Access, Transitions and Equity, Education Policy Unit, University of the Witwatersrand.

Mourshed M, Chijioke C & Barber M (2010) *How the world's most improved school systems keep getting better.* McKinsey & Company. Available at: http://mckinseyonsociety.com/how-the-worlds-most-improved-school-systems-keep-getting-better/.

NPC (National Planning Commission) (2011) *Diagnostic report.* Pretoria: NPC.

Paterson A & Arends F (2009) *Teacher graduate production in South Africa.* Pretoria: HSRC Press.

PMG (Parliamentary Monitoring Group) (2011) *Financial performance of provincial education departments: Briefing by Auditor General South Africa.* Available at: http://www.pmg.org.za/report/20111019-financial-performance-provincial-departments-briefing-office-auditor-.

Raudenbush SW (2004) Schooling, statistics, and poverty: Can we measure school improvement? Ninth Annual William H Angoff Memorial Lecture, presented at Educational Testing Service, Princeton, NJ, 1 April.

Reddy V (2006) *Mathematics and science achievement at South African schools in TIMSS 2003.* Cape Town: HSRC Press.

Sayed Y & Ahmed R (2011) Education quality in post-apartheid South African policy: Balancing equity, diversity, rights and participation. *Comparative Education* 47(1): 103–118.

Simkins C (2010) *The maths and science performance of South Africa's public schools: Some lessons from the past decade.* Johannesburg: CDE.

Simkins C, Rule S & Bernstein A (2007) *Doubling for growth. Addressing the maths and science challenge in South Africa's schools.* Johannesburg: CDE.

Soudien C (2004) 'Constituting the class': An analysis of the process of 'integration' in South African schools. In Chisholm L (ed.) *Changing class: Education and social change in post-apartheid South Africa.* Cape Town: HSRC Press.

Taylor N (2011) Improving the effectiveness of our schools. *HSRC Review* 9(3): 30–31.

Taylor S & Yu D (2009) Socio-economic status and educational achievement: Does education provide a stepping stone out of poverty in South Africa? In Hofmeyr J (ed.) *Transformation audit 2009: Recession and recovery.* Cape Town: IJR.

Tikly L (2011) Towards a framework for researching the quality of education in low-income countries. *Comparative Education* 47(1): 1–23.

Thomas S, Sammons P, Mortimore P & Smees R (1997) Stability and consistency in secondary schools' effects on students' GCSE outcomes over three years. *School Effectiveness and School Improvement* 8(2): 169–197.

UNESCO (United Nations Educational, Scientific and Cultural Organisation) (2011) *EFA Global monitoring report. The hidden crisis. Armed conflict and education.* Paris: UNESCO.

Van der Berg S (2011) Low education quality as a poverty trap: Introduction and welcoming. Unpublished presentation. Programme to Support Pro-Poor Policy Development, University of Stellenbosch.

Von Hippel PT (2009) Achievement, learning, and seasonal impact as measures of school effectiveness: It's better to be valid than reliable. *School Effectiveness and School Improvement* 20(2): 187–213.

Wildeman R (2010) *Resources and outcomes in public schools. The case of South Africa.* Pretoria: IDASA.

Yang M & Woodhouse G (2001) Progress from GCSE to A and AS level: Institutional and gender differences, and trends over time. *British Educational Research Journal* 27(3): 245–67.

CHAPTER 4

Ajam T & Aron J (2009) Transforming fiscal governance. In Aron J, Kahn B & Kingdon G (eds) *South African economic policy under democracy.* Oxford: Oxford University Press.

Anand S & Sen A (1994) Human development index: Methodology and measurement. In Fukuda-Parr S & Shiva Kumar AK (eds) (2003) *Readings in human development.* New York: Oxford University Press.

Argent J (2009) Household income: Report on NIDS Wave 1. NIDS Technical Paper, No. 3, Southern Africa Labour and Development Research Unit, University of Cape Town.

Bhorat H & Van der Westhuizen C (2009) Economic growth, poverty and inequality in South Africa: The first decade of democracy. Unpublished Paper. Development Policy Research Unit, University of Cape Town.

Bhorat H, Naidoo P & Van der Westhuizen C (2006) Shifts in non-income welfare in South Africa, 1993–2004. DPRU conference paper, 18–20 October, Johannesburg.

Bhorat H, Van der Westhuizen C & Cassim A (2009) Findings from NIDS 2008: Access to household services and assets. *NIDS Discussion Paper* No. 4, SALDRU.

Cummings S & Nørgaard O (2004) Conceptualizing state capacity: Comparing Kazakhstan and Kyrgzstan. *Policy Studies* 52(4): 685–708.

DBE (Department of Basic Education) (2010) *Education for All. Country report South Africa*. Pretoria: DBE.

DE (Department of Education) (2005) *Grade 6 systemic evaluation report*. Pretoria: DE.

DE (2006) *Monitoring and evaluation report on the impact and outcomes of the education system on South Africa's population: Evidence from household surveys*. Pretoria: DE.

DE (2008) *Education for all. Country report South Africa*. Pretoria: DE

Fiske EB & Ladd HF (2005) *Elusive equity: Education reform in post-apartheid South Africa*. Cape Town: HSRC Press.

Fukuda-Parr S & Shiva Kumar, AK (eds) (2003). *Readings in human development*. Oxford: Oxford University Press.

Goñi E, Lopez JH & Serven L (2008) Fiscal redistribution and income inequality in Latin America. *World Bank Policy Research Working Paper* No. 4487. Washington DC: World Bank.

Gumede V (2011) Policy-making in South Africa. In Landsberg C & Venter A (4th edition) *South African government and politics*. Pretoria: Van Schaik Publishers.

Haq M (1995) The human development paradigm. In Fukuda-Parr S & Shiva Kumar AK (eds) (2003) *Readings in human development*. New York: Oxford University Press.

Hoogeveen JG & Özler B (2006) Poverty and inequality in post-apartheid South Africa: 1995–2000. In Bhorat H & Kanbur R (eds) *Poverty and policy in post-apartheid South Africa*. Cape Town: HSRC Press.

IMF (International Monetary Fund) (2011) South Africa: Article IV Consultation. *IMF Country Report* No. 11/258. Washington DC: IMF.

Jansen JD (2001) Rethinking education policy making in South Africa: Symbols of change, signals of conflict. In Kraak A & Young M (eds) *Education in retrospect: Policy and implementation since 1990*. Cape Town: HSRC Press.

Lam D, Leibbrandt M & Garlick J (2010) Investing in human capital to reduce inequality. Paper delivered at the Centre for Development Enterprise Workshop, Tackling Inequality in South Africa, 1 March.

Leibbrandt M, Van der Berg S & Bhorat H (2001) Introduction. In Bhorat H, Leibbrandt M, Maziya M, Van der Berg S & Woolard I (eds.) *Fighting poverty: Labour markets and inequality in South Africa*. Cape Town: UCT Press.

Leibbrandt M, Woolard C & Woolard I (2009) Poverty and inequality dynamics in South Africa: Post-apartheid developments in the light of the long-run legacy. In Aron J, Kahn B & Kingdon G (eds) *South African economic policy under democracy*. Oxford: Oxford University Press.

Leibbrandt M, Finn A & Woolard I (2010) Describing and decomposing post-apartheid inequality in South Africa: An analysis based on income and expenditure data from the 1993 Project for Statistics on Living Standards and Development and the 2008 base wave of the National Income Dynamics Study. Paper presented at the Overcoming Inequality and Structural Poverty in South Africa: Toward Inclusive Growth and Development conference, Birchwood Hotel, Johannesburg, 20–22 September.

Leibbrandt M, Finn A, Argent J & Woolard I (2010) Changes in income poverty over the post-apartheid period: An analysis based on data from the 1993 Project for Statistics on Living Standards and Development and the 2008 base wave of the National Income Dynamics Study. *Studies in Economics and Econometrics* 34(3): 25–43.

Leibbrandt M, Woolard I, Finn A & Argent J (2010) Trends in South African income distribution and poverty since the fall of apartheid. *OECD Social, Employment and Migration Working Papers* No. 101, January.

Leibbrandt M, Woolard I, McEwen H & Koep C (2010) Better employment to reduce inequality further in South Africa. In *Tackling inequalities in Brazil, India, China and South Africa: The role of labour market and social policies*. Paris: OECD Publishing.

Leibbrandt M & Levinsohn J (2011) Fifteen years on: Household incomes in South Africa. *National Bureau of Economic Research Working Paper* No. 16661, Cambridge, January.

Mkandawire T (2001) Thinking about developmental states in Africa. *Cambridge Journal of Economics* 24(3): 289–313.

Motala S (2006) Education transformation in South Africa: The impact of finance equity reforms in public schooling after 1998. PhD thesis. University of the Witwatersrand, Johannesburg.

National Treasury (2009) *Provincial budgets and expenditure review 2005/06–2011/12*. Pretoria: National Treasury.

NPC (National Planning Commission) (2011a) *Diagnostic report*. Pretoria: NPC.

NPC (2011b) *National development plan: Vision for 2030*. Pretoria: NPC.

Nunes R (2011) *The other side of 'We're all in it together'.* European Institute for Progressive Kulturepolitik. Available at: http://eipcp.net/n/1313133309/print.

OECD (Organisation for Economic Co-operation and Development) (2008). *Reviews of national policies for education – South Africa*. Available at: http://www.education.gov.za/LinkClick.aspx?fileticket=sKsxhYorWOk%3D&tabid=452&mid=1034.

Reddy V (2006) *Mathematics and science achievement at South African schools in TIMSS 2003*. Cape Town: HSRC Press.

Rensburg I (2001) Reflections from the inside: Key policy assumptions and how they have shaped policy making and implementation in South Africa, 1994–2000. In Kraak A & Young M (eds) *Education in retrospect: Policy and implementation since 1990*. Cape Town: HSRC Press.

Sen A (1993) Capability and well-being. In Sen A & Nussbaum M (eds) *The quality of life*. Oxford: Clarendon Press.

Stiglitz J, Sen A & Fitoussi JP (2010) *Report by the Commission on the Measurement of Economic Performance and Social Progress*. Available at: http://www.stiglitz-sen-fitoussi.fr/documents/rapport_anglais.pdf.

UNDP (United Nations Development Programme) (2011) *Human development report*. New York: Palgrave Macmillan.

Van der Berg S (2005) Fiscal expenditure incidence in South Africa, 1995 and 2000. *A report for the National Treasury*. Available at: www.treasury.gpg.gov.za/docs/Fiscal Incidence Report2005.pdf.

Van der Berg S (2007) Apartheid's enduring legacy: Inequalities in education. *Journal of African Economies* 16(5): 849–880.

Van der Berg S (2009) *Fiscal incidence of social spending in South Africa, 2006*. Working Papers 10/2009, Stellenbosch University, Department of Economics.

Van der Berg S & Siebrits K (2010) *Social assistance reform during a period of fiscal stress*. Working Paper 17/2010, Stellenbosch University, Department of Economics.

Van der Berg S, Louw M & Yu D (2008) Post-transition poverty trends based on an alternative data source. *South African Journal of Economics* 76(1): 58–76.

Wildemann R (2008) Public expenditure on education. In Kraak A & Press K (eds) *Human Resources Development Review 2008*. Cape Town: HSRC Press.

CHAPTER 5

Hindu, The (2011) Corrupt, repressive and stupid. Editorial, *The Hindu*, 17 August. Available at: www.thehindu.com/opinion/editorial/article2362951.ece.

IJR (Institute for Justice and Reconciliation) (2011) *SA Reconciliation Barometer Survey: 2011 Report*, Cape Town: Institute for Justice and Reconciliation.

Moodley-Isaacs N (2011) Bad debt stats 'are worrying'. *Independent Online*. Available at: www.iol.co.za [accessed 2 December 2011].

National Treasury (1999, 2003, 2005, 2007) *Intergovernmental Fiscal Review*. Available at: http://www.treasury.gov.za/publications/igfr/default.aspx.

National Treasury (2010) *Medium-Term Budget Policy Statement 2010*. Available at: http://www.treasury.gov.za/documents/mtbps/2010/default.aspx.

National Treasury (2011) *Medium-Term Budget Policy Statement 2011*. Available at: http://www.treasury.gov.za/documents/mtbps/2011/mtbps/speech.pdf.

OECD (Organisation for Economic Co-operation and Development) (2011) *Perspectives on global development 2012: Social cohesion in a shifting world*. OECD Publishing.

Rachmann G (2011) 2011, the year of global indignation. *Financial Times*, 29 August. Available at: www.ft.com.

Schultz-Herzenberg C (2009) *Elections and accountability in South Africa*. ISS Paper 188. Pretoria: Institute for Security Studies.

Stats SA (Statistics South Africa) (1996–1999) *October Household Surveys*. Pretoria: Stats SA.

Stats SA (2000–2001) *Labour Force Surveys*. Pretoria: Stats SA.

Stats SA (2002–2009) *General Household Surveys*. Pretoria: Stats SA.

Stats SA (2011) *Statistics of liquidations and insolvencies – October 2011*. Pretoria: Stats SA.